MW01486969

HOSPITALITY 2.0

DIGITAL REVOLUTION IN THE HOTEL INDUSTRY

BY IRA VOUK

January 31, 2022

Written by the pool at a fitness club in Downtown San Diego, CA

ISBN: 978-1-716-13778-5

"This book is a must read for industry investors, asset owners, senior executives in operational enterprises and travel intermediaries, academicians, entrepreneurs, and students. It pulls the covers back on key issues causing economic inefficiencies in the travel and hospitality industry and highlights opportunities created by technological advances and their implementation to drive profit, ROI, and consumer value creation. The book is written in a conversational style, devoid of technospeak, that allows readers to hear from some of the best minds in the industry, presenting both issues and economically optimal recommendations for a pathway forward."

Dr. Bill Carroll, *Marketing Economics, Phocuswright, Cornell University*

❧

"Ira really opened my eyes to how and why the Digital Revolution will occur in hospitality. Her practical experience in hotel operations combined with an informed mind on how technology can drive business results is a potent combination. She astutely maps the lodging ecosystem in a way that informs the reader how many stakeholders in that system have competing and non-aligned interests. She approaches this work with the passion of a modern day Joan of Arc. It is a great read."

Carl Winston, *Payne School of Hospitality & Tourism Management, SDSU.*

❧

"Ira Vouk's book is undoubtedly one of the most comprehensive pieces of work on the intersection of the hospitality industry and technology adoption. The book provides a solid overview of all the different challenges and disruptors that are impacting the hotel industry today and moving forward, as well as providing a clear understanding of how we got to the current situation. The colloquial style opens up this space to a wide ranging audience, which is exactly what is needed to affect change."

Wouter Geerts, *Skift*

❧

"Ira's 'Hospitality 2.0' accelerates the reader into a digital journey from re-discovery to monetization, with a host of multi-industry veterans sharing their own transformation stories. Ira humbly offers up new perspectives in her conversations, while encouraging the experts to venture outside their (conversational) comfort zones. Even at more than 200 pages, it's a novel-breezy read but with a better ending - simply that you'll keep coming back to it to remember that last quote or statistic."

Todd Rollin, *Duetto*

"Many hotels are desperately lagging behind as far as technology is concerned: knowledge, devices, applications. Luckily, 'Hospitality 2.0' fills in some major knowledge gaps and outlives a path forward for the digital transformation of our beloved industry."

Max Starkov, *Hospitality Consulting, New York University*

"Anyone entering our industry simply must read 'Hospitality 2.0' as there is no book that can even get close to the comprehensiveness this book provides. I also recommend it to experienced executives in all travel companies that use technology (which doesn't?) as I haven't yet found a book with the same level of depth to give context and sufficient understanding on such a large array of hotel technology subjects."

Dori Stein, *Fornova*

&

"Ira Vouk provides essential context for anyone hoping to understand the complex dynamics of today's lodging industry. This text provides an important and unflinching look into the reasons why the industry lags others in technological sophistication, process workflows and profit optimization. Ira and a cadre of industry leaders reveal the structural conflicts between business models that not only strain relationships across distribution channels with travel sellers, but within hotel operations. Most importantly, this is not simply a passive analysis of an industry's woes, but a call to action for immediate proactive change that will help hoteliers compete against the growing challenges presented by alternative accommodations, technological advancement and labor constraints. Ira covers topics and perspectives the industry desperately needs to hear."

Robert Cole, *RockCheetah, Phocuswright*

&

"I am very impressed by the content and the style of what Ira has written in this book. I have not seen anything like this in the industry for a long time! It is comprehensive and very informative. The content is just great, and everybody in the hospitality industry should get this update on the technology status and trends in our space. I highly recommend it. The value Ira has created by producing this piece is certainly significant!"

Ulrich Pillau, *Apaleo*

&

"Great read. The author's insights and depth of hospitality technology and revenue management make it a must for anyone wanting to proactively compete in today's and tomorrow's hotel business. The inclusion of the various industry and related professionals makes it even more credible and informative. Well done!"

Howard Greenberg, *Trilogy Real Estate Management*

&

FOREWORD

The publication of 'Hospitality 2.0' comes at a pivotal moment for the hotel industry. The pandemic rapidly accelerated the adoption of digital technologies in old-world industries like hospitality and we saw this happening first hand in our data at Hotel Tech Report.

In January of 2020 - 49,050 people researched hotel technology solutions on the HotelTechReport website. In November of 2021 - 177,198 hoteliers visited HotelTechReport to find the right technology for their businesses. So what caused this 261% growth in hoteliers researching tech solutions during such a relatively short period of time?

Despite the fact that there are still fewer travellers staying in hotels than two years ago, the demand for technology in hotels has never been stronger on an absolute basis. That's why we're seeing billions of dollars in venture capital flooding markets. Smart money investors like Tiger Global and Softbank deeply understand the tectonic shift in hospitality, precisely because they've seen leading indicators in adjacent markets as evidenced by Toast's (restaurant software) massive $20B IPO in 2021.

The pandemic forced hotels to reimagine every facet of their businesses. Some hoteliers were forced to work remotely for the first time. Others were forced to quickly cross-train and learn new roles. Marketers couldn't use the same tactics they had used in the past to drive demand, and revenue managers could no longer lean on historical data. The entire game got flipped on its head, and technology was the only path forward regardless of the role. Revenue managers sought out RMS partners that could tap into forward-looking data. Marketers, who historically relied on international travel, had to seek out CRMs that could quickly drum up drive market business. Across the board, hoteliers were forced to think differently, and technology was at the center of every major operational or organizational change.

With the rapid evolution of the hotel technology market, there was no playbook or almanac for how to think about digital transformation - until now.

In her book, Ira Vouk leverages her past experience as both a hotelier and a technologist building products for hoteliers to translate decades of market developments into an easy-to-understand blueprint for those who want a crash course on where we've been and where we're going. Ira is a serial networker, an entrepreneur, and a builder who has spent the last 20 years living and breathing this industry. Despite her deep experience in the space, Ira is constantly tapping her network to augment her knowledge, and this book gives readers a front row ticket to her conversations with top minds in the industry.

A career in hotel technology right now is like a career in marketing in the early days of Facebook. Most of the older generation didn't understand social media, which gave the newer generation a massive advantage. Hoteliers who don't take the time to educate themselves on hotel technology today, will go the way of those marketers who didn't invest energy in social media.

If you're looking for a crash course on the next phase of hospitality and are ready to explore the latest market trends - look no further than 'Hospitality 2.0'.

Jordan Hollander, *Hotel Tech Report*

The future is already here, it's just unevenly distributed.

William Gibson

INTRODUCTION

Who am I and why did I write this book?

I am a former housekeeper who fell in love with the hospitality industry 20 years ago and became dedicated to solving its problems through technology, education, consulting and writing.

Early in my hospitality career, I chose revenue management as my path because I've always been convinced that data is the key to optimal decision making and successful operations, so I started my consulting company. When I realized there were many more hotels that needed help than I could personally manage, I began teaching revenue management - through seminars, webinars, and educational publications. Then I published a book, Revenue Management Made Easy,[1] in 2018 in an attempt to spread awareness about the discipline and the new concepts and techniques I had developed and fine-tuned through years of practice. I have sold thousands of copies to hospitality operators and other industry professionals as well as universities and students in different countries.

At some point in my career, I discovered that my true passion was technology. People who know me personally say I'm an explorer and an innovator at heart. I have dedicated many years to innovating the industry. I have been a huge promoter of technology and have built and brought to market multiple successful and innovative hospitality software solutions. That passion definitely reflected in the way that this book took form. As you will soon see, the path to innovation lies in data and modern technology.

I hope that my efforts throughout these years have helped the industry become slightly more efficient and successful. But I didn't want to stop there. Hence the book you're holding in your hands (or listening to in your car on the way to the office).

This book is about digital transformations in our industry and all the wonderful opportunities that lie ahead of us, because there is just no way hoteliers can continue running their operations the same old way. Technology is critical for all hospitality operators. Most importantly, technology should be modern, agile and should drive hotels forward – it can't be outdated, over complicated and hold them back. It has to be easy-to-use, cloud-native, and seamlessly integrated into their workflows. That is my firm belief and I'm sticking to it, in this book as well as in my consulting practice.

Hoteliers want simple things: to spend less time on routine tasks, to make their operations more efficient, to generate more revenue and profit, and to provide better service to their guests. That is exactly what technology is designed to help them achieve. It is here to help them solve those problems as efficiently and effectively as possible.

---

[1]Revenue Management Made Easy by Ira Vouk (April 2019): https://www.amazon.com/REVENUE-MANAGEMENT-Midscale-Limited-Service-Hotels

If you look at the companies that are succeeding in the travel space, you will notice some things that they all have in common:

- They are heavily reliant on technology (not just any technology - the modern kind that's in the cloud)
- They are agile
- They are continually innovating
- They use data to make decisions, instead of relying on gut instincts

However, as you may be aware, the hospitality industry has been slow in adopting new solutions due to a variety of factors described in the following chapters. One of the main objectives of my book is to address this issue.

Disclaimer: this book is not a typical industry publication. It is offering an unbiased point of view on the state of the industry today, along with a glimpse into what the future holds, from the perspective of someone who has followed the evolution of hospitality for over two decades from every possible angle of observation, including: various operational roles on the property level, a representative of a hotel management company, a franchisee of a major brand, an independent property operator, a product management professional who builds and markets SaaS tools for the industry, a technology founder of a third-party solution that relies on a PMS integration, a researcher, a private consultant, an educator and a writer. I am fortunate to have worn many hats in this industry over the last 20 years. They have provided me with a unique perspective and a holistic view of the challenges that the industry is currently facing as well as possible solutions to overcome them.

What you are reading right now is very different from the original idea of this book. The manuscript was a living organism. It started from one outline and then evolved into something much deeper and broader as I continued my research and conversations with various industry leaders, expanding my horizons and building on the original idea. Somewhere along the way, I started to feel like I no longer had control over how the book evolved and developed. It became an independent entity (just like my other kids). So what you will read in the following pages is mostly what the industry really wanted to convey to you. I had very little to do with it.

Needless to say, I had a lot of fun writing this book. It was perhaps as much fun as when I was developing an algorithm with a team of Russian scientists 12 years ago, when we pioneered machine learning in the revenue management space.

What you should also know is that this book is full of gold. It includes exclusive interviews with industry leaders and tech founders who share their stories about what inspired them to start their businesses, how they overcame the challenges the industry presented, and how they developed their products into key elements of the hospitality ecosystem. I also interviewed major players like Google and Amazon Web Services about their visions for moving the industry forward through technology and what they are already doing in this area.

In this book you will find some brilliant insights from a large number of experts, a description of the major trends that have disrupted the industry in the last decade, quite a bit about the evolution of technology, and of course a lot about where it's all headed and where the main areas of opportunity lie.

By writing this book, I hope to help industry professionals, executives as well as founders, investors, professors, and students understand how to address the main challenges the industry is facing today, and how to apply the lessons we have learned from the past. I also want to show how hotels can implement successful business strategies in this new environment through innovative technology solutions and redesigned operations, and how to prepare for the inevitable disruptions of the next years to come.

As Ravi Mehrota of IDeaS put it, *"Humans always attempt to model their reality."* What we need to keep in mind is that our reality is constantly changing. That means our models need to be continually adjusted. They can't be stagnant. When old concepts and frameworks no longer work - we need to readapt (#agile). When reading this book, you will notice that I am a big fan of agile methodologies.

As a result of recent events (and not just COVID, the elephant in the room, but other disruptors that will be discussed), our old model of reality has been falling apart in front of our eyes like a big old puzzle. So, instead of clinging to the remaining pieces, we need to realize it's time to create a new beginning. As Vadim Zeland says in his famous book Transurfing,[2] *"We're capable of building our own reality."* In the third part of this book, I will attempt to paint the picture of that reality (Hospitality 2.0) and how we can start building it today.

As part of my research, I identified 3 major factors that have been driving transformations in the hospitality industry in the recent decade:

1. The natural evolution of technology (mainly, cloud computing)
2. The growth of the alternative accommodations sector
   and last but not least...
3. The COVID-19 pandemic

We will talk about all of these, and more.

I wish to express my sincere gratitude to those who took part in the interviews and shared their wisdom with me. Every single interaction was fascinating, engaging and educational. Those conversations allowed me to examine the industry from over a dozen additional perspectives and present a more holistic view of the topics covered in these chapters.

When conducting these interviews, each transcript yielded about 10 pages of text in a Google document. As I was incorporating those transcripts into this book, I would often refer to them as "10 pages of gold". The conversations with these amazing, bright, and inspiring individuals provided me with a great deal of wisdom and insight, and it was an absolute honor to connect with them throughout the process of writing these pages. Every

---

[2]Vadim Zeland: Reality Transurfing: https://zelands.com/

single interviewee gave me a whole new perspective on things that are happening in our industry, while in certain areas they were absolutely unanimous. I had the time of my life when scheduling, interacting with them, holding those engaging discussions and seeing the world through their eyes.

Industry leaders interviewed (in alphabetical order, by organization):

Aggregate Intelligence: John Tilly (Founder, CEO)

AirDNA: Scott Shatford (Founder, CEO)

Amazon Web Services: Sekhar Mallipeddi (Global Travel & Hospitality Technology Leader at AWS at the time of writing, recently joined an IT startup company)

Atomize RMS: Leif Jagerbrand (Founder, Chairman of the Board)

CitizenM: Michael Levie (Co-founder, COO)

Duetto RMS: Marco Benvenuti (Co-founder)

Google Cloud: Ravi Simhambhatla (Managing Director/CTO, Digital Transformation - Travel & Transportation)

Hospitality Technology Consulting: John Burns (President)

Hotel Tech Report: Jordan Hollander (Co-founder, CEO)

HSMAI: Bob Gilbert (President, CEO)

HTNG/AHLA: Michael Blake (CTO)

IDeaS RMS: Ravi Mehrotra (Co-founder, President and Chief Scientist)

Son Hospitality Consulting: Mylene Young (Founder, Principal)

Sonder: Francis Davidson (Co-founder, CEO)

STR / CoStar: Jan Freitag (former Senior Vice President at STR, now National Director at CoStar Group)

University of Delaware, Hospitality Business Management: Timothy Webb, PhD (Assistant Professor)

University of Denver, Daniels College of Business, Knoebel School of Hospitality Management: H.G. Parsa, PhD (Barron Hilton Chair in Lodging & Professor)

University of Las Vegas, William F. Harrah College of Hospitality: Amanda Belarmino, PhD (Assistant Professor)

I also have to note that I don't have any financial interest in any of the above mentioned companies. All references are here not for the purpose of advertising, but purely to raise awareness about existing technologies and business practices that I find valuable and that in my opinion have the potential to drive industry innovation. This list was hand-picked based on my previous experience and knowledge of these companies. With that said, there are many more excellent solutions that didn't make it into this book because of various limitations, but I look forward to talking about them in my future podcasts.

I will end my introduction with a quote from one of my interviewees. It gave me the energy to continue working on the manuscript relentlessly and served as an affirmation that my efforts will help push the industry one step closer to being more efficient and successful, which is the very reason why I decided to start this journey.

"What you're putting together is very exciting and the industry definitely needs it. It needs direction, so that things start to gradually unfold, because many of them don't know where to get the right knowledge." Michael Levie, citizenM

I hope this book will serve as a guide for anyone who is interested in understanding what is happening with the hospitality industry today and what to expect in the next 5-10 years.

Happy reading.

PART 1: **CHALLENGES**

Lessons of the past

While the idea behind the layout of this book is to follow the chronology of the industry's evolution with a glimpse into the future, I made a conscious decision to not talk about the history of the hospitality industry here. A lot has been written about it, and this book is already long enough (about four times longer than I expected).

What happened in the past is not as important as the lessons we should learn from it.

This book begins by discussing the major challenges the industry faces today, along with an explanation of how those challenges arose, which can help us learn from those events, as well as find possible solutions to overcome them.

LOW TECHNOLOGY ADOPTION

Sophisticated technology surrounds us in our everyday lives, AI algorithms predict our shopping behavior, social media ads are tailored to our needs based on vast amounts of data gathered and analyzed through the web. Yet at the same time, most hoteliers are still adopting an old-school, manual approach to many aspects of their operations without investing in any (even basic) technology.

I want to start this chapter with a quote from Ravi Simhambhatla (Google Cloud) that absolutely blew my mind:

If you look at our human body, it is mostly useless after 60 years of usage. So in my very humble opinion, as we journey to different planets in the next 100-200 years, I think technology is going to enable us to harvest the brain and augment our bodies or do away with our bodies and to just attach it to some sort of composite structure that will allow us to stay "alive". I think that is going to happen.

You can imagine that after having worked in the hospitality industry for a couple decades, my head nearly exploded after I heard the above. While visionaries like Ravi talk about other planets and synthetic organs, here we are in the hotel industry, thinking about how to price our Queen room for the next Saturday and whether we have enough data and the right algorithm to make that decision.

In this chapter, I'm attempting to explain why this regressive mindset prevails in our industry and whether there is a light at the end of the tunnel for us in the near future.

As we know, technology adoption has been a challenge for hospitality for a very long time. If we take the revenue management discipline for example, according to the recent study by Skift,[3] *"Only 16.5% of hotels in the world use revenue management technology that goes beyond Excel spreadsheets, heuristics and gut feeling."* Isn't it mindblowing?

Marco Benvenuti, one of the founders of Duetto RMS shares how this became a challenge to scale the company:

This is something that I've known from the beginning. When you're selling hotel software, whether it's a Revenue Management System, a PMS or whatever else, you're never going to see hockey stick growth, because hotels are slow. They're slow in buying, they're slow in implementing.

Duetto actually scaled better than I thought, but of course, if you compare it to Uber, the growth trajectory is not the same.

And that's just the nature of the industry. It's the nature of the difficultness of implementing any software that is operational in nature in a hotel. It just takes time, it takes people, it takes data, it takes connectivity and all that.

This is a little bit of a Chicken and the Egg problem. I don't know how it started, but because of the type of buyer that you have in the hotel space and the fact that you cannot get this explosive growth, investors historically have been reluctant to invest in B2B hospitality technology. That creates a bad cycle.

If we take marketing, it is the same. The state of marketing automation in hospitality is currently very basic. In most cases, this is a privilege of upscale independent resorts and casinos staffed with full-time marketing professionals. But the majority of hotels in the world (especially midscale and lower-end segments) are not yet allocating resources for these automated tools. At the same time, OTAs have been successfully using marketing automation for quite some time, reaching high levels of sophistication and customization. As a result, they continue chipping away at the market share and shifting business away from the hotels' direct booking channels.

And this applies to pretty much every other aspect of running a hotel (marketing, sales, operations, customer communication, internal communication, labor management, revenue management, etc.)

At the same time, there are many industries and sectors that are way ahead of where we are right now. We see AI, machine learning, technology and automation everywhere in our daily lives. But when we look at the hospitality industry, sometimes it feels like the Stone Age: excel spreadsheets, calculators and pencils. Hotel owners

---

[3]Skift: The Hotel Revenue Management Landscape 2019 (April 2019): https://research.skift.com/report/the-hotel-revenue-management-landscape-2019/

are obviously the ones who are incentivized the most by revenue or profit growth through automation. Logically, every hotel is owned by someone. Why then, are those owners not pushing towards technology adoption? And what do we need to do to get there in order for those technology tools to become fully adopted, flawlessly integrated and entirely automated?

In my in-depth research, I found that the following reasons are holding us back from adopting innovative solutions more quickly:

1. Natural adoption curve (the human nature to be scared of technology)

This one has to do with the standard tech adoption lifecycle, not pertaining to any particular industry or any particular technology.

Here's the definition from my favorite source of knowledge.

The technology adoption lifecycle is a sociological model that describes the adoption or acceptance of a new product or innovation, according to the demographic and psychological characteristics of defined adopter groups. The process of adoption over time is typically illustrated as a classical normal distribution or "bell curve". The model indicates that the first group of people to use a new product is called "innovators", followed by "early adopters". Next come the "early majority" and the "late majority", and the last group to eventually adopt a product are called "laggards" or "phobics". For example, a phobic may only use a cloud service when it is the only remaining method of performing a required task, but the phobic may not have an in-depth technical knowledge of how to use the service.[4]

As Ravi Mehrotra (IDeaS RMS) explained:

Look at the history of flight as an example. It is filled with mishaps, failures and fatalities. In their efforts to understand the mechanics of flight, would-be inventors mostly tried to mimic the anatomy of birds. As excited and curious as most people were about the possibility of flight before the invention of the airplane, some were downright terrified of the idea, worried about the potentially foolish dangers of flying until Near Kitty Hawk, North Carolina, Orville and Wilbur Wright make the first successful flight in history of a self-propelled, heavier-than-air aircraft. Today we cannot imagine transportation without airplanes!

Now imagine that day comes when self-driving cars are available to you. How many out of 100 people will agree to use it? There will be very few and those who will do it, perhaps will be those who designed it or those who understand how things work.

Interestingly, professor H.G. Parsa (University of Denver, Daniels College of Business) used the same analogy in our conversation:

---

[4]Wikipedia: Technology adoption life cycle: https://en.wikipedia.org/wiki/Technology_adoption_life_cycle

| Professor Parsa

Traditionally, when new technology enters the market, only about 20% of people jump on it, 40% wait and watch what happens, and others never adopt. This adoption curve is observed again and again in many industries. Evolution takes time.

It's the same reason why you and I are scared to death to sit in a driverless car.

| Ira Vouk

Oh no, not me. Mine actually saved my life a couple weeks ago when it stopped because of a huge trash bin in the middle of the freeway - from 75 to zero within a few seconds. There is no way I would have avoided that object if I was the only entity controlling my car at that moment.

I must belong to the "innovator" category on the adoption curve.

So how do we address this? One could say, "Just wait and it will happen," but as Ravi Mehrotra of IDeaS objectively noted, "Patience is not a virtue that you have, Ira," so my proposal is to do a few things:

- Let's make sure that the software products we build actually address the problems that hotel owners and operators have, which is the first rule of Product Management that leads to building products that customers fall in love with. For some reason, not all companies understand that but that's the rule technology companies need to always follow when building solutions for the industry.
- Let's make sure that our technology is user-friendly and seamlessly integrated into the end user's workflows.
- Let's make sure our technology is cloud native (should I even mention this? It really should be the only option these days; no legacy, premise-based systems please!).
- Let's learn how to clearly explain to the end user what the product does and how it will benefit them.
- Let's continue raising awareness about why technology, in general, is a friend and not a foe.

2. Overall conservatism of the industry

While humans in general are naturally hesitant to jump into something new and unknown (as described in the first item), things are much worse in our sector. There's no question about it. Overall conservatism of the hospitality industry is something that needs to be addressed on a larger scale. It is known that hospitality professionals tend to be more reluctant to adopt new technologies, which prevents our industry from developing at the same pace as others.

Michael Blake (CTO of AHLA,[5] former CEO of HTNG[6]) describes what goes into the investment decision of a typical hospitality owner and operator:

[5]American Hotel & Lodging Association: https://www.ahla.com/
[6]Hospitality Technology Next Generation: https://www.htng.org/

You have to understand things from their perspective. And a lot of their perspective is that they manage from a place of "if it ain't broke, don't fix it". So they're looking at technology as a cost or expense line item, not as an investment.

In my attempt to understand why that is the case and what caused the industry to grow into this mindset, I spoke to a few other industry leaders.

John Burns (Hospitality Technology Consulting) phrased it this way:

We have to go back to the beginning and think about the fact that we are in a service industry. And over time, we came to believe that there were two choices: you could be high-touch or high-tech. And if you were high-tech, you could not deliver the high-touch that was appropriate for guest service. And that has not only lingered in our minds, but it's become part of our DNA. So we are not tech forward. Too often, we're tech reluctant, we're "tech hesitant".

In the hotel business we are still fascinated by pop-up toasters. We don't understand technology. We like what happens but that's about as far as we, as general managers or directors, have gotten in terms of technology. So we're still trying to figure out the toaster before we move on to the bigger things in life. That's why we've been distracted and discouraged in terms of the adoption of technology.

Leif Jägerbrand (founder of Atomize RMS) agrees:

That's a question that I thought a lot about during these years. My take is that hospitality people are not tech people. They are absolutely fantastic, they offer great experience to their customers and they are so nice to be around and work with but they are not tech savvy. And they are not math people.

I think that is the main reason for the slow technology adoption rate. In other industries, they have employed data scientists and they understand that they need the systems. But I'm not seeing it happening in hospitality.

How do we address this?

This one is actually relatively easy but requires an organized approach through a united front of technology providers.

Two words: awareness and education.

Hospitality technology providers need to do a better job at raising awareness and educating the market about the importance, benefits, and ROI of such tools. We will also need the help of hospitality academia (we will talk about that in a separate chapter).

As Tim Webb (University of Delaware, Hospitality Business Management) rightly noted:

Technology is an investment for ownership. And until owners recognize the value that a technology solution can provide (incremental to cost), they are not going to invest.

So as I see it, there is definitely a lot of room for improvement for technology vendors in terms of addressing these issues. To make sure their tools aren't perceived as an expense line item, but rather an investment that generates revenue and profit at the end of the day, we must communicate the benefits clearly.

3. Lack of training and lack of education targeted towards tech adoption and the use of technology

This item is closely related to the previous one but has a slightly different aspect. It's not just about the awareness of why technology is important and beneficial, but more about the training.

Professor H. G. Parsa (University of Denver) shared his opinion with me:

People in the hospitality industry are often not very well trained in using technology. You Are. I am. But many others are not. What we call human capital investments - that requires training.

Let's talk about Excel. These days, even fifth graders know how to use Excel. But if we roll back 20 years, they were teaching Excel in colleges. It took 20 years for it to come to high schools. Same thing with technology, for example revenue management tech. We have been teaching revenue management in colleges for the last 5-8 years. It will take more time before everybody uses RM technology. So, the cost of human training and perceived ROI is definitely an obstacle.

So when it comes to education and training, we should differentiate between:

- Formal education (many wonderful hospitality schools exist in different parts of the world)
- Everything else that doesn't involve obtaining an actual hospitality degree (certifications, online webinars, industry events, classes and panel discussions at conferences, industry publications, blogs, promotional materials, etc. etc.)

While we're seeing an increasing demand for hospitality degrees, there will always be a very significant portion of hoteliers without any formal education. And the reason for that is the fragmentation of the industry, which is described in the next item and also in the following chapter, in more detail.

While one might think that if hotel owners from all over the world put pressure on hospitality schools to teach their students about technology, that will solve our problems - the reality is a little bit more complex than that.

One of the problems is that hundreds of thousands of hotels are owned and operated by a single person and that person will never decide to earn a hospitality degree. As Leif Jagerbrand (Atomize RMS) phrased it, *"It's a person that owns a 50 room hotel and they are everything in that hotel: they are the revenue manager and the bartender."*

We see that a lot in the independent space. They may have just inherited that business or decided to open a hotel just like a lot of people wake up one morning with a decision to open a restaurant. They don't have any professional hospitality education and they never will. And that is unlikely to change.

So we need to find ways to educate that type of owner by finding the right channels of communication to raise their awareness and selecting the right language and proper messaging so that they can relate and understand. All my publications from the last 10 years attempt to do just that. And this is also part of the reason why I wrote this book.

On the other hand, it's our job (I still by inertia consider myself part of the "tech vendor" group due to my history of being a hotel tech startup founder) to make sure the tools we make are user-friendly and intuitive so that they don't require extensive training. And from what I'm seeing in the hotel tech space, I think the industry is on the right track. There are many amazing cloud-native younger companies that are entering the market and they are doing a very impressive job with their UI (user interface). As they gain market share, legacy solutions are feeling threatened, so either they improve their tech stack or they will eventually be displaced.

4. Fragmentation of the industry and the conflict of interest among stakeholders

The next (and probably most important) reason for low adoption is the fragmentation of the industry.

First of all, we have different stakeholders: owners, management companies, and brands that are involved in the operation of a hotel as well as tech investment decisions, with each having its own priorities and interests.

And second, when it comes to owners - as mentioned above, there is a significant amount of individual hotels (hundreds of thousands of them) worldwide that are independently owned and they're very small in terms of a business unit.

How does this fragmentation affect technology adoption in our industry? Michael Blake (HTNG) provides an example that illustrates it very well:

When I was working as a CIO for a large brand, a lot of times, there was a big difference between me and my friends over at the banks. In Citibank, they can go ahead and make a change in their tech stack and it'll ripple through all the branches within a week. For me, it was a little more complex than that. I had management groups that I had to talk to. I had asset ownership that I had to talk to. I had our own asset managers within our own portfolio that I had to talk to. So if we ever had to make a change, it was not as easy as those banker guys had it.

Marco Benvenuti of Duetto also shared his perspective which supports the above:

When the industry decided to split the management side versus the brand side versus the real-estate side (which created a lot of value for a lot of people) - it really put a disincentive on investing in technology. Because if you invest in technology, you need to look a little bit more on the longer term. If you're looking at just flipping a hotel, you're better off just replacing the carpet, as they say. And so putting all these players on the same agenda when you're selling technology to them is hard. So that made it hard for new technology to come in as well.

How do we address this?

This is a tough one. A full chapter is dedicated to this problem where I will attempt to paint a picture of how we ended up there and what we can possibly do about it.

5. Lack of data standardization

In order for technology to start taking over the decision-making process for humans so that it can be widely adopted, the following is needed:

- Access to data, lots of data
- Standardization for all of this data

This is also a big issue in our industry and there is also a full chapter dedicated to it further.

6. Complexity of the hospitality technology ecosystem

This one is really a consequence of a few factors listed above (fragmentation of the industry and lack of standardization). All of that has shaped up our tech ecosystem into how it looks today - a very complex and cumbersome environment that is quite hard to comprehend. For many hotel owners and operators, navigating in this space may be extremely challenging. There are not a lot of industry experts and tech consultants, like yours truly, who can help hospitality companies pick an optimal tech stack. Many times, hotel owners and operators are on their own, they get lost in the weeds of different software categories and connectivities - and give up.

In Bob Gilbert's opinion (President and CEO of HSMAI[7]), *"An ideal scenario for a select service is one-stop shopping. You want one software doing your reservations, your check-in, your check-out, your pricing, your distribution, your channel management, your housekeeping, your payroll, and your accounting - all those things."*

But we don't see a lot of those comprehensive one-stop solutions on the market (yet). Just look at the list of exhibitors at the annual HITEC conference.[8] Every year, there are new players as the family of hotel tech vendors keeps evolving. Just the list of categories itself looks intimidating.

And... you guessed it right, there is a separate chapter dedicated to this, where I will attempt to shed some light on the subject.

7. Integration problems

---

[7]Hospitality Sales & Marketing Association International: https://global.hsmai.org/
[8]HITEC Dallas 2021 Exhibitors: https://s23.a2zinc.net/clients/HFTP/HITECDallas2021/Public/Exhibitors.aspx

Lack of reliable and seamless integrations between different components of the complex hospitality ecosystem has been a major obstacle for many hospitality technology companies. Many hotels are still using premise-based legacy PMS systems that intentionally make it nearly impossible to connect to third-party tools.

The good news is that we're seeing more and more user-friendly cloud-based hospitality tech solutions (PMSs, channel managers, booking engines, etc.) that provide more API integration options. However, those companies also face obstacles when trying to gain market share due to various adoption barriers described in this chapter.

And last but not least:

8. Lack of innovative vision among large hospitality corporations

When researching this topic, I had a few conversations with Google and AWS, as those companies mainly work with large hospitality organizations, so I wanted to hear their perspectives on things that pertain to that segment of the industry.

Sekhar Mallipeddi (AWS) describes the challenges of working with those clients:

For us, the biggest challenge is that hotel companies have so much legacy, and they are spending so much money on keeping the lights on rather than innovating because of legacy systems and whatever they built over the last 20 years: mainframe systems, data systems. They are so convoluted because they kept making the same mistakes or they kept repeating certain things that they should not have done and that became basically the norm and now they can't let go of that legacy.

It's all about the fear of the unknown and the fear of cutting loose of that legacy system that has systematically failed them over and over again and yet they keep going back to it.

Similarly, I had an interesting conversation with Ravi Simhambhatla (Managing Director/CTO, Digital Transformation - Travel & Transportation at Google Cloud), who shares the same opinion concerning large hospitality corporations. I'm including an excerpt from this conversation below, as is, because some jewels retain their value better if they remain untouched.

❙ Ravi Simhambhatla

I think the reason why we have been left in the Stone Age in many cases is because corporations have not thought about technology as an enabler for the future. They are thinking about technology as an enabler for the present.

So as a CFO of a large hospitality company, when you're saying, "Okay, I'm going to allocate $X for this technology piece," you know they're only looking at it from a three-year viewpoint. Which is essentially today. Three years just goes like that. So the investments have not been commensurate with the ambitions.

In the airline space, some companies started recognizing that they need to invest because the prize that they see, for example, is a billion dollars in growth. And if they invest a hundred million to make a billion dollars in five years, that's a very good investment of their capital - so they're going to go for it. And so some companies have gone ahead with those investments, they have very innovative thinkers, very open-minded leaders who see the future so to speak. They are actually writing the future as they go along.

And then, the people who lead the companies that lag behind, they see that success and say, "I want to be like that, too." How do they get there? They can't just get there by saying, "I want to be like that." They have to invest in two areas: in people first, then technology.

| Ira Vouk

They have to have the right people who believe in technology.

| Ravi Simhambhatla

Absolutely, people who believe in technology as a tool and as an enabler. Technology is not your enemy. It could become your enemy if you misuse it. But generally speaking, it has only done good. So how do you make it your friend and how do you leverage every nuance of it to take your dreams further? That's becoming much of a reality.

But another reason for slow technology adoption is that many, many corporations are not digital natives and have large, legacy technology ecosystems. These companies are likely very focused on the operational aspects of their business. Like an airline: an airline's goal is to fly airplanes safely from point A to point B and get people to their destinations on time with the baggage.

| Ira Vouk

With their underwear...

| Ravi Simhambhatla

In today's world, even that has become an optional thing.

| Ira Vouk

True that.

| Ravi Simhambhatla

Right. Our kids have changed the world...

So those companies are very focused on that. They cannot fail there, that dictates how you conduct the rest of your business. And the larger your operation is, the greater the probability that you are slow, because everything you do touches every aspect of your operation. And you cannot afford that because you cannot take delays or cancellations, etc. So they've been slow to move. It's because old technology holds them back, it's not that people don't want to change. It's just that they've had such poor experiences in the past with technology, they've been burned so many times that they don't want to take that risk.

Because these people who run operations for example, they're not measured on the effectiveness of the technology they use. They are measured on the effectiveness of the operations they run. Nobody cares about tech. So if you're going to judge me by how many on-time departures I had today, then that's what I'm going to focus on. I'm going to do everything to get on-time departures, even if it means moving away from technology and using my radio.

And the same goes for large hotel companies.

So these are the main macro reasons why you find folks in the Stone Age. But the good news is that companies are starting to realize that. Companies that do not think in terms of data science/analytics and innovation, will disappear because there's a golden saying in the business that says "<u>you cannot cost-cut your way into profitability</u>".

| **Ira Vouk**

That is gold. I'm going to make it a headline in the chapter about evolution of technology.

And so I did.

It appears Ravi was right. Thankfully, we have a few great examples of companies with an innovative mindset that have been very successful in adopting a modern tech stack. Those are the companies that we should benchmark against.

CitizenM is one of my favorite examples and we will talk more about them further in the book. They basically built their entire tech stack from scratch, and found innovative ways to structure it in a way that allowed them to bypass the limitations of legacy solutions and connectivity problems.

Another great example is Sonder - a very unique company and current leader in the alternative accommodations space, also referred to as a "quasi-hotel company", now valued at $2.2 bln.[9]

I had an honor to speak with the Co-founder and CEO of Sonder, Francis Davidson. Most of the material from that conversation can be found in the 'Evolution of the Alternative Accommodations' chapter in Part 2 of this book, but here I wanted to reference Francis' response to my question about tech adoption.

---

[9]Skift: Sonder to Go Public at $2.2 Billion Valuation as Short-Term Rental Sector Stays Hot (April 30, 2021): https://skift.com/2021/04/30/sonder-to-go-public-at-2-2-billion-valuation-as-short-term-rental-sector-stays-hot/

| Ira Vouk

Sonder is one of very few examples of companies that have an innovative mindset and have been leaders in terms of technology adoption in the industry. How have you managed to keep this mindset considering the overall conservatism of the industry in relation to technology adoption?

| Francis Davidson

Like you mentioned, the industry is quite reticent to rethink their models and use technology to improve the guest experience, improve operations, etc. And our view is that it's our opportunity and we're going to just build it ourselves. So we have quite a large technology organization of over 100 people who just work on building our own custom technology stack. And that technology is not being sold to third parties because it's really used to power our differentiated experience and operations.

It's kind of puzzling to me actually why a lot of the industry isn't investing more heavily into it but we think this is our opportunity.

It is very promising that we have these amazing examples of companies like citizenM and Sonder and many others that pave the path to success for the rest of the industry.

Conclusion

To summarize, the hospitality industry has a long history that has shaped it into what it is today: fragmented, slow and conservative but still able to develop into something very dynamic and innovative.

I have heard people compare us to the airline industry but I believe we will follow our own path. One reason why hospitality has not been able to mimic what's being done in the airline space (in terms of technology adoption) is that as our industry has evolved, it has become extremely fragmented, as I outlined above and will explain in greater detail later. In the airline space, you have a few big players and no franchises. In the hospitality space, it's much more segregated, in terms of the number of companies, ownership types, business models, etc.

So while tech adoption rates are not where we would like them to be, there's light at the end of the tunnel. More companies are starting to realize that the potential upside is huge while the technology costs are much less than they thought. As computing costs have dropped over the years (more on that in the second part of the book), software is now accessible to even the smallest boutique hotels and independent properties. We see many new entrants in the hotel tech market every year, which is driven by the evolution of technology and cloud solutions that are made available by Google, AWS and others. We see strategic mergers and acquisitions that are starting to decrease fragmentation. We see a lot of wonderful things happening and it is very promising.

It will also be interesting to see what's going to happen in APAC (specifically, in China). It's accelerating quite quickly when it comes to adopting new technology and rethinking new ways of doing business.

Ravi Mehrotra of IDeaS agrees with me on this point:

My prediction is that we will see an exponentially increasing rate of technology adoption in the industry. These things start to work and many more people will start joining the move towards more tech adoption. People start to catch up and this is because systems that are coming on the market now are actually producing results that are very viable, that are measurable and understandable.

So what can we do to make it a smoother process? What is the best way to bring hotel tech products to market and scale them, considering all these challenges?

I recommend investors and executives of hospitality technology companies take the complexity of the ecosystem seriously as the first and most important step. If you're planning to invest in a hotel tech startup or launch a new product - make sure you do your research to understand the following:

- main target audience
- what critical problems they need solved
- decision makers (is there more than one stakeholder in the picture?)
- competitive landscape
- integration dependencies
- other potential obstacles

Pay attention to all aspects, starting with technology, availability of data and all other nuances described in this and the following chapters. And of course, don't forget the end user experience and distribution. I'm here for you if you need help with the above. As a dedicated innovator, I've assisted many hospitality tech companies with market research and opportunity assessment of new products.

Another critical part is working with the right talent. Make sure you have industry experts on your team, not just "outsiders". It's a critical element of success. After reading this book, you will see that the hospitality industry has many nuances that aren't apparent on the surface. I myself ran into many of them when I sold my first software to hotel owners. Don't make the same mistake. Hire a hospitality tech consultant or do your own research. It will save you a lot of $$$ in the long run.

In addition, look at what has already been discovered in academic circles. A lot of research has been carried out by hospitality academia and a great deal of it is available to the public. I will be happy to connect interested companies with various hospitality schools for potential cooperation. One of the goals of this book is to start bridging the gap between the industry and academia as they should start working closer together.

Finally, establishing a product oriented culture in your organization is key. As I learned from my product management experience, continually improvising, iterating, gathering early feedback from the market and committing to innovation is what will ensure the success of your business.

I am very optimistic about the future of the industry. I share Ravi Simhambhatla's vision on what is coming:

> *When I was in university, robotics, machine learning and AI were all in research papers. Now, it's all become real. As Moore's law slowed down, every step has become so much more powerful than the past step. So I think the adoption of technology and AI is going to increase and you will find far fewer companies who are left in the Stone Age.*

The industry definitely has potential, but there is still a lot of room for improvement in terms of technology adoption. We just need to embrace it. We shouldn't be afraid of it. Artificial intelligence, machine learning, cloud computing... We should learn from the innovations that have taken place over the last decade, embrace them, and build on top of them. I hope that my book will help push the industry in that direction.

FRAGMENTATION OF THE INDUSTRY AND CONFLICT OF INTEREST AMONG STAKEHOLDERS

The reason why this chapter is occupying the honorable second place in the table of contents is because, when conducting my research, I discovered that a lot of challenges described in this book (including the main challenge of low tech adoption) stem from this very problem.

I found confirmation of the above in many conversations with various industry leaders. One example is below.

Amanda Belarmino, PhD (University of Las Vegas, William F. Harrah College of Hospitality):

Low adoption rates of technology that we're seeing across the industry is partially caused by the emergence of franchise companies that resulted in fractionalized ownership. I think that if we still had the model that we had 20 years ago where there were a few franchises but mostly corporate owned properties - you wouldn't see that.

So, let's dig into the roots of this phenomenon.

First of all, as I briefly mentioned earlier, we should never compare the hotel sector to the airline sector because they're very different in structure. Our industry is very fragmented. We have some large hotel ownership groups but a very, very large portion of owners represent individual hotels, hundreds of thousands of them worldwide, and they're very small in terms of the size of a business unit. This results in a very significant fragmentation of the industry itself and, as a consequence, fragmentation of our technology ecosystem due to the emergence of a myriad of tech startup companies that attempt to target a specific use case, or a local region, without an ability to scale quickly. So instead of everything coming together, we have all these players, all these systems, and all these versions that are piled up into a big mess called "the hospitality tech ecosystem".

What caused us to be so different from the airline industry in that sense? You can imagine that it's probably difficult for an independent party to buy a commercial airplane and start flying a large number of people back and forth - those things are done in a centralized manner by a (relatively small) number of large companies. While, in the hotel world (which is much more similar to the restaurant sector in that sense than the airline sector), as an independent party, you can buy a hotel, inherit it, or marry into owning one. That results in the decentralized/fragmented situation that we have now, where an overwhelming amount of these business owners are not professional hoteliers, they lack formal education, training, previous hotel management experience and thus, a deep understanding of how to run their operations.

Following this logical chain, it is very natural that these owners often prefer to hand off the reins to a third-party (with that, they also hand off decision making that affects purchasing technology, which is an important aspect). This explains the emergence of hotel management companies as well as franchises. Franchising became popular in the 60s and 70s, it all started with Holiday Inns. And this is what we're now also starting to see in the alternative accommodations space.

So what happened in our industry is that we ended up with what Bob Gilbert of HSMAI calls "a three-legged stool". Unlike the airline sector, we have different players (stakeholders or entities) that are now in the picture:

- Owners
- Management companies
- Brands (franchisors)

This in many cases, results in a situation when there are multiple stakeholders that are involved in the operation of the same hotel, with each having their own priorities and interests.

Now, why is this important?

One of the major problems that stems from this fragmentation and the presence of different stakeholders is, as discussed, **low tech adoption rates**. As Skift researcher Wouter Geerts put it, "*It is easy to say that hotel operators are over-conservative in their technology investments, but the situation is more complicated than that. Different stakeholders are involved in IT investment decisions.*"[10]

By the way, Wouter is my favorite industry researcher. He has put together such wonderful guides as State of the Hotel Tech Stack, Hotel PMS Landscape, Hotel Revenue Management Landscape and others. Those are by far, the most comprehensive studies I have seen in my entire hospitality career (and I have seen a lot!). You can find them on the Skift[11] website.

Another issue that is caused by the fragmentation and conflict of interest is **lack of ability for owners to properly manage and optimize bottom-line profits** (which is also described further in more detail, in its own dedicated chapter).

First of all, HMA's (Hotel Management Agreements) that are signed with management companies are still based on top-line room revenues, which means that management companies may drive RevPAR even if that hurts the bottom line.

Furthermore, due to conflict of interest, there are occasions when brands (franchisors) force things upon hotels that result in a loss of profit for the hotel owners while being advantageous for the brand: promotions, campaigns, loyalty programs, technology, and even pricing recommendations.

---

[10]Skift: The Hotel Property Management Systems Landscape 2020 (Jan 2020): https://research.skift.com/report/the-hotel-property-management-systems-landscape-2020/
[11]Travel industry news: https://skift.com/

I had a great conversation about it with Bob Gilbert (President and CEO of HSMAI). He was the first person who helped me look at this problem from a bird's eye view.

Bob Gilbert:

You have to look at the fragmentation of the industry as a fact that can't be ignored because you have brands, management companies, and ownership groups. And each one of them has a different culture, they have a different point of view, they have a different ROI on what they measure and what they're willing to invest in.

A brand has a very different objective than an owner has. An owner has a real estate ROI objective. Brands typically are trying to create loyalty and drive market share to their channels.

Let's talk about the first category - owners. They are the ones who need to be convinced to invest in technology and who would ultimately be cutting the check. So we need to learn more about them.

Owners and their types

Proprietary ownership is the direct ownership of one or more properties by a person or company. Small hotels that are owned and operated by a family are a common example of proprietary ownership. A chain is a group of hotels that are owned or managed by one company. In general, three or more units constitute a chain but major hotel chains have from 300 to 5,000 properties. A proprietary chain is owned entirely by one company.

So, there's no one size fits all with ownership.

You can break them down into at least 5 different types:

- **Ownership groups**

Companies like Accor (270 k rooms), Blackstone (130 k rooms), Westmont Hospitality Group (108 k rooms), etc.

- **Institutional owners**

For example, big insurance companies, like Prudential or Aetna. They use a lot of their retirement portfolios and pension portfolios to invest in hotel real estate. So, these are all long-term holds, they have professional asset managers and they know what they are doing for the most part.

- **REIT (Real Estate Investment Trusts)**

REITs own, and in most cases operate, income-producing real estate, which may include hotels. Some examples of such companies are Host Hotels & Resorts and Apple Hospitality.

- **Franchise ownership**

Some franchisors like Marriott, Hilton, Hyatt also have owned portfolios.

- **Family ownership or small ownership companies**

And this is where the most fragmentation is taking place.

Per Bob Gilbert:

The family ownership group, particularly in the Asian American Community, are now in the 2nd, 3rd, and 4th generations. They've gone from a lot of the select service properties to pretty complex and big full service portfolios. But their core culture has always been about cash and driving the bottom line. Cash is king.

And the easiest thing for anybody with an operations mentality is to look at things from the perspective of where I see direct cost savings. They don't see the ROI on future revenue as easily as they see current cost savings. If a case of beer costs me this and you give me a 10% discount - fantastic. But if my forecasted revenue is X and I need to invest Y amount of that, so over the next five years I can make this much more - it's harder for them to comprehend. Although some do. But some are much more cost savings centric versus forward-looking on a return on investment.

So as we see from the above, different ownership types also dictate the management style, the culture and affect a lot of strategic decisions including ones related to technology upgrades.

Different priorities of stakeholders

Bob Gilbert:

The biggest transformation in the hotel industry, at least in the United States, in the last 50 years was that the majority of the industry has pivoted from private ownership to public. And I think some people forget what a paradigm shift that was. The majority of the hotels in the United States were family-owned companies for decades. And the minute they all went public and became Wall Street companies - that totally transformed the objective of why they were in business. They became financial companies.

In addition, most brands today are also financial companies. Many are asset light, they're focused on their stock earnings and they've got to continue to prove their revenue growth performance for the shareholders. And whatever they need to do to get there - they're going to do, while privately owned companies were able to pivot and make decisions that were frequently much more customer-centric and ROI-centric.

And that's where the fragmentation continues to evolve because that's when management companies came into the picture. And then you had this three-legged stool of brands, management companies, and the ownership groups. And they all have different objectives.

33

This is how three types of stakeholders differ when it comes to their priorities.

Owners are interested in maximizing ROI from their assets (with some rare exceptions).

Management companies - they may own assets but usually they just manage and represent an owner. They are interested in driving RevPAR because that's how management agreements are currently structured. With that, it's important to understand that optimized top-line room revenue doesn't always correlate to optimized bottom-line profit (we will talk more about it in one of the following chapters). There may be situations when they go in opposite directions. Hence the conflict of interest between the owner and the operator.

There are some management companies out there that have really perfected the art of working with different types of owners described above. They are the ones who sort their management teams by ownership type. So they would have one team that would manage all the assets by all institutional owners, another one would do all the brands, and another one would do all the family owned groups. They found that they're much more successful at understanding and executing plans and objectives for a portfolio type of hotel, regardless of the product type.

It might seem counterintuitive, but we have seen a number of management companies in the industry that do it this way and they seem to be successful.

Brands. If the brand doesn't manage or own the hotel (which is the case most of the time), they're just trying to drive volume through their direct channel and grow the loyalty club program. Very often, this has nothing to do with driving profit for the franchisee. Hence, the conflict of interest between the owner and the brand.

How this affects tech investment decisions

With technology investment decisions, there are a lot of variables due to fragmentation, which slows adoption rates. Most tech vendors are faced with the complexity of the landscape, lack of clarity about who the decision makers are, lack of interest to invest in technology from some of them, long sales cycles, and last but not least - integration issues (that warrants its own dedicated chapter).

And when it comes to technology adoption, in Bob Gilberts' opinion, "*Hotel Management Companies are normally the ones that really see the opportunity and understand the value in these types of investments. But then they have to convince the owner why they need to invest in technology. And the management company is also the entity that has to integrate the entire tech stack.*"

There is also another opinion that the best case scenario is when the owner and operator are the same company (as we often see in the case with ownership groups). CitizenM is one of my favorite examples of a modern company that supports the above point. I had an honor to speak with Michael Levie (Co-founder and COO of citizenM) and this is how he described it:

A lot of hotels are owned by different people than run the hotel, or have the brand on the building. And as such, you see that it is very difficult to keep a consistency in your tech stack and keep innovating. In our case, as we own and operate, it's extremely easy for us. You know why? Because we say, "This is how we do it" - and then it goes that way.

We will talk more about citizenM's use case further in the book. They have a fascinating story that the industry can certainly learn a lot from. And from the perspective of adopting modern technology in an agile manner, it is definitely clear that the best case scenario is when you have a single stakeholder.

If we look at the types of stakeholders we listed above and if you follow the market cap and the value for the investors in the hospitality industry, where it primarily lies is in the OTAs and the brands, not the management companies. We will leave out OTAs for now, as this is a whole different animal that we will discuss separately. At the same time, brands are the ones that are less susceptible to quick adoption of innovative technologies, mainly due to their size and the legacy tech stack that they operate on. Because it's so expensive and difficult for a large company (a brand) to switch to new technology, they are forced to use those legacy systems.

Francis Davidson (Co-founder and CEO of Sonder) shared his perspective, which is very similar.

Francis Davidson

The brands: if you look at their economic model, they generate nearly all their cash flow from franchise contracts. And franchise contracts take a percentage of top-line revenue, so there's not much of an incentive to look at how to infuse technology into the operation and improve the cost structure.

So for them it's actually fine if everything is done manually in the hospitality industry and done the same way it was done in the 90s. That's actually no big deal for the large chains.

The only thing that matters for them is RevPAR. Actually, you also see that in their investments. They're investing in some advanced stuff like machine learning for optimization of loyalty and promotions. They'd spent tens of millions of dollars on that system.

And there are real investments for things that drive substantial return for the chain, not for the owner. If I'm in the shoes of a large chain, why would I invest money on simplifying the check-in process? Or figuring out a way to run a property with 20% less cost? That might actually translate into lower ADRs in the long run, because a piece of real estate could be just as profitable with less revenue given the cost structure is lower. It might actually deteriorate the value of their franchise contracts, it might be a negative ROI investment for them to make, so it's just not going to make the cut.

It's actually not responsible for these management teams and these boards to approve substantial investments that will modernize the industry given the franchise contract structure. It's not in their interest for hotels to operate more efficiently.

| Ira Vouk

Do you feel that this is the reason why we're seeing most innovation happening in the European market where the majority of hotels are independent and are much more willing to adopt new technology?

| Francis Davidson

Absolutely.

So while we're seeing a lot of innovation happening in that segment, the ecosystem is still very fragmentized due to the fragmented structure of the industry itself (a myriad of small business owners that don't belong to any large company and thus all use their own tech solutions...if any).

I asked Bob Gilbert the same question. This led to an interesting discussion.

| Bob Gilbert

True. Innovation historically has come from the independents because they have the ability to pivot very quickly based upon trends as they see them, or certain customer niches. That's where boutique hotels came from, as well as very many other things.

So, while 70% of hotels in the US may be branded, in most cases they don't manage and they don't own. So they may recommend a certain system. Or if they dictate it - they're not the ones writing the check. The owner still is. So that fragmentation is still going to be a hurdle or it's going to significantly slow down the process of innovation in terms of what systems are used on a per hotel basis.

Think of reservation systems. Marriott to this day uses their own in-house system that's now 50 years old. And that's still what they keep modifying to make sure that it is going to be the reservation system of the future. That's an expensive proposition to make. And as we know, typically somebody who specializes in technology is going to do a better job of developing a platform or solution than a hotel company trying to develop a technology solution.

| Ira Vouk

But most brands dictate the Property Management System and the CRS, right? And if you're using a PMS that doesn't have the integration with a tech vendor you really like - you can't use it.

| Bob Gilbert

Correct. That's certainly a hurdle in the sales process for those vendors.

| Ira Vouk

I know that upgrading their own tech stack and adopting modern solutions is a business decision that those large brands have to make, and this business decision has to be justified for those companies. But I really wish they could be more forward-looking and not rely so much on these old software partners that are much less efficient and outdated, just because it's a safe bet for them. Same goes for moving their own legacy tech to the cloud and modernizing it.

| Bob Gilbert

Right. We definitely start seeing examples when for some hotel companies, their frustration with large brands and dissatisfaction with the provided tech stack is what led them to pull all their owned hotels and basically form a small brand on their own. And they may be able to get a better ROI than what these behemoths are able to deliver.

So ultimately, the owner can make that decision if technology systems don't meet the expectations.

And while brands will always play a role for the foreseeable future, what independents have been able to benefit from recently is the distribution channels and the ability to be positioned anywhere in the world at the same level as a branded hotel is. The only difference is that they may not have that brand recognition. But with a good marketer, an independent hotel can absolutely compete with a branded hotel any day if they're doing the right things.

| Ira Vouk

I noticed that one of the major problems is lack of awareness among hotel owners (specifically franchisees) and lack of understanding about how to do marketing. I've seen that a lot in my practice. That's why those owners fall into a brand trap because they want to completely rely on the franchisor to do marketing for them, without realizing that it would be much more cost effective to hire a good marketing firm instead of giving up 6% of your total room revenue, being forced to use old technology, being limited about tech vendors they can work with, and running brand promotions that hurt their bottom line... and the list goes on.

| Bob Gilbert

Yes. And if you look at the director of a sales and marketing department at an average hotel today, 90% of their job at the unit level has always been direct sales. At branded hotels, it's 90% key account management. That's what a Director of

Sales and Marketing does. There's usually very little classic marketing done at the unit level of a branded hotel. If you compare that to an independent resort - it's totally different, they're normally more sophisticated with their marketing efforts.

So, 50 years ago, when the franchise model grew more popular and brands started to expand, it made sense for hotel owners to become franchised because the bigger brands had more resources, which allowed them to afford better technology.

But now, in the modern world, it looks like being affiliated with a brand is more of a limitation for a lot of owners. Due to the recent disruptions in the tech space (mostly cloud computing) technology has become much less expensive. And due to the obstacles of integrations with the larger legacy players that own the majority of branded market share, right now independent properties have much more options in terms of modern technology solutions than branded properties.

So the situation has flipped from being advantageous for the owners from the technology standpoint in terms of brand affiliation, to the opposite side of the spectrum.

| Ira Vouk

So, considering what we just discussed, do you feel that it would be more beneficial for the industry's development and the technology development if more companies went independent? How does being part of a brand benefit the owners?

| Bob Gilbert

So even all the way through the 1990s, the primary value proposition of a brand was the reservation system. And that's not the primary value prop anymore. Today, it's still a major one, but it's not the primary one. The brands are looking at how they bring economies of scale in terms of purchasing and their loyalty program. They may offer revenue for hire or e-commerce for hire.

So the brands have had to diversify the business they're in. It's not just a reservation center business anymore by any stretch. But that's what it used to be.

| Ira Vouk

And then the loyalty programs. They are expensive. They are introduced by the brands as value props but if you really look at the numbers, those programs really benefit the brand and not the hotel.

| Bob Gilbert

Exactly. That value proposition works if you're the only hotel in the market and they can give you a base of some points of occupancy from that loyalty program. You have to pay for it, it's expensive, but it may be beneficial for the owner. So it's a trade-off.

But if that brand has 30 other brand affiliates in that market - how is that going to be diluted? There may not be as much of a benefit for you as an owner in that case.

So there's a spectrum of advantages of brand affiliation, but it all depends on the education, the culture, the owner's objectives.

Ira Vouk

Education is definitely one of the key components here. I have been digging into this problem for about a decade and I think where we still have a soft spot is clarity for the owners on how to make a decision about branding, rebranding or going independent.

It doesn't seem that owners always have the right tools to be able to measure the potential and ROI from these different options.

Bob Gilbert

Asset managers can give you a financial perspective on strategies for assets in their portfolio. There's a very specific formula for most big ownership groups.

They will tell you, for example, "Our hold on this asset is only going to be five years and therefore, the maximum amount of capital we're going to put in over this window of time is X." So, based on what's already there or what the investment is going to be, this is how they are going to forecast a return.

And so, very few hotel owners have a long-term view of either customer relationship management or technology. They're looking for short-term ROI based upon how long they're going to hold the property.

And those are the elements that anybody who is selling a software solution has to be cognizant of these days. Otherwise, you're going in blind trying to sell to somebody who has no interest in buying if you don't understand what their objective is for that particular asset and how much capital they're willing to invest to get so much return. If you can't prove a return that's within that hold window - the conversation is over. Their decision is based upon that narrow criteria for that particular asset. If it's a 20 year hold or a 30 year hold - it may be a whole different conversation.

At the top of the funnel, those are the issues that drive all these decisions as it relates to technology and capital investments, and who sees the value of a CRM system versus a revenue management system versus system X, Y and Z. It's different based upon where they are in that segmentation or that funnel.

Conclusion

To conclude, based on the research and various use cases analyzed, the most optimal situation that leads to a higher probability of adopting new technologies as well as increased bottom-line profits is a single stakeholder that represents both the owner and the operator and eliminates any conflict of interest.

With that said, it's obvious that this is not always feasible for some owners who may prefer to hire a management company to run their property or a portfolio of properties. In this case, a good level of collaboration is necessary between the owner and the operator to ensure that owners' interests are met and assets are optimized. This requires HMA's (Hotel Management Agreements) to be reformulated, on a large scale, based on profit metrics as opposed to the top-line room revenue.

And the third leg of the stool - brands. Brands are not evil. They have contributed a lot to the development of our industry and helped it leap forward (from the distribution standpoint) when they were introduced. However, it would be much more fair if they were transparent about their priorities and the fact that their actions sometimes go against the interest of a hotel owner who mostly cares about generating profit and maximizing ROI from their assets.

Mike Levie of citizenM shared his perspective on the future trends when it comes to the role of franchises in our industry:

I think that with the ownership paying the bill for COVID, and the chains not being part of the solution, you will see quite a bit of change over the next couple of years in terms of the number of properties being affiliated with brands.

I'm not advocating against brands. But in order for brands to stay relevant and to continue contributing to the evolution of the industry, they need to improve their value proposition. And the only way for them to do it is through technology. They need to upgrade their tech stack to ensure they continue offering value to the franchisees.

Until that happens, hotel owners who decide to stick to a particular flag need to insist on more flexibility in their selection of technology and other decisions that affect their business.

Brands can't keep dragging us back to the Stone Age. They used to do so much good for the industry. They used to be disruptive, building revolutionary software tools that helped hospitality evolve by leaps and bounds (think about the very first in-house RMS software by Marriott and IHG back in the 90s - that was unprecedented!). What happened to that innovative mindset?

I'm also advocating for transparency that ensures that owners are aware of this conflict of interest and operate in a manner that is optimal for them (owners) and not for the franchisor. That would lead to higher profits, more efficiency and more successful businesses overall and allow the industry to evolve in a much more optimal manner.

At the end of the day, it is the hotel owners, not brands or management companies, who determine where innovations go and what companies stick around. Although it takes a long time for the industry to hear them, it will eventually happen, because ultimately the owner is the one writing the check.

The owner should have the right to choose a technology provider without limitations from the PMS integration standpoint or the brand requirement standpoint. Accor would be a good example of that, as they recently announced their plans to adopt a multi-PMS strategy with 8 certified providers, which will allow the owners to select a solution that best suits their region, brand, or category of service.

At the same time, for the owner to be aware of how to make the right decision when it comes to technology investments, more education is certainly needed. In addition, software vendors need to do a much better job at communicating the benefits of their solution and the ROI that they deliver.

INTEGRATION DEPENDENCIES AND CONNECTIVITY ISSUES

Complexity of the ecosystem and who is the king

As discussed in the previous chapter, the hospitality industry is highly fragmented, and that fragmentation pertains to both: the stakeholders that play a role in operating a property as well as technology vendors. So if we look at it from the standpoint of a technology upgrade decision, this results in a very complex situation on the buyer side and even more complexity on the supplier side.

If we look closer at the supplier side (the hospitality technology ecosystem), we see an interesting dynamic that is somewhat discriminating against newer players that creates significant barriers to entry and to scale. Let me explain.

On one end of the hotel tech world are PMS (property management system) companies who own the key element of the data map - reservation/stay data. On the other end are software and application providers. In order for those to function (in most cases) they need to have access to the reservation or stay data, which creates an integration dependency on the PMS vendors. In a simplified view, here's roughly how it looks (I readapted a diagram from a 2018 Skift Research report[12] by adding one missing element to the picture, try to guess which one it is):

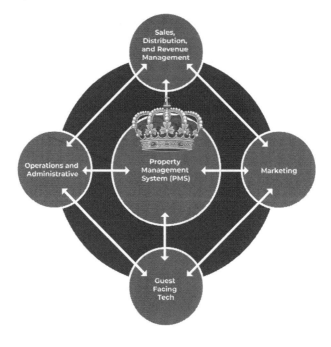

---

[12]Skift: The State of the Hotel Tech Stack 2018 (June 2018): https://research.skift.com/report/the-state-of-the-hotel-tech-stack-2018/

At the same time, to make things worse - the PMS landscape is fragmented as well.

There are myriads of property management systems out there. This is because it's actually relatively easy to build a basic PMS. It's essentially just a database with a pretty face, so many of them are started as in-house solutions and many of them are local regional systems with a very small market share. It is hard to say how many PMS vendors there really are worldwide, but there are various estimates that range from 700 to 1,300.

With that said, there are a relatively small number of PMS leaders that hold a significant share of the total market, with the top 10 vendors representing 34% of the total in terms of rooms. The largest player is Oracle Hospitality with its OPERA suite that has a 16% share[13] of available hotel rooms globally.

Another significant problem is that, unfortunately, many of those dinosaurs haven't yet made it easy for other vendors to connect to them.

This issue creates a major entry barrier for smaller non-PMS players.

Integration barriers

Here's an excerpt from my conversation with Bob Gilbert (President and CEO of HSMAI):

| Ira Vouk

The industry is attempting to move away from an accounting mentality to a more customer-centric approach, and I think that we are on the right path because the newer vendors are really starting to bring this way of thinking to the industry. But the problem is in who sits on the data. PMS is the central element. And what makes it worse is that many of them are these legacy systems that own a very large market share. They don't really have decent APIs or they require a significant amount of money for the "certification" in order to connect to them. So I think this is one of the biggest obstacles that prevent those newer tech non-PMS vendors from scaling. Would you agree?

| Bob Gilbert

You're spot on. That is a big obstacle. Because those legacy companies don't want to lose market share or have their business model usurped by new emerging technologies. So they're going to fight till the end to maintain their market share or they're going to become the Smith Coronas of the future.

---

[13]Skift: The Hotel Property Management Systems Landscape 2020 (Jan 2020): https://research.skift.com/report/the-hotel-property-management-systems-landscape-2020/

Back in 2010, I co-founded a hotel tech company and so I know of these problems firsthand. I went through all the pains of PMS integration dependencies when selling my product. Let me tell you, it wasn't easy, it was surprising and devastating.

As part of the research that I was conducting for this book, I also spoke to a number of other hospitality software founders to see whether they ran into the same issues.

Marco Benvenuti (Co-founder of Duetto) immediately confirmed my perception of this problem:

At the very beginning of Duetto, we had the software but we were kind of dead in the water until we got our first connection, which was with Opera back then. So then we could go sell to their customer base. And then you get connectivity with another PMS and with another one.

And this is where newer providers usually get stuck, it's the connectivity. If you have no data and no ability to push data back - you're dead in the water. And that has always been the constraint for these vendors.

Leif Jägerbrand (Atomize) also supported this point of view. And here I secretly admit that maybe... just maybe, knowing that we weren't the only hotel tech start-up caught by surprise and underestimating the scope of this problem when we started our business, made me feel a little better.

The major problem was, and still is, the legacy PMS systems, because they don't have proper APIs. And without APIs, there's nothing we can do. So that really is the major barrier for the whole industry. And not just for the Revenue Management Systems, but really for anyone who could do anything interesting with data. You need APIs. It's as simple as that. So that really is the major barrier.

Many of these problems stem from contractual restrictions in software licensing and usage, and in the limited willingness or ability of many PMS vendors to support the integration requirements of their hotel customers.

As Wouter Geerts points out in one of the recent Skift research reports,[14] "*Legacy PMS vendors have for too long reaped the rewards without truly pushing the boundaries of what they could offer hoteliers. Now technology has passed them by, and they are playing catch-up.*"

New forward-looking cloud-based hospitality technology companies are more adaptive in terms of targeting the real needs of their consumers. They embrace integrations with third-party providers that complement their suite of products and thus add value for the customers.

---

[14]Skift: The Hotel Property Management Systems Landscape 2020 (Jan 2020): https://research.skift.com/report/the-hotel-property-management-systems-landscape-2020/

Unfortunately, a large majority of hotels still use outdated systems and are reluctant to upgrade. This especially pertains to larger hotel chains and hotel groups. The larger the company, the less flexibility it normally has in adopting innovative solutions (as I already mentioned in the previous chapter). That results in a tech stack that is not optimized, which ultimately results in loss of revenues and profits for those companies and also flows through to the franchisees.

At the same time, not all types of connectivity are made equal. Having a daily data-dump is sold as integration, but this does not provide the ability to make truly dynamic and real-time decisions. And this is exactly what I asked Leif Jägerbrand, founder of Atomize RMS, because one of their main value propositions is real-time pricing updates. It must have made it really hard for them to scale, I thought. And I was not wrong.

| Ira Vouk

So, the real-time aspect of your vision and the way you implement your technology must have made it especially difficult to deal with PMSs, right? Because your technology may be in real time, but most of them are definitely not. Based on my experience, most legacy systems are just not able to consume that much information on a frequent basis. Am I correct?

| Leif Jägerbrand

Yes, exactly, some PMS systems cannot push information to us in real time. Instead, we have to pull information from them. And we cannot pull every second or they will be upset, because their technology won't handle it. We need to pull every 10 minutes or every 20 minutes or less frequently, so then it's no longer true real time. The "pushing back" part has never been a problem in terms of data consumption because there's not as much data going back. It's more the request part that has the major issue. So we prefer to integrate with PMS systems that can push data to us instead of us requesting it.

| Ira Vouk

Which are mostly newer PMS systems, right?

| Leif Jägerbrand

Correct.

I hope that every hotel in the world will switch to a new "open" PMS, a proper one.

| Ira Vouk

Amen to that.

| Leif Jägerbrand

Yes. That would drive so much more innovation in the hospitality industry. Investors would start pouring money into hospitality technology.

Jordan Hollander (Co-founder and CEO of Hotel Tech Report[15]) believes that integration between systems is a common problem in any business. And that's why Zapier and IFTTT have done really well creating that drag-and-drop interface for standard workflows and web hooks.

The biggest challenge that he sees today is that these are all developer tools still. So, there's no consumer facing tool where a hotel could set up a rule that says, for example, "If a guest checks in, send them a message on Whistle and then upsell them via Oaky." They can't go and do the automations themselves. And so that seems to be the biggest challenge in Jordan's opinion.

App marketplaces and platformification

Now, there is another phenomenon that is tightly connected to what we discussed above - emergence of app marketplaces.

While still a relatively new concept in the hotel industry, PMS players (and actually, others as well) are increasingly putting their integrations on marketplaces where integration partners can showcase their products, while hoteliers can access the platform and pick the integration that suits their needs. The main benefit for the end user is that, ideally, hoteliers can instantly switch a system on or off in a user-friendly, automated way, without even talking to a single person on the phone. You know, like the App store on your iPhone, or Google Play store if you're an Android person like me.

Below is the rest of my conversation with Jordan Hollander on this topic. He shared some great insights that I'm generously sharing with you here.

| Ira Vouk

How do you see this evolving in the next few years?

| Jordan Hollander

We've been saying the words "platform" and "platformification" for a while but realistically, it has not happened yet in hotels. There is no Salesforce app store for hotels, there is no Shopify app store for hotels. But I think there's this innate pressure to get there. I think there needs to be a platform where there are standardized data types and there's a commercial model where vendors or entrepreneurs can launch products easier in the market. And that's really where I see this going.

---

[15]Hotel Tech Report: Software Reviews, Technology Trends, and Buying Advice: https://hoteltechreport.com/

You see that early app stores like Mews and Cloudbeds are starting to get a little bit more involved. But it's still very nascent, and for both of those companies, their core business is to promote their own products and neither is at the scale that Shopify has for example, or that Salesforce has in terms of market penetration. And so that's in my opinion why the app stores haven't taken off as much as they should. There's not as much actual attraction within them as they probably would want. But I think the reason for that is because they still have to focus on land grabbing for now.

And I think one of those companies may eventually succeed, or maybe it will be Oracle. Oracle is getting better at those things, they're opening their API and allowing people to build off of it, but I think, ultimately, one or multiple of these companies will get to enough scale and will actually dig in on the app store as a place where they can gain the most amount of incremental revenue.

So the core baseline infrastructure is there. But the incentives are not there yet. And so I think in the next five years, at some point, one of these companies will figure out how to extract an immense amount of value from their marketplaces, and that's going to create a lot more innovation.

Ultimately, we need a more efficient customer acquisition channel in our industry, and platformification is the way to do that. The infrastructure exists but it just takes time to get there. So I am confident that it will happen in the next five years.

Ira Vouk

This is awesome. And I absolutely agree, this is where the future is. Right now, there are about 1000 PMS vendors. After a few of the largest suppliers figure out how to build a decent marketplace and an app store, do you think that many of the smaller PMS vendors will eventually fall off and we will be left with maybe 20-30 top PMS products? And hopefully we can concentrate on them and build to them. Do you think that's where things might be going?

Jordan Hollander

Absolutely. Consumers, who are the same people working in businesses, don't have a tolerance for bad products anymore. There's also an element of what is the succession plan of these smaller regional PMSs. I think there will definitely be a lot of fallout.

To compare, there were a ton of social media platforms in the early days and then there was a huge fallout and everything consolidated. So I think that will happen. We're seeing a lot of M&A already. We're starting to see this game of musical chairs settle a bit.

But then yes, if someone could crack the code on the marketplace side, it would add a lot of value. If I could log into a system and I could set up my apps via a drag-and-drop interface, without ever talking to anyone, those vendor companies wouldn't have to have a sales force because they could just literally be buying clicks within the marketplace to drive customer demand. And as a result, they could invest all their money into innovation and scale faster. And if that happens, there is going to be a vacuum effect that will suck a lot of the oxygen out of the companies that haven't figured that out yet.

A good example of a company that is helping move the industry towards such consolidation is Zucchetti Group.[16] Since 2017, the company acquired 10 different PMS systems, totalling 15000 properties in Europe and the US. Based on an internal source, the goal is to eventually modernize all of them and bring them to one common platform.

And here's more from my conversation with Jordan.

| Ira Vouk

And in order to achieve the platformification, do you think we need to stick with standard API protocols, which is the initiative that HTNG has been trying to address since 2002? Or is it okay for all companies to just build open APIs in whatever format they want to build them?

| Jordan Hollander

I think it depends on the use case but, generally, if you look at other markets (for example, the audio industry has standard audio file types and video has standard video file types), I think you need some level of consistency to build innovation off of. Yes, I think in general, there does need to be coordination and standardization but there's only so much you could do by putting out white papers. I think it has to be regulatory or it has to be really easy for people so that they don't want to touch anything else.

| Ira Vouk

I agree. I think that's one of the things that we need to figure out is how to speak the same language.

| Jordan Hollander

Absolutely.

Integration standards and why they are not followed

Efforts to standardize integrations go back 20 years, when a workgroup of HTNG published a large library of standards to be used by the hotel industry for integrations.

---

[16]Zucchetti Group - software and ICT solutions: https://www.zucchetti.com/

Hotel Technology - Next Generation (HTNG) was founded on June 23, 2002 by a group of nine leading hotel industry technology experts, with global representation of hotel technology management, consulting, and academia.

I have a copy of the original HTNG whitepaper[17] from 2002 in my possession.

PATH TO ACHIEVING

NEXT-GENERATION TECHNOLOGY

FOR THE HOTEL INDUSTRY

White Paper

Prepared by

Hotel Technology – Next Generation

Chicago

June 29, 2002

Here is the summary from the whitepaper (remember, this is 2002!).

"The hotel industry is fundamentally dissatisfied with the effectiveness of its current technology options and their ability to satisfy future business needs. The primary causes of this dissatisfaction are:

- *lack of effective inter-vendor cooperation and systems integration*
- *drawbacks in the current technology financing process, and*
- *poor adoption of modern technologies.*

Further, many segments of the hotel community do not recognize the importance of technology in hotel management. Equally, the industry has been unable to communicate a common and consistent vision of its requirements to the vendor community. A new approach is needed in order to facilitate the development of next-generation, customer-centric systems that will better meet the needs of the global hotel community."

And here we are, 2 decades later, dealing with the very same problems...

And then it continues:

"Few other industries face a technology environment as large and complex as the one found in the hotel industry. There are more than 100 different categories of systems commonly used within hotels, and many of them do (or need to) interact.

---

[17]HTNG 2002 Whitepaper: A Path To Achieving Next-Generation Hotel Technology – Next Generation Technology for the Hotel Industry - White Paper (June 2002): https://www.hospitalitynet.org/file/152000409.pdf

Hotels struggle daily to manage this complexity. They are handicapped by a complex decision-making process for capital spending, and also by a relative lack of third-party providers who can deliver comprehensive solutions on a pay-as-you-go basis. Hotel technology vendors are mostly small and undercapitalized. While there is much in the way of quality products to meet each area of functional need, each product addresses only a very limited set of the total application requirements. Interoperability of systems, with a few notable exceptions, has been an elusive goal."

"Among the existing set of hotel technology vendors, only a few have achieved any significant success with consolidation or partnership strategies, whether by acquisition, through alliances, or through internal development.

The resulting fragmentation of systems and vendors has imposed significant costs and inefficiencies on hotels. At the property level, it requires high levels of management effort to manage the multi-system, multi-vendor environment. For multi-hotel organizations (whether management, ownership, franchise, or membership), it complicates the consolidation of accurate, comprehensive data on guests' profiles, preferences and activities—the lifeblood of any hospitality organization."

What? Nothing changed in 20 years???

So how is it possible that after so many years of HTNG's attempts to bring some sort of order to our chaotic ecosystem, we are still in the same situation?

It was a great initiative. HTNG proposed a set of technical and business standards designed to facilitate the development of stronger, more credible technology vendors who can deliver the technology that hotels need, and many of these standards are still used today, however:

- They have shortcomings and are actively ignored by some of the major and newer PMS vendors

and (what I think is the main issue):

- Our ecosystem is more complex than everyone thought it was

As a result, instead of using those standards, many of the new PMS providers are openly publishing their APIs for third-party vendors to build towards while bypassing the HTNG standards altogether, which ultimately leads to less standardization of integrations. So we find ourselves in a deadly loop.

Numerous workgroups labored hard for years to come up with specs that are publicly available to all on the HTNG website.[18] They cover various scenarios to define message flows between different systems for different use cases.

However, as stated in Skift's PMS Landscape Report from 2020,[19] those standards are in need of upgrading. The report lists 3 main reasons why vendors tend to ignore them:

---

[18]HTNG Technical Specifications: https://www.htng.org/page/technical_specs

[19]Skift: The Hotel Property Management Systems Landscape 2020 (Jan 2020): https://research.skift.com/report/the-hotel-property-management-systems-landscape-2020/

1. Outdated protocols/formats

PMS vendors need to continue innovating to make their systems less rigid and allow for greater customizability and a mobile-first approach. What we are increasingly seeing then, is particularly newer vendors wanting to code their APIs using the REST protocol and JSON data format, but the HTNG standards are based on SOAP and XML. This is a major reason why many APIs today are not in accordance with the HTNG standards.

For reference, Representational State Transfer, or REST, is a design pattern for interacting with resources stored in a server. Each resource has an identity, a data type, and supports a set of actions. The RESTful design pattern is normally used in combination with HTTP, the language of the internet.[20]

2. Interpretability issue

According to some vendors, many fields have no clear description and are interpreted differently by each PMS.

In other words, while technology providers expected to be able to write one integration to the HTNG standards and replicate this across all PMS systems that have adopted the standard, the reality is that each integration continues to be customized. This is because it's necessary to check how each PMS interprets each data field which is certainly a time-consuming task (which I know firsthand... been there, done that).

3. Evolving needs for non-distribution type of data flows

The main focus of the HTNG standards was on integrations applicable to the distribution space, which is understandable, since distribution is a critical piece of the hospitality ecosystem that serves the main purpose of allowing hotels to sell rooms.

But as the ecosystem evolves, more different types of tools are increasingly looking to connect to the PMS as well. Those may include: work order management systems, housekeeping systems, guest messaging, in-room TVs, phone systems, Wi-Fi, or door locks, etc.

In an attempt to dig deeper into this issue, I tracked down Michael Blake, CTO of AHLA (and former CEO of HTNG, before the AHLA merger). I really enjoyed our conversation. Michael was kind enough to share some details from the history of how the organization was formed and also his perspective on the problems we're dealing with. I'm dropping a big portion of this discussion below. Enjoy!

| Michael Blake

The industry itself is highly fragmented both from the supplier side and the buyer side.

So now we get to "Where does HTNG play and why were we formed?" Well, a lot of it surrounded this issue of high fragmentation.

---

[20]REST API Tutorial: What is JSON (September 2021): https://restfulapi.net/introduction-to-json

The original whitepaper was published by HTNG in 2002. That was the original construct. And although some of the underlying technologies have changed, many of the concepts and precepts are there. And it was written in 2002. So you have to remember life before an iPad or life before any of those things and you'll see how kind of seminal this work was, it's fascinating. What were you doing in 2002?

| **Ira Vouk**

I was still in Belarus, my home country, studying for my first Masters degree. That was before I fell in love with the hospitality industry.

| **Michael Blake**

Here you go. So when you think back to those days and where technology was... A lot of things were still done on mainframe processing. We were barely talking about two-tier architecture and stuff like that. That was when HTNG started forming and a lot of the issues that it was attacking were around integration and issues around messaging, and those kinds of things.

HTNG is about solving industry problems and issues. And we do that through workgroups. And this workgroup concept brings vendors and hoteliers and anybody else who is interested in solving problems together, to get those issues resolved.

So you ask me about our plan for updating standards because there are folks that are steering away from our APIs, some of our standards. Why? Because they're old. Most people have a hard time spelling XML these days. So standards should be more of RESTful JSON and what have you. They need to be updated.

| **Ira Vouk**

What does it take to make it happen?

| **Michael Blake**

We need to start bringing this light messaging into the core.

The PMS is the heart of hospitality architecture. So if we could start getting light messages around the PMS, then I think you're going to start finding other light messaging around the core. And then before long, it's all replaced and you're done. It's not something that happens overnight, but it's happening as we speak.

A lot of the standards came from Open Travel and we kind of repackaged them for the hotel world.

In the meantime, what we also did was build out an API library.

Things move so quickly that you have to make the standards evolve as quickly. And the best way we've been able to do that, is through the workgroups, which gives us the ability to take a very disciplined approach to problem-solving.

Sometimes it takes a while to work our way through things.

That old adage, "If you want to run fast, you run by yourself. But if you want to run far, you have to run with the team." And that's where we take that adage pretty seriously because you got to bring a lot of people with you on that journey. And I got to tell you that sometimes the journey is more important than the destination.

Because you're taking all the legacy companies along with you, all these big players. And of course, each one of them has their secret sauce and what they want to do with it. But there are some areas you just don't want folks to argue about because a last name field is a last name field. Someone doesn't have to do that differently.

So our organization was formed to solve some of these issues. But I think what our organization is evolving more towards is to inspire and help innovation and to really help people who are trying to get into our industry, which is so difficult. So think of yourself as an entrepreneur who is trying to sell into this hospitality ecosystem.

| Ira Vouk

I was one, about 10 years ago. And I went through all the pains of the PMS integrations. It hurt.

| Michael Blake

So great. You know how hard it is, you know, a lot of PMS providers can tell you "no and no" and there are not a lot of folks who say "yes".

And many vendors just don't understand how to navigate through our complex environment. Do I talk to the CIO? How do I sell this new widget which I know will be effective for the hotels? How do I get this new algo exposed? What can I do? Who do I partner with?

So at HTNG, we're trying to help people navigate that.

If I was to look at our charter today at HTNG, number one is to continue problem solving, number two is to help and push innovation, and the third one is to educate and inform the senior leadership team. Because this digital transformation stuff is really hard for some people to grasp.

| Ira Vouk

I absolutely agree. Is that what drove your merger with AHLA?[21]

---

[21]AHLA integrates HTNG, Strengthening Technology Expertise, Advocacy, Focus (March 2021): https://www.ahla.com/press-release/ahla-integrates-htng-strengthening-technology-expertise-advocacy-focus

| Michael Blake

AHLA is all about advocating. It's all about moving the industry, and it does it extremely well with the lawmakers and what have you. And the people that participate in AHLA are the target market that we want to help and educate. We want those CEOs. We want those asset managers. We want those owners to understand technology, though not at a detailed level. I would have failed if they actually knew what XML-based messaging brokers are. I don't want to get them in that space. I want to get them into a space on why something makes sense, why we should be moving this way versus that way. Why cybersecurity is important. Why you shouldn't be making trade-offs between your front lobby and a new firewall.

So our role now is in that point of education.

| Ira Vouk

Do you believe that the effort by HTNG to standardize integration protocols was a necessary initiative?

| Michael Blake

If HTNG didn't exist, I would say, somebody else would have invented some standards because it's such a necessary component to bring all these disparate pieces together so that people can conclude on areas that aren't competitively different.

There are areas out there where we don't need to compete on: what a form size is or what the last name field is.

If that initiative didn't exist, we would have continued to solve industry issues, they just wouldn't have been as organized.

| Ira Vouk

What do you think would prevent the majority of vendors in the industry from adopting HTNG standards?

| Michael Blake

What we're talking about is a complex ecosystem. And what you're going to have are people who are going to just not be part of the process at all. And they're going to be successful, for a short period of time. They're going to be the ones who run fast. So they're going to run fast, but they're going to run by themselves because the whole ecosystem isn't going to adjust, and so eventually, it'll reject it. It's just the way complex systems work. Eventually these fast running things fall off unless they get adopted or picked up by another entity. Because another form of assimilation is through consolidation. And if they don't get assimilated, they'll be off on their own. I've seen many companies try and fail, try and fail. Maybe you'll have one or two boutiques that'll pick you up but that's about as far as you'll go.

| Ira Vouk

But don't we need those fast runners to show us where the innovation path is and bring the industry forward?

| Michael Blake

Absolutely, I think you need some of those fast runners but they have to be running in the same race because there's going to be some that'll be fast running, but they'll be running on stuff that may not make sense at all. And they think they're inventing something new, but they are really not.

| Ira Vouk

I think it happens because a lot of times, founders of these different startup companies are not from the industry, so they don't understand the context of how we operate and they run into these things like integration issues. Or, they thought it would be a good use case for our industry because they saw it work in a different sector, but it just doesn't apply here because of A, B, and C...

So what would you want to communicate to the industry through my book based on what we discussed in order to promote innovation and awareness among the readers?

| Michael Blake

I would continue to emphasize the need to be part of the organization and run with the group. It is this concept of being part of an organization and a group and changing the industry as opposed to just kind of running off doing your own thing.

Some people want to compete on different aspects. I get that. But there are others who find the areas where you can find commonality. And let's just make sure that we can work that and we have the organization (HTNG) to do that. We're not one that takes forever to do stuff. We move pretty quickly and we do it through workgroups.

| Ira Vouk

So what's the result of their work? Is that a white paper? Is it a webinar or a publication of some kind?

| Michael Blake

Generally, it's all of the above. Most of the time, it's a best-practice document or a white paper.

But it's one of those situations when the journey is as important as the destination. Just going along for the journey keeps people engaged and aligned and working on problems together.

So each one of our workgroups can be a journey and at any given point in time, there are 12 to 15 workgroups in flight that folks are working on. Most of the time, the workgroups are only established for six to eighteen months, tops.

Ira Vouk

And if there's somebody who wants to participate and contribute to the work that is done within HTNG, how do you recruit people for the workgroups? What's the main channel of communication there?

Michael Blake

Unfortunately, a lot of it is hand-to-hand combat because what we generally do is bring people together and they say, "You know what, I think the right person to talk to is this person and that person and that person," and a lot of people get excited.

Ira Vouk

So in regards to the financial aspect, from what I remember when I was running my company and we were trying to get certified with HTNG standards, there was a financial transaction involved.

Michael Blake

We're not in that business anymore, so we're not certifying anybody because we don't think that that's a good model. We are a membership based organization and that's kind of why we moved more towards AHLA. Because that is a membership organization, primarily for hotels.

Hotel companies that are already AHLA members, don't have to pay anything more.

So we are actually bringing over our vendor members into AHLA to start working with them, because most of them are small companies, they don't have their own advocacy group. So we're going to be able to offer more to individual companies and we actually have a nice startup program where I think the initial buy-in is $1000 a year.

Ira Vouk

So in order for a vendor to have access to the guides and to all the resources, they need to be a member of HTNG or a member of AHLA?

Michael Blake

They don't have to be a member at all because most of the standards we just make available. So the only thing that we don't do is some of the new workgroups that are still working on stuff. We don't make that available to the public until it's done.

But most of the stuff we publish is not behind a paywall so it's all out there, you can consume it.

| Ira Vouk

So why is the membership needed? What additional access does it provide?

| Michael Blake

So you hit it right on the head. What the membership allows you to do is have access, so you can be part of those workgroups. That's what membership gives you the ability to do, the ability to have a voice.

So, my personal conclusions from the above would be the following:

- The ecosystem is very complex (on the buyer's side and on the supplier's side).
- While being conservative, the industry is still very dynamic, and things change quickly, so the needs for data flows change quickly, too.
- This requires integration protocols to be constantly enhanced and updated in order to catch up to the evolving data environment.
- HTNG is currently the only party that has been attempting to approach the standardization issue in an organized manner and it doesn't look like anybody else wants to take on this role because it's a daunting task.
- Technically, anyone can be part of an HTNG workgroup that defines and suggests the standards (as long as they're a member of either HTNG or AHLA), but mostly people who participate in those workgroups come from 2 categories:
  - Representatives of larger hospitality organizations
  - Fanatics, like myself, who are passionate about the topic of standardization, even though they don't have any particular business interest

I did join HTNG right after talking to Michael, now I'm a strategic advisor for the Marketing Pillar (on behalf of HSMAI) and a member of the "AI for Hospitality" workgroup. It doesn't appear that a lot of the newer vendors, who complain the most about lack of updated protocols, actually participate in those discussions.

With that said, I would encourage younger hospitality tech companies, who have a dependency on those PMS integrations, to join HTNG and start bringing their fresh perspectives to these discussions. I believe that together we can make progress on moving towards the ubiquity of API standards.

Success story: how to avoid PMS integration dependency

So while the industry is attempting to take some steps to improve integration, it's clearly a slow process. It's still a big issue for many players today, which is a primary reason for larger hotel companies to develop systems in-house, tailored to their specific needs that require the entire tech stack to come into play. Seamless connections between the property management system, the central reservation system, the revenue management system, etc. are vital. Any customer-facing tech such as mobile applications or IoT (Internet of Things) enabled devices in the guest room can further enhance hotels' understanding of their guests, generate additional revenue streams, improve efficiencies and increase customer satisfaction. Seamless integrations are paramount.

As promised, let's talk about an example of such a company that successfully implemented that approach. CitizenM is a unicorn in the hospitality industry. I had an honor and an absolute pleasure to meet with Michael Levie, its Co-founder and COO. When Michael shared the details of how their tech stack was evolving and what they have been able to achieve as they were building it out and growing the company, I was absolutely blown away. I'm sharing this with the industry so other companies can see that anything is possible and, in particular, PMS dependency can be avoided. However, it does require the right people with the right mindset, a forward-looking, technologically oriented, data-driven one, like Michael's. I wish we could clone him.

❘ Michael Levie

Very early on, when we understood that we needed a more in-depth tech architecture, we wanted middleware to diminish the role of the PMS. Through Microsoft we were introduced to Ireckon[22] in Amsterdam who built the middleware. CitizenM became the launching partner.

(Note from the author: founded in 2008, Ireckon provides hotels with a core platform or middleware, for seamless software integration and complete flexibility in process management.[23])

❘ Ira Vouk

This is amazing...

Can you tell me more about the middleware?

❘ Michael Levie

The middleware is just intelligent plumbing. So the RMS, POS, the door lock system, the website, the app, you name it, only connects to the middleware. Nobody connects directly to the PMS, everybody connects to the middleware.

❘ Ira Vouk

Whoaaa...

❘ Michael Levie

---

[22]Ireconu: Hospitality's First Customer Data Platform (CDP): https://www.ireckonu.com/
[23]HospitalityNet Marketplace: Ireckon: https://www.hospitalitynet.org/organization/17020843/ireckon.html

All connections to the middleware take place through API's, which are not just transactional-like interfaces, but capture all micro-details between the systems.

And then we started to create dashboarding on the middleware, so that if we want to look at reports from that data - we can. For instance, for our shareholders, we have a finance app. So that finance app sits on our mobile phones and we can see to-date, last minute, exactly what's going on with our revenue. And we're updating it even with the full P&L data that also stays up-to-date. It's all possible because all that information travels throughout the same pipe. So now I can build a dashboard on it.

All data traveling through the middleware can be assigned to a system of record. This is important for the guest profiles and cleanliness of that data.

We are building our own CDP (customer data platform) which will become the system of record. And that just means that we have the golden guest profile, and everything gets mirrored from there. Why? Because the CDPs today suck information out of not only your own systems, but many other systems and because of that, the data becomes so much richer. You could set up the system of record to be your PMS or a CRM, or the middleware could do it. The middleware is perfectly capable of being the system of record.

Ira Vouk

This is fascinating. Now you have a middleware that is essentially "the head" and then you have other systems that are connected to this middleware, and then you gather data from all these other systems and you build dashboards on top of this huge pile of data. And that means you can slice and dice the data however you want. So, whoever the stakeholder is, they would have their own dashboard, for example, one for the finance department, one for the revenue management department, one for the housekeeping, etc. - they would each have their own. Am I understanding correctly?

Michael Levie

You got it.

But I think that you should use "the heart", not "the head" for the middleware because, really, it uses all the veins to pump the blood, which is our data. And the CDP (customer data platform) is "the head". Because we're setting up the CDP as the intelligence piece.

Ira Vouk

I see. And how is it going to look?

Michael Levie

The CDP is basically a more contemporary kind of a CRM. And what CDP does differently than a CRM is the following. CRM gets connected and gets the data delivered from all the systems. And then it processes and refiles it. A CDP basically sucks all the information in from your own systems, but can also obtain information from outside, from third parties, and then it goes through the method of enriching your guest profile. And that is the key to solid digital.

So why Amazon and Google can do predictive thinking and suggestive selling to you is because they have the right data and they have it in volumes on you.

And that is basically what a CDP does. It has so much volume that we know with 97-98% certainty (or even better in some cases) that we are actually communicating with you, with that specific person. Current hotel CRM systems, I would say, are somewhere in the 30% accuracy realm. Why? Because they have the first name, the last name and maybe the email address. And that's where it ends. But if you enrich your guest profiles to a couple of hundred fields and you start to cross-reference them and it becomes a different ballgame, then you can start having a digital conversation with your client.

| Ira Vouk

Basically, you will be collaborating with third-party providers in order to obtain that external information that would enrich the CDP data?

| Michael Levie

So, we have our own data lake and whatever the CDP wants to suck out of there - by all means. But yes, it could also be from a third party. I'm not saying it has to be but it could be. And you know that data is actually relatively cheap. So at times, it makes sense. And we have data analysts that are on top of that and it's quite interesting what they come up with. That has been very enriching.

| Ira Vouk

So, because your middleware is the "heart", if you want to hook up a Revenue Management System or any other tool you don't have yet, you would connect it to the middleware, not the PMS?

| Michael Levie

Yes, they always have to connect to the middleware. They can never connect to the PMS directly.

| Ira Vouk

So you completely bypass the PMS when it comes to integrations?

| Michael Levie

Yes, basically what the middleware does is picks up and delivers packages. These packages all contain data, which in its turn, the middleware can organize and display.

Also speed is important here. It's much faster because the PMS interfaces are bypassed and all data is centered around the guest and not the room, like in PMS.

| Ira Vouk

This is a whole different world.

| Michael Levie

It is. We do this differently because we are obsessed with these types of processes, with understanding them and setting them up differently.

And only now, 15-16 years later, I see in the industry that people are starting to understand the middleware concept and getting out of the dependency on the PMS.

| Ira Vouk

Yes, it's very very interesting to see where this takes us five years from now.

Looking at your story, the main reason citizenM is now what it is and where it is in terms of sophistication and technology adoption is because, from the very beginning, you understood the importance of technology in your organization and you built your entire tech stack from scratch because you weren't satisfied with legacy tools. So from the very beginning, you had an understanding that it would be a better route for you?

| Michael Levie

Yeah, but it is also a very lonely journey. Because a lot of times, solutions that we needed, didn't exist. A lot of times, we had to bring them to life. And sometimes it failed. So it has been a long journey but it is very gratifying to see that today, companies that need to switch to digital efficiency, understand that their tech architecture is the main piece and that they need to switch. And that is interesting if you see what we're capable of doing already, and we are ahead of the curve.

| Ira Vouk

What advice would you give to other hotel companies out there who are starting their tech innovation journey?

| Michael Levie

I think that today, if you have a legacy set up, just figure out what it is that you want to be. And then one day switch off the old system and switch on the new one because otherwise you do not make the true transformation. And that's where people's thinking stops. They want to do it little by little. But there is no easy way *to fix it. <u>The legacy component, PMS, needs to be brought back to its original inventory and administrative functions only and leave connectivity to platforms and middleware</u>. There's nothing else you can do.*

| **Ira Vouk**

I will print it out and frame it.

The move towards open API

Historically, the legacy PMS systems were built on the assumption that the PMS needs to have an endless list of features. One large customer asked for a custom feature - they built it. Another customer asked for something that they considered a gap in the functionality for their specific use case - that was added to the list, too. As a result, they have developed into these "heavy" bulky solutions

As Wouter Geerts notes in one of the Skift reports, *"Over many years, PMSs like Oracle OPERA, Protel, and Guestline have built up a huge array of features they can offer their hotel clients."*[24]

In the past few years, however, we have started to see the rise of integration-heavy PMSs, like Mews[25] or Apaleo[26], the trend that Michael Levie calls "platform plumbing" and what Jordan Hollander of Hotel Tech Report calls "platformification".

"Apaleo is the Open Hotel Management Platform. Their API-based cloud technologies help hospitality companies manage their multiple properties, connect their desired apps, and run their daily operations in entirely new ways. Apaleo is different from traditional PMS solutions because it was built on their API-first philosophy. This creates a different type of tech, where integrations that are free, fast, and scalable are at its core and tie perfectly to their marketplace of cloud-based apps."[27]

So companies like Apaleo have the plumbing, the connection, and an app store with anything and everything that you can add to your stack. You can even download APIs if you want to build something on top of it yourself. And it's all open source, so it is a very different type of thinking from the legacy mindset. But those are very young companies that are still developing.

From the same Skift report, *"This is not to say that players like Oracle and Protel have few integrations, they have probably the most extensive lists of integrations built up over many years, but their emphasis is on offering both in-house and integrated solutions. With the rise of cloud technology and the ability to have better and faster*

---

[24]Skift: The Hotel Property Management Systems Landscape 2020 (Jan 2020): https://research.skift.com/report/the-hotel-property-management-systems-landscape-2020/

[25]Mews: Property Management System: https://www.mews.com/en

[26]Apaleo: API-first Technology for Hospitality Companies: https://apaleo.com/

[27]Hotel Tech Report: Apaleo PMS: https://hoteltechreport.com/operations/property-management-systems/apaleo-pms

integrations, younger players like Mews and Apaleo are instead focusing increasingly on offering only the core functionalities of the PMS as in-house features, while spending a lot of time and effort in optimizing integrations with third-party providers, often in the form of marketplaces."

So as we know, there are about 1000 PMSs out there. And of course, there are older market share leaders who have built this incredible amount of functionality. But what we are currently observing is a shift toward having a stripped-down version of a PMS with only the functionality needed for check-in/check-out, billing, etc., with open APIs for vendors that can be connected to them to achieve flexibility in building a customized solution for the specific company. That is in contrast with having this giant with features that you don't use, which is incredibly expensive and difficult to operate and to update.

Jordan Hollander (Co-founder and CEO of Hotel Tech Report) agrees with me but also adds an important aspect about the enterprise use case (which explains why companies like citizenM and Sonder have to essentially build out there own stack):

Absolutely. I think the open API infrastructure works at the small business level where you can integrate apps together. But once you get to a certain level of enterprise scale, there's a budget to invest in customization and building out more specialized workflows for specific business needs that might go beyond the existing software players.

So then we hear everyday that Sonder is going out to messaging companies and upsell companies asking for specialized requirements and those software companies can't possibly build something custom for Sonder who has this one use case and maybe there's four other Sonders in the world. So they'll probably end up building some sort of functionality themselves and they might try to pull some other functionality from some of these players that already exist so they don't need to maintain that code base.

I think you're right. Ultimately, it mirrors what we see in all enterprise software. For example, we all use Slack and it doesn't matter whether you're at JP Morgan or at Hotel Tech Report or you are at a smaller startup level. Ultimately, you're going to be using Slack to communicate with teammates. Software is starting to look much more like it looks in your personal life - tools that you use outside work, like Tiktok and Snapchat, which are easy to use, to understand and learn.

And so I think in the hospitality business, we have these very clunky, very feature heavy, often feature bloated systems and we realize that there's not a ton of need for a lot of this stuff anymore and it was more of some key customer having an idea for something they wanted to do special and they went ahead and built it for them and added it to the extensive list of their features.

Hapi[28] seems to be doing some interesting things as well. Hapi is a platform for fast and cost-effective connectivity between technology systems. It was named Best Hotel Marketplace & Integrator by Hotel Tech Report in Jan 2021.[29]

Michael Blake (HTNG) also provided his perspective on this topic:

It's interesting to see what some of these new API fabrics are becoming. Even Opera has re-architected to get to a lighter messaging and faster kind of thing. So it'll be interesting to see how this plays out. I am fascinated by the whole PMS marketplace and who comes in bold and I watch them wash two years later. So it'll be interesting to see as more of these come out. But hey, let them run. Because eventually they drop a shoe and the industry is like, "Oh yeah, I could use that."

So yes, the good news is that a few companies are making progress in the right direction.

The industry is adopting open APIs to make connecting systems easier and facilitate data transfer, which will further benefit connectivity and ultimately, innovation.

However, there's a caveat. While the technical functionality and the platform may already exist, our business standards and agreements are still conservative in many ways and prevent those open connections from happening. Updated business standards are needed to ensure that hotel companies have the contractual right to license and integrate systems as they see fit, even where competing vendors are involved, and using whatever means of integration are available and appropriate.

Once this process becomes easier to handle, in combination with reduced development costs for applications (which we have already achieved thanks to cloud platforms like AWS or Google) - the tech development will skyrocket.

So to conclude, if a couple of strong PMS vendors (not just any but those that are in the cloud) who own a large market share, are able to design reliable API connections for all (or at least major) necessary use cases in an open source form (an app marketplace approach) - this would solve the PMS dependency problem for the industry. These platforms would then be able to benefit from massive network effects. It would also allow new entrants in the hotel tech market to grow and expand without the existing integration barriers. It would additionally provide huge value to the end users: hotel owners and operators as well as the traveler. They would benefit from the ability to select the vendor of their choice instead of being limited by the existing number of integrations or having to switch to another PMS provider because the current one doesn't have that one connection that is needed for their operation.

I believe this bright future is ahead of us and it will be here sooner than we think because technology is not planning to stop evolving.

---

[28] Hapi Cloud: Data Streaming & Integration for Travel & Hospitality: https://www.hapicloud.io/

[29] Hapi Named Best Hotel Marketplace & Integrator by Hotel Tech Report (January 2021): https://www.hospitalitynet.org/news/4102449.html

DATA STANDARDIZATION

In the previous chapter, we spoke a lot about API standards. This chapter is devoted to a slightly different aspect - standardization of the data itself, naming conventions, formulas for calculations of various metrics, and interpretation of data fields.

To illustrate the difference: API standards may define, for example, what fields need to be transmitted from a PMS to a CRM, how the message should be structured, and how to call the fields that carry that information (i.e. "lastname" or "last_name" or "surname" or what have you).

But here we will be talking about how we code and manage data internally, so things like:

- Whether we all understand in the same way what CPOR means (cost per occupied room) and how it's calculated
- What goes into the formula of occupancy (for example, do you include out-of-order rooms and comps, or do you exclude them)
- How we split our segments and what names we use for them
- Whether a "Standard room type" means the same thing for different companies

and the list goes on...

"Why is this so important?" you ask.

1. First of all, for the purpose of **benchmarking**. It is crucial for businesses (hotel businesses in our case) to be able to measure their performance against the market or a subset of properties in it, in order to assess the effectiveness of their operations. Without standardized data norms, it becomes very difficult to achieve.

2. Second, even within the same company, different properties in the portfolio may be using different interpretations of various fields and different naming conventions, which makes it impossible to **aggregate data** for a group of properties or compare how hotels perform in different regions, different classes, or under different DORM's who manage them. So instead of apples to apples you end up comparing apples to kangaroos.

3. And last but not least. As technology evolves and we enter the digital age where data becomes the center of our universe, and **machines start to take over our decision-making process**, data standards and norms become more and more critical.

Uniform System of Accounts

Let me start from the good news. At least we have USALI! God bless the hearts of those people who put that thing together, so at least we all agree on how to pay our taxes... at least in the US.

USALI (Uniform System of Accounts for the Lodging Industry) was first published in 1926. The primary purpose of this publication is to offer operating statements formatted to provide hotel owners, managers and other interested parties with operational information pertinent to the lodging industry. In 2018, HFTP acquired the copyright to the USALI. which was previously owned by the Hotel Association of New York City. Revisions to the USALI are overseen by the Financial Management Committee (FMC) of the American Hotel & Lodging Association (AHLA), a majority of which are also HFTP members.[30]

Jan Freitag (National Director at CoStar[31] Group, which owns STR[32]) also shares my excitement about this valuable publication:

Let me start by saying that in the United States we are so, so, so, so fortunate that we have this Uniform System of Accounts for the US Lodging Industry. That is extremely valuable because what you call revenue and what I call revenue is very, very clearly defined. It goes into excruciating detail as it should. Luckily, that's not my job, but we have somebody from STR who is on the committee that writes USALI. It doesn't exist in a lot of other industries. But the good news is that for global brands, when they get their revenues from other non-US hotels, they often try to break it into USALI for uniformity.

So, the good news is that in the US, we already have a leg up to a lot of other industries. Now when I get asked from peers in other industries (for example multi-family housing) to do benchmarking and I ask them, "Well, what's revenue?" And they're, "Well, it depends..." And so I say, "Well, then we can't talk because it can't depend." You have to be very clear and if you don't have this playbook, then it's really, really hard to start benchmarking. So we have that in our industry in the US, which is great.

However, USALI doesn't solve all our problems unfortunately. Lack of standardization is still a huge issue in our industry. While we have some common understanding of some things like "revenue" (at least in the US), this is not the case when it comes to many other things. For example, segments, room types, market codes, rate plans, etc. are currently free text fields in many systems with every hotel company having their own naming convention (if any).

And that pertains to many different things that prevent us from scaling our benchmarking solutions globally and to all types of properties, not just the US and not just branded hotels that are more normalized in terms of standardization of certain data points across the whole portfolio of properties. There are still so many things that are just randomly named by different hotels and companies without any uniform guidelines.

---

[30]Uniform System of Accounts for the Lodging Industry (USALI): https://www.hftp.org/hospitality_resources/usali_guide/

[31]CoStar: Provider of Commercial Real Estate Data: https://www.costar.com/

[32]STR: Hospitality Data, Analytics & Insights: https://str.com/

As always, when digging deep into issues that bother me, I turn to people who are wiser and more knowledgeable. So I called Mylene Young, Co-founder and Principal of Son Hospitality Consulting who has nearly 3 decades of industry experience, including working with large brands and hotel companies (like Hilton, Marriott and Sonesta). Mylene was kind enough to share her vision with me:

When the Uniform System of Accounts for the Lodging Industry created the green book for all lodging in North America, the idea was that when you post something in your system, you post it a certain way on the P&L or the income statement and it should look the same for all companies, and then for tax purposes your reports should look exactly the same way.

And then they created an edition for standardized market segmentation in North America (their 11th Edition in 2014[33]). I think that was a good start because at least they had something. The more sophisticated hotelier will take on this and say, "It makes a lot of sense." But it hasn't been widely adopted. I think we have started doing that but we have not done it universally yet.

Again, it's about education and raising awareness. Currently, different hotel companies invent their own names for everything. This should not happen when we have 20 different names for one thing. So back to my accounting example, where they tell you what should be posted where and how and where you have to follow some kind of standardized way of doing your accounting - we have to do the same for the rest of our data.

Right now, for example, when you subscribe for Travelclick products, for their forward-looking competitive data - they have their own way of segmenting. So you could be a hotel that has a completely different segmentation, so that product is useless for you because you can't benchmark against it.

So there's definitely a need for standardization. There is a lot of work to be done from that perspective and I think that at least revenue management system vendors and PMS vendors should start agreeing on those naming conventions.

The importance of being able to benchmark and compare data fields between different properties or groups of companies cannot be overstated, as this is currently a substantial challenge for all hospitality companies. But how do we solve this problem to achieve data consistency?

As Tim Webb (University of Delaware, Hospitality Business Management) points out:

On the one hand, you could force a standardization naming convention that all firms would adopt. In this case, the hotel companies are limited in their flexibility. On the other hand, you could allow them to categorize how they want and then force them to reassign into predetermined groupings that function for the RMS or other solutions. I'm not sure which approach would be more adequate but this is a topic that needs to be considered and addressed across the industry.

---

[33]HFTP: USALI, 11TH Revised Edition: https://www.hftp.org/hospitality⊠resources/usali⊠guide/usali⊠ access/

Application of Machine Learning for data standardization

It is obvious that as we move into the new world full of data, we need some sort of dictionary to understand how to read the data, how to interpret it, how different data points are mapped between different systems, etc.

I agree with others that this topic is definitely critical and requires an organized effort by the whole industry. But I believe there could be another way that doesn't require forcing companies to abide by strict standards that limit their flexibility. I truly believe this is where Artificial Intelligence can help us, as this is one of those perfect use cases for it.

Unfortunately, I can't take any credit for this idea. Jan Freitag (CoStar / STR) suggested that solution and I absolutely loved it. I believe there is a lot of potential to make it happen as our technology evolves, computing power increases and AI/ML algorithms develop further. Here's how Jan phrased it:

The light at the end of the tunnel is just a huge data dictionary that connects the dots: this is what Marriot calls this, which is actually what Hilton calls that, which is what Hyatt calls that.

It's not pretty. And it's unfortunately going to be a long time before things get actually standardized. Because for a variety of reasons, people feel that their rate code is the right code.

That said, it is not impossible. As computing power increases, you can make a lot of assumptions about certain things that are likely the same. For example, when it comes to room types, there are no standards because every hotel is a little different. But you can probably come out with the top five buckets and group 90% of rooms in those buckets. You can have an algorithm read the description and say, "This looks and feels very much like this," and put it together.

So I hope that technology will be a helper in this question of standardization.

I really like the idea of this type of analysis which is where machine learning can be applied to analyze data and assign/tag/group them in major buckets to achieve standardization. I believe it's impossible to expect all hospitality companies to abide by strict and limiting data groupings or naming conventions, and so this new AI approach allows us to solve this problem without forcing everyone to squeeze their square pegs into one perfectly round hole, which is not going to happen.

Our new BI tools are getting better at ingesting data from different sources (not just PMS) and standardizing them. So I think business intelligence is one of the areas where data will start to become more standardized. It's on those players to give hoteliers the ability to normalize and organize those data points across different databases, tools, and companies.

Data is the new king

Data standards and norms become even more critical as technology evolves and we enter the digital age where data becomes the center of our universe, and machines start to take over our decision-making process.

Some companies are starting to understand the value of mining data (we don't have to go too far, take my favorite examples for Sonder or citizenM). And with that awareness comes a lot of opportunities - opportunities for more optimal and timely decision-making, for increased profits, additional revenue streams, improved customer service, and the list goes on.

Once companies start understanding how much value is locked up in this data that is just sitting there unused right now, they will start realizing how to monetize it and use it effectively.

However, it is clear at this point that the existing data infrastructure is not ready for the exponential growth of the hotel tech. There are still significant challenges today with the information infrastructure in our industry, especially considering that we're expecting the data volumes to increase a hundredfold, if not more. There is really currently no information architecture standard out there.

For example, when it comes to STR and how they gather data from hotels, it's clearly easier for a branded hotel to share this data because it's all centralized (through CRS). So the franchise normally collects the data and sends it to STR in one batch. But for individual independent properties, what is the process? Sadly, it's still mostly manual.

Jan Freitag:

We connect to large and some small PMSs but some data comes to us via the website, you know, because it's only three numbers. It can be done through the night audit process. But yes, it's hard. It's a lot easier to say, "We connected into a system and transferred it," versus saying, "Hey, have your night auditor type it in."

As we move into the new, digital world of data, the industry needs to solve the problem of proper real-time data sharing in order to be able to take advantage of all the opportunities that the new age presents.

If we have a dictionary and the right infrastructure, then we can create massive amounts of residual value out of all this data by being able to organize insanely huge amounts of data and business models. We can do things to optimize guest experience along the whole reservation journey, including pre-booking, booking, pre-stay, stay, post-stay, and coming back to our properties. We can optimize hotel pricing on the fly by digesting numerous data points from different sources in real time. Our systems would be so much more state-based and real-time aware, and our products and services would naturally become more efficient and of higher quality.

Based on the above, information brokerage is one of the most significant opportunities in the hotel tech space right now. This would allow us to achieve homogeneity of information across multiple platforms and take the industry to the next level.

What needs to (and I believe, will) happen is more information sharing among companies, organizations and software vendors. The more open a system, the more innovation will be possible as others discover the value of information and build applications around it. There's a huge opportunity in open data sharing.

Of course, this is only possible with presumed security and clearly defined rules about permissions for data access. The company that figures it out will become the next industry leader. And we will talk about this in more detail in Part 3 of this book. There are some solutions available on the market that can help us solve this problem. However, a lot still needs to happen in terms of regulation and standardization in order for us to get there.

LOVE-HATE RELATIONSHIPS WITH OTAS

- Relationship status?

- It's complicated...

An OTA is an acronym for Online Travel Agency and refers to a travel agency whose primary presence is on digital channels, such as a website or a mobile app, where consumers can research and book travel on their own without assistance from a traditional agent.

Hotel Tech Report recently published The Complete Guide to Online Travel Agencies in 2021[34] that lists all major players on the OTA arena and their affiliates.

For many years, hoteliers have been dependent on OTAs to drive business to their properties. OTAs have become a necessary evil. Regardless of the property type (branded or independent), being listed on all major online travel websites is a must these days. Some hotels rely entirely on OTAs to drive their bookings without even having a booking engine of their own. That channel provides a steady source of hotel bookings without much effort for the hotelier, however that business comes with a price - hefty commissions, all the way up to 25%.

According to the Lodging Magazine,[35] commissions are often a hotel's second largest expense after labor. The result is that nearly every hotelier dreams of shifting their business to direct channels while remaining diligent in providing inventory to Booking.com, Expedia and the like, because right now they don't have a choice. That's why Jordan Hollander at Hotel Tech Report refers to the relationship between travel industry suppliers and online travel agencies (OTAs) as "frenemies".[36]

Online Travel Agencies gained their strength in the early 2000's riding the wave of increasing internet penetration in the home.

Currently, there are three major holding groups of OTAs and related travel sites, controlling 95% of the market:

Booking Holdings - the company started as Priceline, which acquired Booking.com in 2005 and now owns Agoda, Kayak, Cheapflights, Rentalcars.com, Momondo, OpenTable, among others.

Expedia Group - started as a division of Microsoft in 1996 and was spun off in 1999 into a public company, and also owns Hotels.com, Hotwire.com, Orbitz, Travelocity, Trivago, Wotif, Venere.com and Vrbo.

---

[34]Hotel Tech Report: The Complete Guide to Online Travel Agencies in 2021 (August 2021): https://hoteltechreport.com/news/online-travel-agencies

[35]Lodging Magazine: Paying the Intermediaries: An Analysis of Hotel Commissions (May 2017): https://lodgingmagazine.com/paying-the-intermediaries-an-analysis-of-hotel-commissions/

[36]Hotel Tech Report: The Evolution of OTAs in the Hotel Industry (May 2021): https://hoteltechreport.com/news/otas-problems

Ctrip - a Chinese multinational online travel company founded in 1999 that provides services including accommodation reservation, transportation ticketing, packaged tours, and corporate travel management. It owns and operates Trip.com, Skyscanner, Qunar, and Ctrip, all of which are online travel agencies.

And last but not least, the newest player:

Airbnb - a company founded in 2008 that operates an online marketplace for lodging, mainly homestays and tourism activities, and is now gaining traction in the hotel sector. Its acquisition of Hotel Tonight in 2018 accelerated its expansion into hotel supply and its ongoing investments in Experiences support its stated ambition to compete globally as an OTA.

Conflict of interest

So, while the existence of OTAs make consumers' lives more comfortable (there is a lot of good that comes out of it from the customer experience perspective), that's not the case with hotels. Selling inventory through that channel can be detrimental to hotels' profitability and not just because of the hefty commissions. There's much more to it.

Here is a brief explanation of conflict of interest between Online Travel Agencies and hotels and why it leads to long-term negative effects for asset owners and operators.

In simple language, the conflict lies mainly in the difference between how OTAs and hotels make their money.

1. First and foremost, there is the obvious one. OTAs are not interested in helping hotels become more profitable. Hotels measure their profitability based on the Net rate (exclusive of distribution expenses), which goes to the bottom line. OTAs charge their commission on the top line, the Sell rate. The more business is shifted away from commissionable OTA channels to direct – the more money goes to the bottom line.

2. Hotels have limited capacity, so the highest potential in growing revenue lies in the growth of the ADR. OTAs don't have such limited capacity (one hotel sells out - they send their customers to the one next door). OTAs thrive on volume, so therefore they're not interested in helping hotels maximize their ADR through increased prices, even when demand is strong. Their goal is the cumulative growth of bookings for the region, driven through their channels. That's why OTAs are all about promotions, promotions and... promotions! Making travel enticing and affordable (not necessarily profitable for the hotelier) with the ultimate goal of increasing volume.

3. OTAs don't exactly care whether those customers go to you or your competitor, as long as the reservation is booked on their website and their commission is paid. They have their own competitors, which include hotels' direct non-commissionable channels. They're very well versed in taking business away from those channels, through sophisticated marketing campaigns.

4. OTAs have been known to push hotels to run exclusive deals on their websites, fully aware that this contradicts the concept of optimal revenue management and negatively affects hotels' profit levels. They do know that this teaches customers to look for best deals on their website and not the hotel's direct channel. They show hotels how much money the campaign generated but they don't say how much of that is displaced business from less expensive channels that would have brought higher ADR and thus more profit. All this ultimately drives profit down. And what's even worse is that it has a long-term effect because it takes months and sometimes years for hotels to earn that customer loyalty back.

5. OTAs often undercut hotels' prices causing parity issues. Because OTAs' main goal is to convert customers, they sometimes resort to actions like reducing their commissions to offer a lower rate and thus capture a booking that may have otherwise gone directly to a hotel, which is pure breach of parity agreements and is often hard to catch due to the complex distribution ecosystem.

If you're old enough, you may recall the days when OTAs dictated the prices at which hotels sold their rooms allocated to them. Those times are long gone, but based on what we discussed above, can we conclude that we are still faced with OTAs' attempts to control the market for their benefit through the tools they offer to hoteliers? I will let each reader decide for themselves.

As Francis Davidson of Sonder put it, "*OTAs are there to match buyer and seller and to optimize their transactions. So, to improve the operations and profitability of hotels and the guest experience of hotels - it's not the business they're in.*"

Nevertheless, the industry has become so dependent on that booking channel that it wouldn't even occur to anyone to close off inventory on any major OTA because the hoteliers know: it will hurt like having an arm chopped off. Remember the big battle[37] between Choice Hotels and Expedia back in 2009 when all Choice branded properties were removed from all Expedia affiliated websites for weeks? I was representing a Choice franchisee at that time. Oh boy, did it hurt! As always, when parents are fighting, kids are the ones suffering the most.

As travel industry analyst Henry Harteveldt once said, "*Expedia wants to play God and tends to think too much of itself and not enough of its partners.*"[38]

Why are OTAs so powerful?

It's becoming increasingly difficult for hotel companies to compete with those OTA giants, even for brands (franchisors) that for the most part don't own any brick and mortar assets and who, just like OTAs, make their money out of thin air.

---

[37]Breaking Travel News: Choice Hotels and Expedia: We've Seen this Movie Before (October 2009): https://www.breakingtravelnews.com/focus/article/choice-hotels-and-expedia-weve-seen-this-movie-before/

[38]Travelweekly: Expedia drops Choice amid feud (Nov 2009): https://www.travelweekly.com/Travel-News/Online-Travel/Expedia-drops-Choice-amid-feud

Look at the graph below from a 2020 Skift research report:[39]

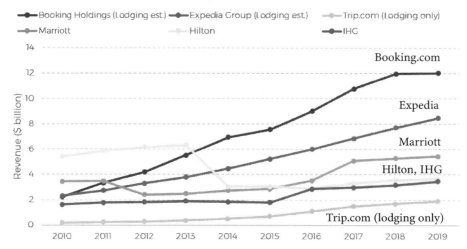

Source: Skift Research from company filings and own estimates

The main reason? OTAs have ridiculous marketing budgets. From the same Skift report:

Source: Skift Research from company filings and own estimates

---

[39]Skift: Hotel Distribution 2020 Part I: The Channel Mix (Nov 2020): https://research.skift.com/report/hotel-distribution-2020-part-i-the-channel-mix/

As seen on that graph, together, top 3 OTAs spent over $14 billion on sales and marketing in 2019.

So I did my research and discovered that $14 billion is more than the annual government budget of the country of Panama, or Latvia... or 140 other countries![40] Just think about it!

In comparison, Marriott, the largest hotel chain by far, spends around $1 billion annually on sales and marketing, a lot of it focused on its direct booking and loyalty campaigns.

So, at this point, it's obvious that there are no hotel companies that would be strong enough to change the dynamics of this relationship or lessen the dependency of hoteliers on the OTA channels. Clearly, it has to be another giant.

And interestingly, there is one candidate...

How does Google fit in the picture?

Google moved into the hotel metasearch space in 2010 when it started showing sponsored hotel prices in Google Maps.

With the merging of Hotel Ads platform into the broader Google Ads platform in 2018, small players and hoteliers were able to manage their ad spend and bidding more easily.

What we have as a result is Google now being the largest metasearch player in our space.

For reference: **a metasearch engine** (or search aggregator) is an online information retrieval tool that uses the data of multiple web search engines to produce its own results. Metasearch engines take input from a user (for example, "hotels in Los Angeles for tonight") and immediately queries search engines (a bunch of travel websites, including OTAs) for results, using those search parameters. Sufficient data is gathered, ranked, and presented to the user.[41]

This is how it looks, visually:

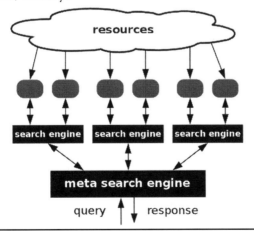

[40]Wikipedia: List of countries by government budget: https://en.wikipedia.org/wiki/List_of_countries_by_government_budget

[41]Wikipedia: Metasearch Engine: https://en.wikipedia.org/wiki/Metasearch_engine

Altexsoft team put together a nice overview of the existing metasearch engines:[42]

METASEARCH ENGINES OVERVIEW

	Customer reach	Industry	Cost model	Connectivity options	Direct booking
Google Hotel Ads	Unavailable	Hotels	CPC, CPA, PPS	Through connectivity partner or via APIs	✓
TripAdvisor	Almost 500 million active monthly users	Hotels, restaurants, attractions	CPC, CPA, PPS	Through connectivity partner	✓
Trivago	More than 120 million monthly users	Hotels	CPC, CPA	Through connectivity partner or via APIs	✓
Kayak	About 15 million visits monthly	Flights, hotels, car rentals	CPC, CPA, CPI	Through connectivity partner	✗
HotelsCombined	About 17 million monthly users	Flights, hotels, car rentals	CPC	Through connectivity partner	✗
Skyscanner	More than 100 million monthly users	Flights, hotels, car rentals	CPC, CPA	Unavailable	✓

altexsoft
software r&d engineering

Note that this only includes Google Hotel Ads, but as we know, Google also has representation in all other travel and hospitality segments.

As you see, metasearch works with a number of different models.

CPC (cost-per-click), which is most common, where hotels and OTAs bid a per-set amount on specified search terms. The bid amount, together with other factors like the room rate, will determine the ranking order on the results page. Hotels and OTAs only pay if the consumer clicks on their link.

CPA (cost-per-acquisition), where a hotel or an OTA only pays if a booking is made. All the major metasearch engines offer this alternative.

Now, this is where it becomes interesting… In response to high cancellation rates due to the pandemic, Google has made its commissionable model available to all Hotel Ads customers.

CPS, aka PPS (commission-per-stay or pay-per-stay) is the model where hoteliers and OTAs only pay Google after the stay has actually happened, which essentially resembles a typical commissionable model that travel agencies (including OTAs) have been using for decades.

---

[42]Altexsoft: Metasearch in Hospitality: an Overview of Hotel Search Engines (March 2021): https://www.altexsoft.com/blog/hotel-search-engines/

Today, Google's share in the search engine market is about 92 percent[43], making it an absolute leader, travel sector included. So what we're seeing is that it is (slowly but surely) also becoming our main distribution channel.

If you ask Google, they say[44] they have no plans to become an OTA. What does that really mean? It means they're not (at least not yet) willing to get into handling transactions between the customer (the traveler) and the supplier (the hotel). In fact, Amazon is much more comfortable with that business model because that's essentially how they built their entire business (as a double-sided marketplace[45]), but Google has a different way of monetizing traffic - through ads.

So while Google is not ready to crawl down the reservation funnel, their main goal and the ultimate North Star (when it comes to their hotel vertical search product) is to have "the best place for travelers to make their booking decision".[46] And the way they're planning to achieve that is by having the best, most comprehensive, most up-to-date, and most accurate information about the availability and prices in the market.

With that ambition in mind, Google is actively reaching out to hotel companies asking for direct integration and bypassing OTAs. Currently, not many hotel companies are directly connected to Google's vertical hotel search (we will discuss that product further in a dedicated chapter) so most reservations are still made through OTAs. But as more and more large hotel companies, as well as booking engines that work with independent hotels, get connected directly to Google hotel search, the more the scale will lean towards Google and away from OTAs. Cloudbeds for example recently announced[47] their connectivity with Google. Great move. Many followed.

It won't be long before we start noticing the change. Google has a very strong potential to start helping hoteliers funnel more traffic to direct channels in the very near future. Note (and this is very important) that listing your hotel on Google's hotel vertical search page is FREE. Yes, FREE! Remember, their goal is to have the most comprehensive marketplace and that's the only way they can achieve that. Naturally though, paid options have a preferred placement over free listings, which appear under the "View more options" section. Mirai estimates[48] that free booking links get on average 17% of overall clicks and about 11% of overall sales volumes.

For those who would like to boost visibility and increase conversion, Google offers an option to pay for ads and the commission (CPS) is flexible, which I predict will eventually become part of RMS (Revenue Management Systems) optimization decisions.

[43]Statcounter: Search Engine Market Share Worldwide: https://gs.statcounter.com/search-engine-market-share

[44]PhocusWire: Q&A with Google's Richard Holden (May 2018): https://www.phocuswire.com/Richard-Holden-Google-Phocuswright-Europe-2018

[45]Wikipedia: Two-sided market: https://en.wikipedia.org/wiki/Two-sided_market

[46]From a conversation with a Google Travel product manager who requested to remain anonymous, at a recent industry event.

[47]Cloudbeds: Google just changed the game. Cloudbeds gives you access: https://www.cloudbeds.com/google-hotel-search/

[48]Mirai: Google free booking links impact; time for the numbers (June 2021): https://www.mirai.com/blog/google-free-booking-links-impact-time-for-the-numbers/

So eventually Google will become the ultimate travel decision-making platform, and nobody will be able to compete. Google will own metasearch, because they own the search, period. Other metasearch engines like Tripadvisor and Trivago still rely on search traffic coming through Google.

So, if I'm a hotelier, should I embrace Google and list my property on their website to book directly? Hell, yes! Here's why:

1. First of all, again, organic listing on Google Hotels is free. So if you have to choose between "free" and what OTAs ask for (which is "around 20% of your top-line revenue, plus your second child")... hmmm, let me think... what would you pick?

    By the way, Google swears they will never start charging for those organic listings.[49] Their perspective is: let's get all hotels in the world on our platform "and then we'll figure out how to monetize that".

2. Google won't mind if you have different rates on different channels, since this is essentially what the business model of a Metasearch Engine depends on (otherwise the consumer has no reason to use it). Though some investigations show that Google does score the quality of direct ARI feeds and may potentially block your free listing if your rates or availability are really out of whack. We will talk about rate parity in more detail further in this chapter.

3. Third, you can be flexible with the amount of commission you pay, depending on your needs. If demand is high and you can fill all your rooms through direct channels without any help - by all means, don't allocate any budget to the ads, just use that organic free search funnel. During need dates - crank up the CPS and see the heads magically appear in your beds. Even in the latter scenario, you possibly won't have to pay as much as what you're currently giving away to the OTA giants.

Considering the above, theoretically that model (Google as the main distribution channel) might be much more optimal for hotels that may drive a higher return on investment. Furthermore, **we also need to start considering how we can bring the revenue management discipline and the marketing discipline together as Hotel Ads become a part of our revenue and profit optimization strategy** in the same way revenue managers have been overseeing OTA distribution for the last two decades. Sorry, DORMs, you now have another thing on your plate.

Rate Parity

When we're talking about OTAs, we can't ignore the topic of rate parity. This discussion has also been around for a while as it is pretty controversial, like many things in our industry. And like many things in our industry, the controversy is caused by the fragmentation of the market.

---

[49]From a fireside chat with a Google Travel representative who requested to remain anonymous, at BookDirect Summit organized by TripTease in San Diego, CA in October 2021.

Typical agreements that hotels have with online travel agencies in the US call for rate parity across all distribution channels. This means that if a hotel lists a certain rate on its website for a room on a given night, that same room type and rate has to be available to the public on partner OTAs. Same goes for franchise agreements.

The concept of Rate Parity was invented by hospitality companies whose business model revolves around generating revenues through commissions, margins or fees on hotel bookings, without actually owning or operating the assets (like OTAs, franchisors, etc.). This prevents hotels from limiting how many rooms they can sell through those channels and from offering a price that is higher than elsewhere. What is interesting is that the inventors themselves often break the parity agreements in their favor through sophisticated mechanisms. OTAs often undercut hotels' prices causing parity issues by reducing their commissions to offer a lower rate. Both the OTAs and major hotel brands complicated the issue even further when they began offering out-of-parity, member-only rates, hidden behind an easily obtained loyalty program password.

The good news is that things are gradually changing.

Passed in July 2015 by the National Assembly, France's new Macron Law is designed to eliminate barriers to free competition in the lodging industry, as well as implement reforms across the board. It explicitly bans rate parity clauses, granting hotels the right to price rooms as they please, including below the rates given to distribution partners. In response, both Expedia and Booking.com eliminated the offending parity clauses in contracts with hotels throughout Europe.

So as a result, in some countries, rate parity clauses are strictly prohibited (such as France, Austria, Italy, and Belgium), in some - partially prohibited (Germany and Sweden), and in others they are still unregulated (like the US and Latin America).

While rate parity in itself does not benefit hotel operations financially, as the OTAs and franchisors grew in size and strength, hoteliers became dependent on them and began complying with the parity clauses in fear of losing a big chunk of their bookings as a form of punishment for those parity violations.

As we discussed earlier, it is definitely unhealthy for hotel operators to be dependent on those players so much that they have to operate in a manner that results in profit losses. As part of optimal revenue and profit management, hotels must have full control over how they operate their businesses, including channel management (limiting availability, setting stay restrictions on certain channels or varying prices) based on the profitability of those channels, in order to maximize their (hotels') profits.

Metasearch engines are actively advocating for rate parity clauses and regulations to be disbanded, as their entire business model is based upon different rates being available on different channels. Consumers will only use metasearch engines if they believe that there is a wide range of pricing options out there.

Mylene Young (Son Hospitality Consulting) suggests:

Considering the changes to the once seemingly inevitable laws of rate parity, it is an opportunity for hotels and their revenue managers to take a hard look at their current revenue strategy. What is working at your hotel and what is not? And what are the proactive steps you can take while the rate parity issue plays itself out?

Based on her opinion, a more optimal and, therefore, profitable strategy would involve more aggressive funneling of customers to direct booking channels, better control of hotels' channel management and pricing, focusing on value rather than simple discounting to give consumers a more compelling reason to book direct, implementing loyalty programs and aiming for balanced distribution. It will also include wisely spreading inventory among multiple channels while gradually moving toward consolidation - focusing on the channels that bring you the most distribution and at the best cost.

With that said, even if rate parity clauses are completely banned globally, it doesn't mean hoteliers can (or should) run to their desks and immediately start discriminating against OTAs across the board with higher rates and lower availability.

Unfortunately, hotels still need the OTAs, especially in the periods of weak demand. It's like a drug that the entire industry is hooked on: if you go cold turkey - you will experience painful withdrawal symptoms. Ask Choice franchisees, they know.

Will COVID change the hotel/OTA relationship?

Skift Research analysis[50] shows that the economic crisis in 2008/09 boosted the number of independent hotels joining the major OTA platforms, despite higher commission rates.

The take rate of incremental bookings made through Booking.com in 2009 (i.e. bookings made beyond what was made the previous year) shows a major spike, indicating that many independent hotels joined the platform at a high commission rate.

Will this time be different? Probably not. Looks like OTAs will continue to be a necessary evil for a while. With their marketing budgets, they still remain powerful distribution players.

---

[50]Skift: Hotel Distribution 2020 Part I: The Channel Mix (November 2020): https://research.skift.com/report/hotel-distribution-2020-part-i-the-channel-mix/

PROFIT MANAGEMENT VS REVENUE MANAGEMENT

"Since we don't know how to measure what we want,

we settle for wanting what we know how to measure."

Jeffrey Campbell

This is a very important and controversial topic that has been gaining traction lately, although many (including myself) have been talking about it for a decade or two.

As part of writing this book, I wanted to dive deeper into this subject and conducted thorough research to put this chapter together.

For those of you who are unaware of this issue in our industry, I will sum it up:

- Most hotels still **measure** their performance using top-line room revenue, not profit, for various reasons that will be explained further
- Many hospitality companies don't know how to **aggregate** profit-oriented metrics across different properties in their portfolio
- Majority of the industry doesn't have a way to **benchmark** the profit of different properties against each other
- And more importantly, almost no one knows how to properly **maximize** profit

It goes without saying that measuring profit levels is an extremely important part of managing a hotel, like any other business. Profitability impacts whether a company can secure financing from a bank, attract investors to fund its operations and grow. It's very hard to remain in business without turning a profit.

Even though it is crucial for any business to be aware of its profitability levels, the hospitality industry has been largely concentrated only on top-line revenue measurements, mainly through RevPAR (Revenue Per Available Room) being a de facto metric, which doesn't allow to assess profit levels.

Unfortunately, from the very beginning, the revenue management discipline didn't evolve in the right direction when it comes to the aspect of profit maximization. In the 1990s, when revenue management came on the scene, hoteliers started thinking about managing top-line revenue, which (wrongly) assumed direct correlation between top line and bottom line. So for decades, the whole industry has been measuring and maximizing a wrong metric - that is, RevPAR.

Breaking news: **top-line room revenue DOES NOT always correlate with profit.** There are situations when RevPAR and profit may actually be moving in **opposite directions.**

Let's shed some light on that subject. There was research conducted on this topic in 2016 by a group of hospitality professors, the results were published in the Journal of

Revenue and Pricing Management.[51] As part of the research, 1000 lodging properties were examined over a period of 6 years on the basis of annual data, as STR collects HOST data once a year.

Here are some excerpts from that paper:

"Since its early days, the practice of optimizing performance in the airline industry, and later in the lodging industry was centered on yield and revenues. Although most hotels' ultimate goal was always to maximize profits, for various reasons, the employed management science methods of optimization were and for the most part still are, mostly revenue oriented.

The main reason was that optimization of revenues (that is, the mathematical maximization calculations) is considerably less complicated than optimization of net contribution (price minus the incremental cost) or profits. The approach of revenue maximization was justified on the basis of the assumption that, when revenues are optimized, profits follow suit and are sufficiently close to being maximal. But it's not always the case."

"Despite its widespread use, both industry practitioners and academics have long questioned the adequacy and reliability of RevPAR as a key metric for benchmarking hotel performance, mainly because it accounts for revenue derived from room rentals only.

RevPAR cannot be used as a measure of financial performance, either to assess the efficiency of operations or to predict market-based performance of the organization."

"Using RevPAR as a proxy for GOPPAR (or other GOP-based measures) as the hotel's performance measure has two related major drawbacks:

- ***Suboptimality***: *If the optimization is RevPAR based (that is, if revenue management controls are set such that the hotel maximizes its revenues or RevPAR), GOPPAR, which more appropriately represents the 'true target function' of hotel owners and investors, <u>is not necessarily optimized</u>.*

- ***Bidirectionality***: *Using RevPAR to assess the impact of setting certain levels of controls (such as the revenue management decisions on room rates and the allocation of rooms to rate levels and to distribution channels) might be a misleading practice... <u>The two performance measures (RevPAR and GOPPAR) might be moving in opposite directions. That is, within certain levels of rates and sold rooms, when RevPAR indicates an improvement, the GOPPAR measure indicates a decline in the hotel's performance.</u>"*

---

[51]"Performance measures for strategic revenue management: RevPAR versus GOPPAR", Zvi Schwartz, Mehmet Altin and Manisha Singal, 2016 Macmillan Publishers Ltd. 1476-6930 Journal of Revenue and Pricing Management 1–19 www.palgrave-journals.com/rpm/

To illustrate the mistake that hoteliers constantly make when using traditional RevPAR as an ultimate indicator for their decision-making, let's look at 2 scenarios (the scenarios are extreme and that is done on purpose, to better illustrate the point I'm trying to make).

Imagine a 100-room hotel.

Scenario 1:
- 100 rooms sold at $10 each
- Revenue = $1000
- RevPAR = $10

Scenario 2:
- 10 rooms sold at $100 each
- Revenue = $1000
- RevPAR = $10

RevPAR is the same in both cases, even though Scenario 2 is clearly much more profitable for the hotel. It is exactly because RevPAR is not the best index for measuring a hotel's actual productivity.

So there's that.

The above referenced academic paper was published in 2016. I released my article Things you didn't know about RevPAR[52] where I explained these drawbacks, back in 2014. But the majority of the industry still uses RevPAR as the major guideline.

Why is that the case? As you may have guessed, just like with many other issues we are facing today, the fragmentation of our industry is at the core of the problem. Conflict of interest among stakeholders (owners vs operators vs franchisors… and let's add OTAs to the pile) doesn't make it easy for the industry to advance in the area of profit optimization.

When it comes to **operators**, Hotel Management Agreements (which are contracts between hotel owners and hotel operators controlling the management of a hotel property) have a performance clause that is based on the top-line revenue and not on bottom-line metrics. In order to manage and maximize profit efficiently, those contracts need to be updated to align objectives around profit.

There's a similar situation with franchise agreements that dictate the relationships between the owner and the **brand**. Royalty fees are charged based on the top-line room revenues. While it is unlikely that this will change, it is important that hotel owners are aware of this and consider it when making strategic decisions that affect profit levels (such as accepting promotions and campaigns initiated by the brand or pricing recommendations from the brand revenue management team). Those recommendations need to be run through a profit analysis on the property level before a decision is made.

OTAs are definitely not interested in maximizing hotel profits either, because they make their money on the top line as well.

---

[52]HospitalityNet: Things you didn't know about RevPAR by Ira Vouk (September 2014): https://www.hospitalitynet.org/opinion/4066863.html

Due to that fragmentation of the ecosystem that we discussed in detail in the previous chapters, nobody except for the owner, wants to maximize profit (meaning the hotel's profit, because brands and OTAs are very good at maximizing theirs).

But the **owners** of the hotels are the ones who are picking up the tab when it comes to costs associated with running their businesses. Those are the people who actually own the assets. Without assets, there wouldn't be any business for other stakeholders (management companies, brands, OTAs, tech vendors, etc). Obviously, most owners care about profit and cash flow and they are interested in maximizing that.

Now, many owners are not even aware of the problem and it's a big issue that I'm trying to address in this chapter.

But there's another, bigger, issue. Even if the owner understands that RevPar is really not the core metric that needs to be tracked and maximized and that their current model is far from optimal - there are currently not a lot of options for them to move away from it. Our processes and tools in the industry are still revolving around RevPAR, and there are no standardization and widely accepted workflows that would make profit management a user friendly task for those who care about profit (which is pretty much the majority of asset owners in the world, with some rare exceptions).

There are two major reasons for that problem:

- **Technology**

Our current reality is that hoteliers are offered a very minimal amount of technical functionality that would make profit maximization and reporting a user-friendly task. Current systems (as well as integrations and data flows between those systems) are limited by only concentrating on the top-line room revenue.

In addition, existing automated revenue management solutions don't account for cost factors and ancillary (non-room) revenues when determining optimal room pricing, while still aiming for the same thing in their algorithms - RevPAR.

We need better tools that would allow the industry as a whole to track or forecast total revenue, manage and optimize expenses, and easily benchmark performance against each other in a standardized manner, for different regions, sizes or types of hotel properties. We need tools that will allow asset owners to maximize profit. That's not much to ask, really.

- **Education**

The reason why we don't have proper technology on the market is because there hasn't been a lot of demand for it. And the key factor here is that there is still not enough awareness in the industry about the drawbacks of RevPAR, about issues with our management agreements and franchise agreements, about which metrics should be tracked and maximized and how to achieve profit maximization through technology.

In addition, not all hotel schools have a profit-oriented approach in their revenue management courses.

84

As John Burns phrased it:

This idea of revenue management going further into profit management is one that we have never successfully addressed yet. We've been talking about this for 20 years but we have made little progress.

The irony is that the difference between revenue and profit is not mysterious. We know exactly the line items that are responsible for that difference. Those line items are very finance focused. So the controller understands them, but they've never been part of the education of a hotel manager (and revenue manager in particular).

Hoteliers don't even realize how much more optimal their operations could be (from the efficiency and profit standpoint) with the right profit-oriented approach. The lack of this understanding also contributes to the problem of different departments working in silos as they don't use the same metrics to assess their performance and often contradict each other in their initiatives:

- **Revenue managers** are still incentivised based on RevPAR. This results in situations when their actions are not aligned with ownership's desire to maximize profit: for example, dropping rates in an effort to drive RevPAR through increased occupancy, which may ultimately hurt the bottom-line performance.

- **Sales departments** currently don't look at profit levels when taking group business. They're also incentivised on the top-line revenue, and profit isn't their focus.

- Same goes for the **marketing departments** when it comes to performance of campaigns and promotions.

We lack tools that will aid different operational departments in understanding what actions to take in their daily activities that will lead to profit maximization, which is the ultimate goal of running a business.

What is changing

On July 30, 2021 (one day before my birthday) I helped facilitate a roundtable discussion[53] that was open to the Cornell's Center for Hospitality Research[54] advisory board members and invited experts who represented various sectors of the hospitality industry. It was a very engaging conversation that aimed to start shifting the industry from talking about why we can't do it (that is, to embrace profit-oriented benchmarking and optimization) to actually implementing it. The summary of that discussion can be found via the link in the footnote.

---

[53]Cornell SC Johnson College of Business: Roundtable Recap: Finding the Balance Between Driving Revenue & Managing Costs by Ira Vouk (August 2021): https://business.cornell.edu/hub/2021/09/15/roundtable-recap-finding-the-balance-between-driving-revenue-managing-costs/

[54]Cornell SC Johnson College of Business: Center for Hospitality Research: https://sha.cornell.edu/faculty-research/centers-institutes/chr/

So the good news is that the conversations are happening and the industry is now finally becoming more and more aware of the limitations of the traditional RevPAR-oriented approach, which drives the profit-oriented initiative. And COVID-19 is to thank for that. Unfortunately, it took a major disruptive force to get us on the right track.

As a result of the pandemic, proper cost control became a matter of survival for many. The industry was also forced to start innovating by developing new sources of revenue, improving efficiencies, while at the same time, it also incurred additional costs related to employee and guest health concerns. Hence, hotel revenue levels and structure, as well as expense levels and structure, have drastically changed for many businesses. This impacts break-even levels to cover interest expenses, debt repayment and a reasonable return to equity holders. So this now drives the need to redesign our approach to running our businesses, tracking our performance and benchmarking, and as a result, reimagine the revenue management discipline.

Whether we like it or not, every single decision revenue managers take on a daily basis has an impact on the bottom line. That dictates the need for the revenue management discipline to not just concentrate on optimizing the room revenue stream, but ultimately on increasing profitability. That's why revenue management has to be the central piece of the profitability puzzle, as it has the power to solve the problem of profit maximization.

Some of you may remember the times when hotels were targeting occupancy in their revenue strategy (that was before "dynamic pricing" became a thing). Then, at the next stage of its evolution, the revenue management discipline started revolving around RevPAR. And now is the time to move on to another level by accepting the drawbacks of the old RevPAR-centric approach and embracing the new profit-oriented paradigm.

Here's how I visualized the evolution of the revenue management discipline (soon to be renamed to something more adequate):

Evolution of Revenue Management

Occupancy » RevPAR » Profit

It is not just about revenue - it's about profit. And it's not just management - it's optimization. **"Revenue and Profit Optimization"** seems to be a good candidate for the new name of the discipline.

I also recently participated in a roundtable organized by STR SHARE Center[55] and RevME (in August 2021) where we discussed opportunities for future research and how the industry and academia can collaborate to help discover better ways for hotels to operate as we recover from the pandemic. Among the topics of our discussion was, of course, revenue and profit maximization. One of the participants (Breffni Noone, Associate Professor at The Pennsylvania State University) mentioned that they are renaming their revenue management course to "Revenue and Profit Optimization" and that's what I'm seeing happening a lot in the industry. We are definitely witnessing a shift in awareness towards a more profit-oriented approach and this is great news, though we still have a long journey ahead of us.

I would like to dig deeper into the subject of profit optimization as I find this topic extremely important for the evolution of the industry. Again, if hotel businesses are not successful, there is no business for everyone else: OTAs, management companies, brands, and technology players.

Disclaimer: the next few sections are quite geeky. If you're not friends with basic accounting principles - feel free to skip to the next chapter, or you'll be bored to tears.

Drawbacks of RevPAR

While the whole industry has been using RevPAR to measure its performance since I was born, it is definitely not a good indicator of profit levels as we now (hopefully) agree. Let me explain what exactly makes RevPAR ~~defective~~ imperfect when it comes to profit targeting.

There are a few very important components missing in RevPAR's formula, which (as mentioned earlier) results in situations when RevPAR and profit may actually go in different directions, which is why it cannot be used as an indicator of profit. More details to follow on that, but first, let's talk about one of the three key financial statements, profit and loss (P&L), that tells the narrative of your business over a specific period of time. For most hoteliers, accounting software generates these automatically.

As discussed in one of the previous chapters, a significant proportion of the hospitality industry in the US follows guidelines laid out in the Uniform System of Accounts for the Lodging Industry (USALI), now in its 11th edition. All USALI-based P&L statements look alike. So that's good news.

Here's the list of line items in a typical P&L statement:

- **Revenues**
  - Rooms

---

[55]STR: SHARE Center: Hospitality Industry Data for Students: https://str.com/training/academic-resources/share-center

- ○ Food
- ○ Beverage
- ○ Other F&B
- ○ Other operated departments revenue
- ○ Miscellaneous income

- **Departmental Expenses**
  - ○ Labor costs (broken out by department)
  - ○ Rooms departmental expenses
  - ○ Food expense
  - ○ Beverage expense
  - ○ Other departmental

- **Undistributed Expenses** (those that are not directly linked to the hotel operation)
  - ○ Administrative & General
  - ○ Information & Telecommunication
  - ○ Marketing expense
  - ○ Utility costs
  - ○ Property Operations & Maintenance
  - ○ Management Fees

- **Gross Operating Profit - GOP** (revenue left after subtracting Departmental and Undistributed expenses)

- **Fixed Expenses** (those that do not vary with number of guests)
  - ○ Non-operating income
  - ○ Rent
  - ○ Property Taxes
  - ○ Insurance
  - ○ Reserve for Capital Replacement

- **NET INCOME** (This is the final bottom-line profit number of a business, after all expenses have been deducted from revenues. From this value, hotels can view their net profit or loss. It is essentially the remaining amount once they've paid for everything that the hotel requires in order to operate. Or, in simpler terms, what the owner takes back.)

Many P&L reports finish with the operating earnings (EBIT) because this item does not include interest expense and income tax expense (items that are generally the responsibility of financial executives).

So, if you're wondering why RevPAR is not the right metric to assess your property's performance… See the very first line item in the Revenue section, "Rooms"? That's the only thing that RevPAR reflects. What is it missing? Everything else. There's the answer.

So while the difference between room revenue and bottom-line profit is relatively clear as it's explained by USALI, where we've been hitting the wall is:

1. How do we use that knowledge to learn how to be more efficient in our operations (to ultimately maximize our profit)?

2. How do we use that knowledge to benchmark our performance against each other?

I will attempt to answer these questions in the following sections.

Maximizing profit instead of maximizing RevPAR

Let's start with the first question. How do we maximize profit? Because *profit = revenues - expenses* (as you're well aware I'm sure), in order to increase profit, we need to aim for increasing our revenues while lowering our costs.

What **revenues**? This one is easy. All of them! Not just the Rooms department.

What **costs**? And this is where it gets tricky.

First of all, there are 2 main types of costs associated with running a hospitality business:

1. **Fixed** (which are not affected by the operations of the property).

2. **Variable** (which vary with occupancy, and this is important because these are the expenses that can be directly affected by the management strategy).

It's clear that in our daily operations (from a position of a revenue manager) there's nothing we can do with fixed costs (hence the name) so we'll leave them alone when talking about profit maximization.

Now, from the aspect of what actions can be taken to increase the bottom line, when it comes to variable expenses, it's important to differentiate between 2 major categories. And the reason why we haven't yet found a good way to build an optimal profit-oriented strategy is because they're not clearly defined by USALI in our P&L statements. They are kind of all over the place.

The two major types of variable expenses that can be affected by the operator and thus improve the bottom line are:

1. **Variable operating costs**

These are all variable expenses that fluctuate with occupancy (or rather, with the number of guests).

In the profit and loss statement (as we see above), two big buckets (Departmental and Undistributed) both fall under non-fixed expenses. I would argue that this division is too generic as it doesn't separate true variable operating costs from fixed operating costs. There are operating costs which hotels incur that don't increase if you sell an extra room. For example, a hotel may always have 1 manager on duty, regardless of the level of occupancy. I'm not suggesting we should change the way we report expenses in our P&L's (the industry has gone through years and years of standardizing those statements and let's just be thankful for what we have). But it would be good to find a reliable way to differentiate between true fixed and true variable expenses, at least approximately.

There is also a metric called CPOR (Cost per Occupied Room) that was created to solve for it. Technically, CPOR is supposed to define expenses that are associated with a guest occupying a room for 1 night, i.e. the difference between an empty or occupied room from the cost standpoint.

The traditional formula of CPOR is the following:

CPOR = Total Rooms Departments Cost / Number of Rooms Sold

However, it doesn't take into account the fact that certain Department Costs may be fixed and at the same time, certain Undistributed expenses may be variable and fluctuate with the number of guests (for example, utility bill). Though there is definitely room for improvement, this is still the best metric we have so far, as it's the most reflective of the variable operating costs I'm describing in this section. The good news is that CPOR is normally a relatively stable value, which doesn't change often.

2. Distribution costs

The second big bucket is expenses related to obtaining a reservation through different channels. And as we know, there is no single channel that is free. Every source of bookings has a cost associated with it, which is reflected in a form of commissions, markups, royalty fees, loyalty fees, GDS fees, marketing expenses, and also discounts.

What makes it cumbersome is that currently, the industry doesn't really have an agreement on how to properly record distribution expenses, which is a big line item (in fact, second largest after labor expense). This is a factor that significantly affects profit levels and should strongly influence your revenue and profit optimization strategy. Some of those are bundled in the "Marketing" category in the P&L (as franchise fees and marketing expenses), some are lumped into the Rooms Departmental Expenses, while others are not recorded anywhere.

Channel commissions and fees may be paid either pre- or post-stay, which defines how they are reflected in the property reports.

- Pre-stay (for example the ones generated by "OTA collect" types of reservations) are not reflected anywhere in property reports as they're deducted before the reservation even hits the PMS.

- Post-stay (OTAs call them "hotel collect" but this also includes any commissionable bookings, be it transient or group). These are (hopefully) recorded because you eventually have to reconcile and pay the agency their share of the booking value. But even if a hotel keeps track of these in their accounting software, this information is not attached to the corresponding reservation in the PMS, which makes it impossible to populate comprehensive analytic reports with this data.

- Then there are also GDS fees, marketing expenses, call center fees, franchise fees. They are recorded in different financial reports, while again, not being attached to the actual reservation in the PMS.

As you can see, currently there is no single source of truth for Distribution expenses. If one wants to understand how much was paid to each channel during a given date range, in most cases, they would need to manually compose that from multiple sources of information and then add extra manipulations (including creative guesstimation) to fill gaps in data. There are BI tools out there that aid hoteliers in gathering that information, but they are not widely adopted. They are still very basic and not truly accurate (which is not their fault but mainly a result of the issues with recording and tracking this data).

So at this point, we should all agree that **this is still a huge gap** in the revenue management (or, revenue and profit optimization) discipline and in our industry in general.

The following paragraph is for real nerds like me. If you're not one of them - feel free to ignore it.

An important note is that currently, the most accurate way of measuring Distribution expenses is on the rate plan level, not on a segment or market code level, as each segment or market code may be composed of different rate plans that have different discounts or markups. However, even rate plans don't carry the information about the actual value of the commission. The most optimal (from the standpoint of wholeness, solidity and consistency of data) approach would be for the reservation to carry this information as an additional field. This would flow from the booking channel, to the CRS or a channel manager, and end up in the hotel's PMS, to then be consumed by the end user (human or analytical software). Though, the PMS part is actually optional if you have a CRS. If you're worried about overburdening the reservation with an extra field, please don't. It currently carries about 400 of them, it won't feel the difference if we throw one more at it.

So, to summarize and visualize what we just spoke about - here are the critical components that are not reflected in RevPAR but are important from the profit maximization standpoint, and should dictate the operating strategy of a hotel property:

One important note here (it's common sense but I thought I should mention for clarity): what you're looking at above, is not the formula of profit. It simply aims to show the elements over which property managers (and revenue/profit managers in particular) have influence in their daily practice and what elements can be optimized in order to achieve profitability.

Formulas of profit metrics (GOP, Net Income, EBIT, EBITDA) can be found in financial literature, and that is outside of the topic of this chapter, which is already geeky enough.

And another note: introducing new metrics and ways to measure profitability will not reduce the importance of RevPAR in the industry because currently, it's still the only metric that can be used to benchmark hotels' performance against each other on a global scale. It will continue being our key benchmarking metric until the practice of sharing hotels' cost data with data aggregators becomes widely adopted (which is currently not the case, as there is a very small portion of hotels that are willing to share their financial numbers with these companies). We will talk about it later in this chapter.

Adjusted RevPAR

For the purpose of profit optimization, a new index was invented back in 2014 (by someone I personally know) that incorporates all of those elements that you see in the illustration above. The index has been adopted by hospitality professionals all over the world (though, unfortunately, not widely enough). It was called Adjusted RevPAR (for the lack of a better term) and you can find it on wikipedia.[56]

Unlike traditional RevPAR, Adjusted RevPAR is a much better indicator of the bottom-line profits, not just top-line revenue. This is incredibly useful for helping hotels understand the effectiveness of their revenue management and profit optimization strategy. And this focus is right in line with the lodging industry's current shift from high-occupancy revenue management strategies to those that maximize profits.

Adjusted RevPAR can be calculated in a few different ways (depending on what measurements you want to use in your calculations). And you can find those formulas on the wiki page I referenced above. But the simplest way to express it is the following:

Adjusted RevPAR

=

(ADR + Additional revenues per occupied room – Variable costs per occupied room)

x Occupancy

The good news is that Adjusted RevPAR can be calculated fairly easily, as soon as you measure your average variable expenses (per occupied room) based on historical accounting data, as well as average additional income (per occupied room) from other revenue-generating departments (if any). These values can then be considered (roughly) constant and used for any future calculations. Recalculation is only needed after dramatic changes that significantly affect average variable costs or average additional revenues (like renovation or rebranding).

If we apply this formula to the scenarios referenced in the beginning of this chapter, here's what happens. And for simplicity of calculations, let's assume we're talking about a limited-service hotel that doesn't have any additional revenue-generating departments, and variable expenses are equal to $10 per occupied room.

---

[56]Wikipedia: Adjusted RevPAR: https://en.wikipedia.org/wiki/Adjusted_RevPAR

Imagine the same 100-room hotel.

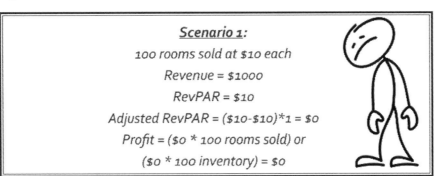

Scenario 1:
100 rooms sold at $10 each
Revenue = $1000
RevPAR = $10
Adjusted RevPAR = ($10-$10)*1 = $0
Profit = ($0 * 100 rooms sold) or
($0 * 100 inventory) = $0

Scenario 2:
10 rooms sold at $100 each
Revenue = $1000
RevPAR = $10
Adjusted RevPAR = ($100 - $10)*0.1 = $9
Profit = ($90 * 10 rooms sold) or
($9 * 100 inventory) = $900

As you now hopefully see, concentrating on just maximizing RevPAR can lead to significant profit losses, since sometimes an increase in room revenue may actually mean a decrease in final profits (as was also discovered in the academic paper[57] I referenced earlier). But if you set Adjusted RevPAR maximization as your main goal – this will directly lead to increased profit. Of course, this is easier to do algorithmically through technology than trying to calculate it manually.

To conclude this section, there are a variety of performance metrics that hotels use to understand the success of their operations and to guide their revenue and profit strategy. But when you're concerned with whether your strategy is adding to the bottom line or hurting it, and whether you're using the right optimization target, Adjusted RevPAR gives you a much clearer picture than any other KPI. Knowing this will help the industry make better decisions and generate more consistent profits going forward, with the help of technology.

Profit-oriented benchmarking

So, we talked about profit maximization. Now, let's talk about benchmarking.

---

[57]"Performance measures for strategic revenue management: RevPAR versus GOPPAR", Zvi Schwartz, Mehmet Altin and Manisha Singal, 2016 Macmillan Publishers Ltd. 1476-6930 Journal of Revenue and Pricing Management 1–19 www.palgrave-journals.com/rpm/

I had a very engaging conversation with Jan Freitag at CoStar Group (which now owns STR). He provided an update on STR's most recent initiatives in this area, and the barriers that they're facing when trying to scale their new benchmarking solutions.

Here's an excerpt from that discussion:

| Ira Vouk

So now that the revenue management discipline, and the hospitality industry in general, has evolved from looking at the top-line room revenue to understanding that profit is important for any business, we are starting to pay attention to the bottom-line values.

I know that the industry has been really struggling with benchmarking in this area. And I know that you have an initiative to start scaling your product there. And there are a few companies that are also doing that, trying to gather these insights from different hotels for benchmarking purposes, but it seems that it's still hard for the industry to embrace the concept of profit management and profit benchmarking. Why do you think that is? And also can you elaborate a little bit on what initiatives you have at STR that will help us solve that?

| Jan Freitag

Some people already get nervous when we ask for the basic 3 numbers (Rooms sold, Revenue and Capacity). When it comes to profit metrics - now we're asking for the total revenue, for expenses and department level revenues, and GOPPAR and EBITDA, and that gets very, very personal for some hoteliers. The good thing is that I think the value of benchmarking outweighs the hesitancy to share, especially with a global provider, like we are. If large players such as Hilton and Marriot trust us, then other hotels should trust us as well.

So we also offer the P&L benchmarking product. We're publishing it monthly, globally and in the United States, and it keeps growing, especially in these days after COVID, because people really want to know how everybody else is doing in terms of revenues or expenses, or what other departments look like from the standpoint of expenses, etc. So we feel that this is the time to grow participation.

| Ira Vouk

Absolutely. I agree that this is the right time for the industry to start embracing the concept of looking at the bottom-line profits by paying attention to their expenses and all revenue streams. It should have been done a long time ago, but better late than never, right? There are a few good things that came out of COVID, and that would be one of them - profit oriented operations. That, and less traffic on the roads.

| Jan Freitag

Right. What we said after 9/11 and after 2009 is "never let a good crisis go to waste". I think what this crisis has shown us is that total revenue matters, additional revenue streams matter. Suddenly rooftop restaurants started generating auxiliary F&B revenues from people who live in town, when you don't have anybody traveling, but local people still want to go out. Or take housekeeping. What's the expense? Is it worth it? Do people really want it? If they really want it - would they pay for it? I think those are all interesting discussions that are coming out of COVID and the P&L reports could allow you to answer some of these questions.

STR has recently introduced new products that target profit-oriented benchmarking. I believe this initiative is really beneficial for the industry and I'm happy to see it grow.

Here is a brief description of those products.

1. 2021 Profitability Study[58]

"The Hotel Profitability Study is designed to provide you with annual P&L data and trends for the entire world, all in one concise deliverable. This report contains profitability insights on a macro level, but with additional focus on regions, countries, markets, classes and service types, you can also gain an understanding of the micro-level trends affecting your hotel operation.

Key features:

- *A global view of profitability, covering 53 countries and 269 markets*
- *Regional overviews and highlights*
- *Metrics include total revenue, GOP, EBITDA, labor costs, etc."*

More details about this product can be found via the link in the footnote.

2. Custom Profit & Loss report[59]

"Build custom hotel sets to benchmark your monthly and annual profitability against the competition. With more than 100 individual line items, this two-year report delivers insight into hotel revenue, expenses, labor costs by department, and more."

The list of metrics that are being gathered and benchmarked are based on USALI standard P&L line items outlined earlier in this chapter.

More details about this product from Joseph Rael, Senior Director, Financial Performance, STR: *"Monthly benchmarking is the main goal. We have an online benchmarking product planned to be released in 2022. We are currently reporting data and*

---

[58]STR: Hotel Profitability Study Report: https://str.com/data-solutions/hotel-profitability-study-report

[59]STR: Custom Profit & Loss Report: https://str.com/data-solutions/custom-pl-report

sending clients data files and a set of dashboards. The monthly program is still very new (launched last year), although we do have annual P&L data for over 30 years."

More details about this product can be found via the link in the footnote.

3. Monthly Profit and Loss review[60]

This product is aimed to dig deeper into the data with a monthly overview of U.S. hotel profitability metrics. It also includes details on top markets, bottom markets, performance by industry segment (chain scale, class, region, location) and other data.

More details about this product can be found via the link in the footnote.

Action plan

To conclude this chapter, I will attempt to outline some steps that should help the industry eventually move the conversation from managing top-line room revenues (with RevPAR as the de facto performance metric) to actually optimizing profit.

Below is what needs to happen before we start seeing the change:

1. Update Hotel Management Agreements to reflect profit-oriented metrics as the basis for performance management and compensation

2. Align objectives on the property (or the cluster) level across departments to target profit maximization

3. Use the right data and the right metrics for decision making (that requires understanding your cost structure and all revenue streams)

4. Implement Business Intelligence technology that generates actionable insights targeted towards profit optimization

5. Ensure that at the property level, or at the cluster level, you have the right people in the revenue and profit optimization roles who understand data and have strategic skills that can aid in aligning all departments towards profit goals, using the outputs from the BI solutions and adding the human touch and strategic expertise to those decisions

6. Ensure that people in those roles are engaged and growing as well as properly compensated

Some of you will say, "Easier said than done! We have known this for decades but we haven't made any progress, why even try?" Well, this time around it's different. Truly different. This time we actually have a chance.

---

[60]STR: US Monthly Profit & Loss Review Report: https://str.com/data-solutions/monthly-profit-and-loss-review

First of all, we all went through the pains of 2020 and many hotel owners are scared and willing to do anything to prevent the crisis from happening again. And for that, they need better tools to understand how to manage their cash flows so they will be more willing to adopt those new tools. Let's take advantage of this window of opportunity.

Secondly, I agree that there are obvious challenges with our existing processes and the way we run operations that prevent the industry from easily adopting the profit optimization paradigm. But where the process is broken, we need to turn to technology to help us solve the problem.

So what's different now than when we were trying to tackle this after 9/11 or in 2009 - is technology. Data gathering and data analysis are the core aspects of this problem, which can (and should) be addressed through tech. This time around, we have better technology (way better technology!) that we can utilize to build amazing user-friendly and intuitive, cloud-based, ML-based software solutions that will solve the profit optimization problem for the industry.

So how do we approach this? It will take time and many iterations but we can do this, step-by-step. Here's what's needed:

1. Let's get more **clarity and uniformity** across organizations about who owns the data, what the format is, and how we interpret it. There is a need for a **data standardization initiative** by hospitality organizations to address the frequency at which certain expenses and revenues are recorded, as well as the consistency and completeness of this reporting.

The general understanding about the existing data sources related to this topic is the following:

   a. In order to make progress toward proper profit optimization and benchmarking, hotels need to have their profit & loss (P&L) statements securely uploaded to the cloud, automatically, which would enable data collection of all revenue streams and cost categories. Then those statements need to be analyzed.

   b. Because P&L data alone won't solve all our problems, we need to ensure that we have that automated upload for other relevant data sources, including some tables from PMS. For example, to report on ancillary revenues, we can turn to the General Ledger (GL) report.

   c. To start gathering distribution costs data in a comprehensive manner, we may need to rethink how this information is communicated from the booking channel to the property. One way of solving this would be attaching those values as an additional field to the reservation.

2. Taking advantage of the new opportunities resulting from the previous step and access to the right data, **technology vendors will start introducing better functionalities**. These will be solutions that will allow hotel operators to properly

measure, track and forecast profit-related metrics as well as build optimal revenue management strategy that maximizes overall profit and not just top-line room revenue. This new functionality will also target breaking the silos and allow for closer collaboration between the Revenue Management department and Operations, Finance, Marketing and Sales, as they will all be working together towards one common goal and will use the same language and the same metrics to track their performance.

3. While we can't solve the fragmentation problem overnight, what we can do is educate the key stakeholder of our ecosystem who writes the checks - the owner. **Raising awareness among hotel owners and operators** about the necessity of profit-oriented data sharing is crucial in order for those tech companies to scale and build better tools for the industry. That communication needs to be framed around positive outcomes and how hoteliers will benefit from this initiative.

4. We also need to continue conversations about **privacy and security of data** in the cloud to address lack of trust and owners' unwillingness to share profit-level data. It is necessary to clearly communicate that data gathering is secure and confidential.

The good news is that we already have examples of hotel companies that have implemented profit-oriented data analysis successfully. They are doing things manually for the most part (as proper tools don't yet exist) but thanks to those successful examples, we already know that this is achievable. Now, we need to create a scaled solution using the right cloud-based technology.

And once scaled, **this information can be used for benchmarking across the industry,** to help hotels measure their level of competitiveness with other hotels in their market and spot potential performance issues. This type of benchmarking is extremely valuable, regardless of property size and type, as long as the data is standardized, normalized and consistent, and gathered regularly and automatically. There are a few companies in the industry (e.g. the data providers like Smith Travel Research, Kalibri Labs, CBRE) that have made some progress toward profit-oriented data gathering. However, there is more progress to be made to enable automated daily updates of this information on a large scale across the industry.

What we also need to consider is that scaling and automation is easier to achieve for chains, but a very large share of hotels in the world are independent. We need a good technology solution that could address both segments. And like I said earlier, this time we actually have a chance to pull it off.

THE FORECASTING PROBLEM

Speaking about revenue and profit optimization (what helps hoteliers keep the lights on), one key condition is the ability of hospitality operators to be able to anticipate demand levels for every day in the future (365 days out or even further) because that's the basis for any profit optimization strategy and budget planning. And in our current situation of uncertainty, it is even more crucial than ever.

The pandemic made it obvious (and painful) to hoteliers that in any situation that poses uncertainty, it is crucial to quickly develop and deploy strategies to adapt to both short- and long-term shifts in demand. But here's the thing. Travel demand has always been uncertain, and history never repeats itself. Recent events just highlighted this fact for all of us and pushed the industry towards more innovations in the areas of forecasting and optimization.

I love how Ravi Mehrotra of IDeaS phrased it:

In revenue management, we're always focused on solving a real world problem.

So, what is it that you have to do in order to solve a real word problem? Especially if you are going to use scientific reasoning models and algorithms and so on. You have to find a way to capture that reality through a model. Once you capture that reality through a model, then you will do whatever it is to the model and you will take the output of the model to control the real world.

Now, if some problems seem to be very difficult or impossible, the question is: does that complexity lie in the real world or in the way that you have chosen to model the real world?

And unfortunately, I find that 9 out of 10 times, the flaw is in how people model the real world. They take some very deterministic aspects of it and model it in great detail. And then give themselves a pat on the back and forget the very basic thing that all business people know: that no matter what you think, no matter what you forecast, ultimately, the reality is uncertain.

This particular topic is mostly related to the revenue management discipline but does ultimately affect the overall performance of hotels that use the traditional demand forecasting approach that is no longer relevant in our new environment and that is why I wanted to highlight it in this book. I recently published an article[61] on this topic where readers can find more details if needed (link is referenced in the footnote).

Without going into too many details, I will explain what the problem is, and how to address it.

---

[61] HospitalityNet: Constrained/Unconstrained Forecasting is Obsolete (August 2021): https://www.hospitalitynet.org/opinion/4106201.html

Right now, the industry is just starting to realize how uncertain the market is. But it's always been this way. Maybe it was just less hectic and less chaotic, but it's always been uncertain.

Now that the industry has come to this understanding, it's time to build a better "model of our reality" that can incorporate the uncertainty in a more optimal manner. It's time to rebuild our forecasting methods. I will soon publish another book where this topic will be discussed in a more detailed manner for those who are interested, but here I will provide a brief explanation.

There are two major problems with the traditional forecasting approach. The first one has to do with the traditional Constrained / Unconstrained forecasting model that is described below.

Constrained demand forecasting is obsolete

The traditional revenue management discipline revolves around four pillars: Measure, Forecast, Optimize, and Collaborate (via actionable Insights). They're further explained below.

1. **Measure**

   Look at the right/relevant data

2. **Forecast**

   Estimate true demand strength and market opportunity for every day in the range (at least 365 days out)

3. **Optimize**

   Using the results from the previous steps (as well as additional data points), build the optimal pricing, restriction and segmentation strategy to achieve the highest total revenue potential as well as maximize profits. This can (and should) also drive marketing and sales strategy optimization, and dictate the actions taken to manage the property as a whole across different departments (finance, operations, etc.).

4. **Collaborate (via actionable insights)**

   Using internal and external data, as well as intelligence gathered from the previous steps, provide insightful visualizations to support the decision-making process of various stakeholders.

As some of the readers may be aware, traditionally, the second (Forecasting) pillar assumes constrained and unconstrained demand forecasting that **estimates the quantity of rooms to be sold, using historic reservation data**. If you dig a bit deeper, you will notice that essentially, the whole revenue management discipline as we know it today is built on that concept, and everything is derived from it. Almost any revenue management book or guide refers to this concept as the foundation of the discipline.

These forecasts are then traditionally used in the revenue management discipline for further planning of the optimal revenue strategy, as part of the Optimize pillar, as well as generating insights that are related to the strength of demand for further use by various stakeholders.

While the traditional forecasting approach served us well for a few decades, it's time to let it go and build a new one because it is no longer relevant. Because proper forecasting is the foundation of revenue and profit optimization, the discipline (and the industry overall) can't continue evolving optimally until we realize that we need a new way to forecast that reflects our new reality.

Essentially, what revenue managers are doing today (and what we're still teaching the new generation) is **using historical internal occupancy data to predict the number of expected booked rooms**. Let's be honest with ourselves: with this approach, we're not predicting *demand*, we're predicting *occupancy*.

In addition, we are absolutely ignoring the hotel's pricing strategy, and this is a big problem. **The price set by the hotel fully controls the resulting occupancy levels**. This is a basic principle that we're currently not taking into account for some reason. **Forecasting occupancy irrespective of pricing is irrelevant in today's world**.

To visualize, this is how the traditional approach of *occupancy* forecasts (described above) compares to true *demand* forecasting.

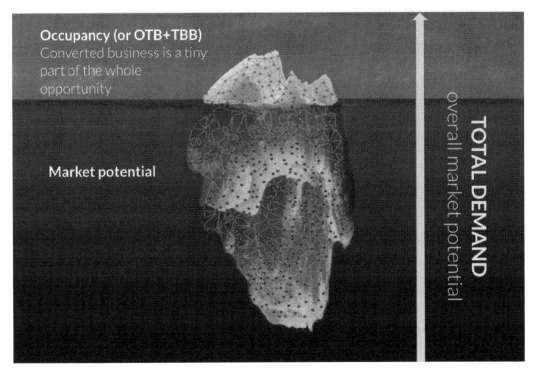

The top portion of the iceberg (predicted and actualized occupancy) is largely dependent on the user's actions (mostly, pricing), not only on the strength of demand (the whole iceberg).

Thus, occupancy forecasts can no longer be used to build revenue management and profit optimization strategy because:

- Occupancy is a result of the user's actions (pricing, restrictions, promotions, etc.)
- Occupancy data does not contain information about travelers' price expectations (elasticity)

Why did this model work before?

A long-long time ago, when dinosaurs roamed around the Earth, humanity didn't know about the concept of Dynamic Pricing. With a static price (let's say $119 set for every single day), occupancy fluctuated between 10% and 100% **following the fluctuations of demand**. So when the revenue management discipline was born, forecasting occupancy totally made sense because it was literally **a direct reflection of the market demand**.

But it was then.

Now... or, actually, more than a decade ago... The concept of Dynamic Pricing (where rates fluctuate based upon demand conditions) emerged and revolutionized the discipline of revenue management and the whole industry along with it.

In our current reality, when prices change every day (and in many cases, every hour) occupancy no longer correlates with market demand because it's affected by our pricing strategy. Most hotels will strive for higher occupancy numbers (due to the perishable nature of their goods) and drop the rate when demand is low, and vice versa. This is why we may see examples of occupancy sometimes reaching higher values for days with low demand than days with high demand.

Moral of the story: **it doesn't really matter what occupancy we forecast. Humans (and machines) can build strategies to reach whatever occupancy targets they prefer.**

My main goal here is to communicate to the industry that it simply does not make sense to continue forecasting occupancy (our traditional approach), due to the reasons described above.

Now, the million dollar question: how do we build an optimal revenue management and profit optimization strategy using measurements of true market potential?

Well, I'm glad you asked! Certainly, not through historic internal booking curves.

1. First of all: demand measurement and demand forecasting need to **take into account price expectations and price elasticity.** So we need to move from measuring *"my hotel's booking volumes"* to *"all hotels' booking volumes and customers' price expectations"*.

2. Second: true market Demand measurements are only possible when **external forward-looking market** data is available.

And this leads to the second problem with the traditional forecasting approach explained below.

Using external forward-looking market data to measure overall demand potential

The next logical question is: **how do we properly track market demand?** There are various data points that hoteliers and different technology vendors have been collecting to attempt assessing demand fluctuations for any given day in the future, but in general, they can be grouped into 2 main categories:

1. **Internal hotel data** (in the form of daily statistics, booking pace, etc.). This data is available at the hotel level, through access to the property's PMS or CRS system. The traditional approach to forecasting involves building booking curves only from this internal historic reservation data, which is not nearly comprehensive enough, as we discussed earlier.

2. **External market data.** That is data gathered from the market (outside of the hotel). And it's not just compset rates. What I'm talking about here is comprehensive market data that allows you to get as close to measuring market potential (and as far away from internal booking curves) as possible.

Examples of such data could be (in addition to published rates of all hotels in the area/region, which is still valuable): observed volumes of online searches/bookings for future dates in the market (obtained from OTAs or MSEs), events data, air searches and booking volumes, car rental searches and booking volumes, competitive performance, including alternative accommodations, etc.

At the start of the COVID-19 pandemic, I was having conversations with industry experts and hotel company executives who were sharing their frustrations about how the RMS (Revenue Management System) tools they were using completely fell apart in a highly unstable environment. Many of those tools had rigid algorithms that were using the same approach and logic that was built in from the beginning, specifically: extrapolating STLY (same time last year) internal data onto the future to make forecasting and optimization decisions.

And this is the main reason why the majority of those algorithms fell apart when the pandemic hit the world in Q1 of 2020 - they were relying on the consistent patterns of those historic internal booking curves instead of attempting to measure true market conditions, and of course they failed because 2020 was like no other year.

And as it's now obvious for everyone, last year's data quickly became irrelevant when it comes to forecasting. In addition to that, it's also clear that as we go into recovery, any hotel looking at last year's COVID-drained numbers for guidance in predicting demand, isn't going to get any reasonable results.

But there's more. Last year's internal data will never again be enough to rely solely on it for strategic and tactical revenue and profit optimization decisions, because demand has always been uncertain, and history never repeats itself. In the new world, we as an industry need to find a better way to forecast and optimize.

To date, the upper funnel, forward-looking data, like online search volumes for example, have not been properly utilized in our forecasting algorithms, mainly due to lack of access to this data. The above forced the industry to attempt to derive demand fluctuations from other data points (mostly internal), none of which reflect true market conditions. And when it comes to external (market) data, it was poor and not very helpful, which generated many opponents of using this data in forecasting (the founders of Pace RMS, for example).

Thankfully, due to the development of cloud computing in recent years, more and more market data is becoming available from various providers.

One major source that is still very much underutilized is MSE (metasearch engines) upper funnel search volumes. Out of all known data sources available in the industry today, MSEs' (like Google, Trivago, TripAdvisor) search volumes data currently represents one of the most objective ways of proactively and dynamically measuring forward-looking market demand. Being able to access this data presents a unique opportunity to use those insights for building adequate demand patterns, aid the hospitality industry in building much more accurate forecasts, and significantly improve performance.

Those who get their hands first on Google hotels' search volumes will win the forecasting battle.

In addition, there are many other types of external market data that have become or are becoming widely available: OTA search volumes, flight search and booking volumes, car rental search and booking volumes, Google traffic data, events intel, OTA ranking and visibility, parity insights, AirDNA data, and more.

I'm also a big advocate for data-sharing between industries. For example, we can look at search volumes and booking curves from the airline industry to inform demand forecasting and optimization decisions for hotels, and vice versa. The possibilities are infinite.

Clearly, there is no way that humans will be able to digest all this information and come up with reasonable optimization decisions, so we will have to rely on automated revenue and profit management tools for that (but this is a whole separate discussion, which you can read in my next book, stay tuned).

This is not to say that all the data types mentioned above should be thrown into an RMS algorithm for forecasting. In an ideal world, each one of them should be run against an individual hotel's historic performance data and added to the forecasting "formula" for that hotel, only if a correlation is found. I'm using quotation marks for the world "formula" because I really hope that very soon, there won't be any RMS tools left that are not using machine learning algorithms.

Okay, that was a lot. But this is not all.

Here is the last, but a very important aspect regarding the dawn of traditional demand forecasting.

Forecasting accuracy is not as important as adaptability

The primary goal of a revenue and profit manager, as well as any RMS, is performance through proper adjustments of your strategy, not through accurate forecasts.

I'm ready to catch a few rotten tomatoes with this one. It's okay, I'm used to that.

The industry has been talking about forecasting accuracy for too long, and many strategies and tools are founded with that target in mind, so I anticipate it to take quite a bit of time for our industry to grasp that concept (many have already caught up but they're still a minority).

Forecasting accuracy is not our primary target. You can have an occupancy forecast that is 100% accurate (of course, because you can hit whatever occupancy target you'd like, as we discussed earlier) and make less money at the end of the day, than having a less accurate original forecast with more money as a result, if your strategy is adaptive enough that it always readjusts with demand fluctuations.

Key takeaways

So, to summarize what we discussed in this chapter:
- The main goal of a revenue and profit optimization strategy is to help hotels be more successful and profitable
- The main value of demand forecasting is to assist with the above
- Forecasts help establish goals and provide alerts. They play an important role in decision making, but they are just an input and not the decision.
- Variations in occupancy are caused both by outside forces and by businesses themselves. Businesses create volatility in occupancy when they change prices and implement promotions to meet targets.
- Demand forecasts are always wrong. No one has a crystal ball or perfect vision.
- And that is why it's important to be able to readjust quickly and adaptively, and that is exactly what makes a difference in your strategy.
- The best way to improve performance is not by accurately forecasting occupancy but by properly measuring demand and being adaptive (#agile).

Having said that, we can of course continue to estimate occupancy for the purposes of budgeting (because that's what we've done since forever and that's what asset owners and operators expect to see every quarter). But we must recognize that the balance between occupancy and ADR is largely determined by the person (or the tool) who controls pricing and other revenue strategies (like promotions, stay restrictions, channel strategy). DORMs (directors of revenue management) can hit any occupancy forecast they'd like through various manipulations. So, if you need to plan your budget, the idea is to predict revenue (because that's what has the highest correlation with true market demand strength), and then derive occupancy and ADR from that, and not the other way around.

The main moral of the story: **we should never again use occupancy forecasts to drive our revenue and profit optimization decisions** (like pricing and others). **We should use the true estimation of demand at any given point in time, utilizing external forward-looking market data, and then adaptively adjust as it changes. This leads to reaching your maximum revenue and profit potential.**

After all, the goal of running a hotel business is not hitting occupancy targets. The goal is maximizing profit.

THE DISCONNECT BETWEEN THE INDUSTRY AND HOSPITALITY ACADEMIA

Throughout my entire hospitality career, I've been very curious about finding better ways to solve the industry's problems. In parallel with building technology solutions and bringing them to market, I have also been doing my own research, developing ideas (such as Adjusted RevPAR index), generating numerous educational publications on various subjects, as well as teaching. Also, recently I have been participating in research with a few universities on the subject of machine learning applications in demand forecasting and others.

So my background puts me in a position that essentially lies between the two worlds: the industry and academia. My passion for both is driving the desire to figure out how to connect the two.

That is why one of the goals of this book is to bring the knowledge from those two areas together, and see if we can start establishing a reliable channel of communication between them, so that we can drive the industry forward more efficiently and optimally.

There is currently a big gap between hospitality academia and the industry. On one hand, there is a lot of great research done by professors at various universities worldwide, and there are many great discoveries, however those findings are rarely communicated to the industry (and if they are - the language is very hard to digest as those are purely scientific publications). At the same time, hospitality companies hardly ever reach out to the academic circles with information about what research is relevant and what problems need to be solved. As a result, professors continue to generate papers that are not necessarily always related to what the industry really needs. At the same time, they often continue teaching their students the same old concepts that are no longer applicable.

It appears there are a few reasons for the problem of the two worlds being drastically out of sync, as many professors shared with me in our conversations.

The main reason is the **structure of incentives for academics**. They are judged and compensated based on certain things that they do, and none of them is working with the industry.

They need to publish papers and they need to be good teachers. They need to bring grants, and the grants are unfortunately not coming from the industry. In other industries, we see examples where things are not as gloomy. In accounting, millions of dollars are invested in academia because they understand the importance of it. The same goes for chemistry, and others.

But in hospitality, that's not the case unfortunately. So there's no incentive for academics to be truly "connected" to real world problems. Some of them still do research for the industry and that is because they are passionate and because they came from the field. On the other hand, many do not, as they have no interest in advancing the field and solving real business problems. Sometimes you find people that are intrinsically curious,

107

interested, want to learn more and want to progress their own understanding and apply their knowledge in the field, but they are rare.

Here's an excerpt from a discussion with professor H.G. Parsa (University of Denver, Daniels College of Business, Hospitality Management):

The key aspect of this is that reward and recognition systems in the industry are different from academia. In the industry, I'm rewarded for my revenues and for my profits, plus for developing the skills of my employees.

Take American football for example. They're not rewarded for how they play the game. They're rewarded for whether they win or lose. They don't care how the game was played. That's what the industry is all about. Academia is all about how you play the game. We study the game. The role of a coach is to take this game knowledge and put it on the field, so they can win. That's what we're missing in the industry and academia, there's no link.

Secondly, in academia, we are rewarded for basic research, not applications.

But if I want to do research, for example, on the response of the world hospitality leaders to COVID - my University would not care.

And as Amanda Belarmino (University of Las Vegas, William F. Harrah College of Hospitality) pointed out:

Obviously I think we'd all love to have a closer relationship with the industry and find ways to do this. But there has to be that dual benefit.

As it appears, when it comes to the disconnect between the industry and academia, there are 2 sides of this coin: **research** and **education**.

I had conversations with a few hospitality professors from different universities, as well as some industry representatives, to try and shed some light on this subject. I provide excerpts from those discussions below, organized in a few main sections that describe the problems we are dealing with, as well as suggested action plans on how to remedy them.

Research

Communication from the industry to academics

Let's start from this angle.

Below are my conversations with various professors from different universities related to this subject.

Ira Vouk

Do hospitality companies ever reach out to you with requests to do research in a specific area?

Amanda Belarmino *(University of Las Vegas, William F. Harrah College of Hospitality)*

Occasionally, but not as much as one would think.

Sometimes they come to you and then they realize they don't have funding to do it, or we want access to data that they don't want to give us. So there are a lot of different complications.

Tim Webb *(University of Delaware, Hospitality Business Management)*

In general no, they don't reach out. However, I have been fortunate enough to establish collaborations with hospitality companies to investigate a mutually interesting topic for both parties, such as new forecasting algorithms. In the same sense, I was approached to join one as an academic partner to help develop their training simulation for university students, however not for the development of any functionality.

Ira Vouk

What portion of your research would you say is used by the hospitality companies or tech companies in the field?

Tim Webb

I would guess no more than 5% but it is unclear what each company's practices are.

When trying to find a way to address this, I had an engaging discussion with professor H. G. Parsa (University of Denver) that led to an interesting discovery that could serve as an opportunity to build a bridge between the industry and academia in our sector.

Ira Vouk

Are you aware of research happening in the industry, outside of the academic circles? Does the industry communicate this to you?

H. G. Parsa

No, I am not. Companies like Marriott and Hilton invest heavily in research and they don't tell us about their discoveries. Industry is not telling us what they do, though we ask them all the time. They want to keep their competitive edge. That's another part of the dilemma.

Ira Vouk

So if we leave out companies like Marriott or Hilton, who have extensive resources for their own research, and consider the myriad of hospitality startup companies that are emerging in the market right now, or smaller hotel companies. They don't have a lot of resources to invest in research and discovery but may need some scientific basis for their products, or to figure out how to solve a business problem through science. They might not even have any industry expertise, which happens often where founders come from other industries. They get into hospitality because they see a gap in a specific area.

So those companies don't always have proper scientific talent. Is there a way for them to use your knowledge or, for example, get you interested in research that is relevant to them? Can a group of professors from different universities collaborate on solving a specific problem, if this is an important problem and solving it has the potential to make the industry more evolved?

| H. G. Parsa

It's achievable and we have successful examples in other sectors.

In the marketing discipline, they had exactly the same problem in the 1980s. Marketing research was so far ahead, and the industry was not using any of it. Academia did whatever it did, nobody read it, the industry was going in its own direction. So, what happened then? The Marketing Science Institute was created, funded by the industry partly. The Marketing Institute put out a call for papers all over the country: here are 10 problems that we want to research. Give us results in two years. And that's how the Marketing Institute brought the industry and academia together. Though of course, it is not that simple and there is a whole lot more to it.

A wonderful idea for our industry would be to create a Hospitality Research Consortium. For example, if a company wants a particular paid research to be done but they want to remain anonymous - they contact you, you come to us, we come together and do it. That's one way of helping the industry and academia to work together.

We need a pioneer who can say, "I'm willing to be the head of that Consortium." Someone like you. They trust you. And we trust you. You're in the middle. You're the person who can make that happen.

I promised professor Parsa to think about it... If someone is interested in having more discussions around this topic - please reach out to me on LinkedIn and we can start this conversation. I'll be happy to entertain ideas on how to create such a Consortium and aid in organizing efforts to make research more industry relevant.

Another professor who requested to remain anonymous shared his vision on how the industry could help hotel schools to do better research that is more applicable to the real environment.

It was my dream to open up a lab at my university. Where you have software companies come in and establish their demo in the lab. So our students and also people from the industry could come and test things and see how they work, and compare and run them. And then if somebody is interested in buying a particular solution - we could connect them with the sales person.

Another layer would be for academics to look more deeply into those solutions and try to compare what one is doing compared to another, test things, research things. For example, if we take a revenue management solution - test their ability to forecast and optimize and how things are connected to each other, etc. The big challenge right now is how to make one system talk to another. So that would be a nice academic lab that could really help the industry.

I believe that through organized efforts, we can achieve a certain level of collaboration between the industry and universities worldwide. I will start thinking in that direction to see who I can pull into this discussion to start making progress. If you're interested in participating or have any ideas that could help with this initiative - please reach out.

Selecting research topics by academics

A big part of a professor's job is conducting research in the area of their expertise.

Now that we have established that in most cases, hospitality professors are not drawing their research ideas from the industry, due to the reasons outlined above, I was curious to understand how they decide what topics to study. So I asked around. Here are the results of those discussions.

Ira Vouk

Recently, I've been working with some professors from a few universities on a topic that was relevant and interesting to me and to the company that I worked at, and I believe the results of the research have a lot of potential to actually be applied in the real world. But what I'm seeing and hearing is that it's not always the case. Often, research conducted by hospitality professors is not something that the industry would be interested in using in the future. Can you describe how you normally select the topics for your research? Do you make the decision or is it dictated by the university?

Amanda Belarmino *(University of Las Vegas, William F. Harrah College of Hospitality)*

We do actually get to decide what we want to do, the school doesn't dictate it. Ideally, you try to have a specialty that you stick with so that you're an expert in that area. But because I find something interesting and it's publishable, it doesn't necessarily mean that it's needed by the industry.

There are a lot of different things that go into that decision. One is that we keep our jobs based on how many things we get published. So the appetite within academic literature is all there. We need to be extending theory and for that, we should be

111

filling gaps in the literature. So I think that's why sometimes unfortunately we create these things that are more theoretically interesting than necessarily are practically applicable.

So I have to have a certain number of publications done in a mix of these certain journals by 2023 or I won't keep my job. But I worked in the industry for a while and I want to do things that are more industry applicable. So I try to find something that's going to be both theoretically interesting and have potential to be applied in the real world.

The things I've done that I think are the most industry relevant are also the hardest things for us to publish, because it may not be viewed as relevant theoretically. So I think that there's just that gap of what we need to do to be here.

Communicating research results from academics to the industry

Another problem that I've been witnessing is the delivery of the information from academia to the industry. So the next question was related to that.

| **Ira Vouk**

So let's say you conduct some research that has a practical application and it's distilled into some end result and is ready to be used by the industry or at least by the pioneers. What is the best way of communicating this information to the industry?

Does the industry even know where to look for this information or who to reach out to?

For example, there's a tech founder trying to invest in a profit optimization system for hotels and they're assembling a team of scientists and engineers to develop an algorithm, they're building everything from scratch. Wouldn't they want to take advantage of the work you have already done in that area? Wouldn't they want to go to you because you've already done all the research for them?

| **Tim Webb** (*University of Delaware, Hospitality Business Management*)

In general, I don't believe there is a good outlet to share information at this point. It is really up to the academics to try and start a conversation or self-promote the findings of the research to generate interest, awareness, or future collaboration. In some instances, STR may provide the opportunity to share results through their news sites.

| **Amanda Belarmino** (*University of Las Vegas, William F. Harrah College of Hospitality*)

Another thing to keep in mind is that when we're writing a paper, we're writing it for academics, so it's not written in a way that's approachable.

And there are things that are in those articles that aren't really industry relevant, they are more theoretically relevant. And then of course it's also hard to get access to some of these. If you don't have access to the University Library, you have to pay for it. Is it worth paying for the subscription? That's a whole other conversation.

And then, for us to get something published, it can take six months to a year. I have a paper that might finally get published this year that I wrote five years ago. So how relevant is that now? It may take 6 to 15 months, from the start of a paper to the time it gets published in academia, and you can't rely on that in the industry.

Based on what I heard above, I believe one of the possible solutions could be for professors to write a short executive summary describing key points of the research and publish it on an industry portal that is accessible to all without any fees. If we have a publicly available library of such summaries with open access for all, this would help the industry stay up-to-date on the conducted research and find topics that are of interest and could be helpful for their business case. This would also facilitate communication between hotel companies and academia in such cases where there's an interest in a particular subject and a company needs more details on the topic or would like to order a deeper study in that area.

And to wrap up our discussion about research topics, I asked one last clarifying question that led to opening up another aspect of the problem we're dealing with.

Ira Vouk

So I'm trying to understand what the benefit is of doing research for the purpose of filling a gap in theory. Logically, research for an industry should be done in order to make that industry more improved and efficient, not just for the purpose of the research itself, right?

Amanda Belarmino

I think where we really try to use our research is in teaching. Ideally, research is done to improve what you're teaching in the classroom.

So I think that more of our purpose in research is creating education rather than because we want to help hospitality companies.

We all want something that's so generalizable that we can teach this to our students. So, our main purpose of our research is to say, "These are the things that I think are interesting that will help me teach and make me a better educator."

And that leads us to another aspect of our discussion - education.

Education and curriculum

Another side of the disconnect between the industry and academia is related to what we teach and how we teach it.

One issue is that in the past, there hasn't been a huge demand for formal hospitality education. But that is now changing.

Michael Levie of citizenM commented on that:

Unfortunately we're an undereducated industry.

A lot of people end up in the industry by default. You see bachelor degrees only in about 15% of cases. Master degrees - single digits. We're an industry that is governed by people that have learned from operations. And that was okay when it was not sophisticated, but it is getting very sophisticated, so you need a more academic approach, you need more knowledge in order to get "to the other side".

And so we run into another problem. In many cases, our curricula are old and not (yet) adapted to modern reality. Considering that the industry is constantly readapting to the changing environment (look at what 2020 alone did to transform the way we operate), we need to ensure that the curricula in hospitality schools are constantly updated so that they can stay relevant.

For example, I'm firm that we absolutely have to have a dedicated class on hospitality technology in hotel schools. The hospitality tech ecosystem is very fragmented, and there are many different players and different categories, and to make things worse - they overlap and intertwine. So navigating in this complex space can be challenging (take the distribution category alone!). And it's absolutely necessary to teach future hospitality leaders how to be fluent in that space and to structure their knowledge about various software categories in the industry and their applications. Technology is our future and very soon, it's going to take over a big portion of what we currently do manually, whether we like it or not. So we need to make sure students have the right knowledge and skills to be comfortable in that environment. But currently, we don't see that in a lot of curricula and it's still a huge gap.

I spoke to a few industry leaders, as well as professors to gather their opinions on that subject.

| Ira Vouk

Do you think the curriculum and what they actually teach in hospitality schools is close to real life?

| **Marco Benvenuti** *(Co-founder of Duetto)*

There's a general problem that the world changes very fast. And academia doesn't change fast for a lot of different reasons. And now sometimes academia is still teaching the same thing they were teaching a decade ago or they're behind on how the industry is evolving, and it's very challenging to keep the two in sync. Very, very challenging. But this is also where the hotel community and hotel companies can help. Because in the end, we have to have somebody who keeps the two worlds connected. So I tried to do that during my years at Duetto as much as I could. I invested a lot of time and effort in doing that.

| **Tim Webb** *(University of Delaware)*

I think academics may lack a firm understanding of what students MUST know to be successful in the field. In revenue management for example, this ranges from important concepts such as segmentation and price discrimination, to skills such as forecasting, and implementing rate restrictions. I believe that there could be immense opportunities to collaborate between the two groups on important topics that are relevant to both the industry but also academia.

Some interviewees had great suggestions in regard to collaboration between hospitality companies and hospitality schools to help improve education.

| **H. G. Parsa**

Smith Travel Research (STR) 10-15 years ago made a deliberate choice to make their data available to all teachers. Guess what? Every major hotel school in the country now uses STR reports. Now STR is universal. Everybody teaches STR.

So, I really wish technology vendors could take the same approach someday so we can teach our students with real software, even if it's a diluted version. They can keep their Cadillacs and Lamborghinis for themselves and give us Chevys, so we can use their software as teaching tools.

| **Ira Vouk**

Let the future leaders learn fast and learn the right thing, using a real product, right?

| **H. G. Parsa**

Exactly. In other industries, we see many examples of free demos, free sampling used for education. Unfortunately, our software companies are not open-minded enough yet to do the same. For example, Microsoft gives away MS Office bundles to universities at throw away prices. They see it as an investment in the future users and cost of customer acquisition but not as losses. Hospitality technology companies should learn from Microsoft and be the leaders that transform the industry.

The good news is that we are gradually starting to see more examples of such collaboration in the industry. I recently connected representatives from OTA Insight to some hotel schools to initiate a conversation that will hopefully result in sharing market data from the industry to the universities to aid in research and education. In addition,

Cloudbeds just announced[62] the launch of Cloudbeds Horizon, a new educational partners program that partners with hospitality schools and universities worldwide to educate students using the Cloudbeds platform and empower hospitality's future leaders with modern technology skills.

I'm also hoping that this book will draw more attention to this subject and help us move in the right direction.

Clearly, this initiative to connect the industry and academia requires close collaboration between hotel schools and hospitality representatives - those who care about the future of the industry. A great example is what Marco Benvenuti of Duetto shared from his past experience:

> When running Duetto, I spent a tremendous amount of time and energy on revenue management education at Cornell because that's where I came from and I tried to foster that. I also pushed UNLV to bring revenue management classes into the curriculum.

> But the industry has to do more to keep the momentum going and have more of a talent pool to hire from. And then they need to make sure that they foster and grow these people, and give them a career path, and compensate them appropriately, because these people are the ones that are going to make or break your profit.

Michael Levie of citizenM shared his opinion on the topic and also generated a great idea about how we could approach this in an organized manner:

> Our curriculums are old. To make new ones, we really don't have a lot of professors that have the new practical knowledge. So before you build a new curriculum, there are another two or three years. Then you need to teach people for four years. And then those people need to still grow in the industry before they start becoming useful to us. So we're talking about 12-14 years total.

> That's not feasible. So we need to attack that differently. The industry and the specialists in the industry need to assist the professors and the schools to get the curriculum together.

> We really need to gather all the industry experts, build it together and put it out there to the industry because we need to turbo-boost it. We really need a concentrated effort in order to move that forward.

I think it's a great idea and an amazing initiative and I will be happy to participate and fully support it.

---

[62]Cloudbeds: Cloudbeds Horizon launches to empower hospitality schools to upskill students in cloud technology (December 2021): https://www.cloudbeds.com/articles/cloudbeds-horizon-launches-to-empower-hospitality-schools-to-upskill-students-in-cloud-technology/

Conclusions and action plan

As we have concluded, the two worlds (the industry and academia) are not talking to each other very well, not yet at least. There is no established channel of 2-way communication and it's a known problem.

We need to find ways to build that bridge to help the industry advance further, a bridge that, on one hand, will help represent hospitality academia and make their research and findings more accessible to those who are interested in learning about them, and on the other hand, will allow us to communicate our needs to them (related to both: research and education). In these rough times, we could absolutely use their help to solve our business challenges, but they will require our help to understand what those challenges are.

I am proposing a few ideas as well as referencing successful examples that have been implemented in the past to fix the "information asymmetry" and ensure that research becomes useful for the industry and lessons learned from the market are plowed back into education and learning:

1. **Industry representatives and academics need to collaborate more on connecting for research ideas.**

I recently participated in a roundtable organized by STR SHARE center for a discussion on relevant industry research around post-COVID recovery. There are some other successful examples that I have seen, but we can (and should) do more to make further progress in that direction.

Some professors already take the initiative to stay up-to-speed on what is happening in the field and I hope we can see more of this in our practice.

2. **Establish a portal where academics can publish executive summaries of their research in a short and easy-to-read format to make it accessible for the industry.**

This needs to be a centralized effort, and it also requires collaboration to ensure that, on one hand, professors from different universities are incentivized to submit these summaries with each research and, on the other hand, that the channel is well maintained and supported.

HNN (Hotel News Now) could possibly be that portal. I will be happy to contribute from my side to organize these efforts.

3. **Organize events that connect academia with the field (invite professors to speak at industry conferences, roundtable discussions).**

Many professors are eager to engage in more discussions with us. We need to find better ways to let them participate and contribute to the development of the industry.

This is from a hospitality professor who requested to remain anonymous:

I believe that the only way forward is a collaboration between academia and the industry. I always thought that the industry isn't thinking nor paying enough attention to the discoveries and the research conducted by the academics... We would be delighted to engage in a discussion on this level with the industry and are looking forward to collaborating.

4. Tech vendors need to be more engaged with hotel schools and provide samples of their products.

It would be very beneficial for hospitality students to practice using real software products. The more hospitality tech companies provide demo versions of their solutions to hotel schools, the more adapted students will be to the real life environment when they graduate. Unfortunately, not a lot of companies are currently engaged on that level.

It would be great if software vendors became more interested in connecting with hotel schools proactively and offering their solutions to be used in classes. Hopefully, this book will help with raising awareness among those vendors and emphasize the importance of that initiative for the future of our industry.

Though I believe in order to bring this initiative to a larger scale, and to be able to cover all major software categories, this also requires an organized approach where a representative from the academic circles would need to proactively reach out to software vendors for the purpose of gaining access to their demo versions.

5. Hospitality companies need to be able to share data (anonymous and aggregated) with academia for the purpose of research.

It has been a big problem for hotel schools to source industry data for their research, regardless of the fact that the data is only used for the purpose of the study and is never made publicly available. It's always used in an anonymous and aggregated manner.

The more data the industry shares with academics, the more the industry will benefit from that.

6. Data providers need to partner with universities to use data for problem solving.

In addition to hotel companies and tech vendors, we also have industry players that have their hands on huge amounts of data - for example, companies that gather market intelligence. Availability of that data could drive a lot of research in that field.

7. Organize a Consortium.

As proposed by professor H. G. Parsa, similar to what was done in the marketing sector, we could benefit from an organization that serves as a middle layer between our industry and the universities and is formed for the purpose of targeted research on the topics that are relevant and applicable and for the purpose of establishing a centralized channel of communication between the two worlds.

8. Education: constantly update curricula.

It is necessary to update curricula to ensure that education is connected to the current needs of the industry, and for students to be able to actually apply that knowledge when they go into the field and when they become future leaders in the hospitality space.

We need to ensure that the syllabus is not just based on the research in the area of the professor's interest, but that they gather feedback from the industry when putting those programs together.

There are some good examples of this already happening, but this needs to be universally adopted by all schools to ensure curricula are built and constantly updated (#agile) using feedback from subject matter experts in the field. The "Consortium" could also be an entity that helps find subject matter experts in relevant areas and establish contact with them.

And there's an initiative driven by Michael Levie (citizenM) that I believe is amazing and has a lot of potential to turbo-boost the injection of real industry knowledge into our education. Michael is working with a group of industry leaders to find five urgent subjects in hospitality, come up with a week's curriculum, bring it to hotel schools and teach it with the help of industry specialists.

9. Certifications, online educational content, etc.

Updating curricula at hotel schools is an important initiative, but it will not solve all of our education problems because still a relatively small portion of people in our industry begin their careers with formal education. In the majority of cases, they make it to the leadership roles by climbing the organizational ladder, sometimes starting from the very bottom (just like yours, truly: neither of my 2 degrees are formal hospitality diplomas, my hospitality career started from making beds). Some industry professionals may decide to obtain a degree later, to advance in their career, but many will never choose to do so.

We need a way to continue educating them with relevant knowledge that is up-to-date, and practically applicable but also supported by research. One way of doing it is offering certifications by hotel schools. We don't see many examples of that yet in our industry, and I believe this is another area where we can improve.

To summarize, it looks like we have quite a few challenges to address (both from a research and education standpoint). But I believe that through organized efforts, we definitely have the potential to achieve a more optimal and synchronized collaboration between the industry and hotel schools to help hospitality evolve at a much faster pace and in a more efficient manner.

PART 2: **RECENT DISRUPTIONS**

When doing my research and conducting interviews with industry leaders, I asked whether, in their opinion, the industry has significantly changed in the last 10 years. All of them were unanimous in regard to the fact that the last decade has made a big impact on the way hospitality has been shaped and where we are now.

I identified 3 major factors that have been driving transformations in the industry in the recent years:

1. Natural evolution of technology (mainly, cloud computing)

2. Growth of the alternative accommodations sector

   and last but not least...

3. The COVID-19 pandemic.

Let's discuss each of them in more detail, starting with my favorite topic.

EVOLUTION OF TECHNOLOGY

"You cannot cost-cut your way into profitability."

Ravi Simhambhatla (Google Cloud)

There is no doubt that technology is going to play the main role in the next 5 to 10 years (and most likely forever in the future) in transforming our industry to being more efficient and profitable. More and more companies are starting to look at it as an investment rather than an expense line item - an investment in their future success.

While adoption rates are still very, very low (as discussed in the first part of this book) and there's a lot of room for improvement in that area, if we look back at where we were just 10 years ago, we will realize how much has changed in the tech landscape since then. Regardless of the fact that the industry is very slow in embracing new tech, it is actually mind blowing to see what we have been able to achieve in just a decade in terms of advancements in technology and what it is now able to do for us.

I had a very engaging discussion with Ravi Simhambhatla (Managing Director/CTO, Digital Transformation - Travel & Transportation at Google Cloud), a true visionary who shared a lot of great insights into the role technology plays in the travel industry. You will see a lot from this discussion in this chapter, but I'd like to start with one quote that paints a picture of how much has changed in the industry in recent years.

Ravi Simhambhatla:

I've been in this industry for 32 years. It's been an amazing journey. I've seen it from token ring networks to what we have now. We moved from one megabit per second to 10 to 100, to a gig, to 10 gigs higher. Can you imagine what that enables? It's mind-boggling. It enables the production and consumption of vast volumes of data. IoT sensors are everywhere now. Not because IoT sensors on their own enable something, but because they generate data continuously, and you have the network capacity to gather that in real time, then behind that you have the compute and storage capacity to absorb all of that in real time and drive insights in real time.

That completely changed the paradigm.

And now you can also go to any of the PC suppliers and buy yourself a workstation class desktop that is more powerful than some of the big and very expensive computers that you could buy 15 years ago.

Evolution of technology is inevitable and unstoppable. In this part of the book, we will talk about how this has been shaping the hospitality industry and what the future holds in terms of main areas of application and opportunities for further advancement.

Wide adoption of cloud computing was certainly the major driving factor in speeding up the development of tech in our industry as well as many others. I have a separate chapter dedicated to cloud computing where we will talk about it in more detail. There are also other factors that we will be discussing.

But first, let's see how "tech on steroids" has shaped the hospitality ecosystem into a dazzling mosaic.

As my favorite researcher Wouter Geerts (Skift) pointed out, *"Hotel tech tends to be characterized by piecemeal solutions by a myriad of tech vendors, all offering a few pieces of the puzzle."*[63]

---

[63]Skift: Hotel Distribution 2020 Part II: The Tech Landscape (November 2020): https://research.skift.com/report/hotel-distribution-2020-part-ii-the-tech-landscape/

The vendor map and main categories

Those of you who have been in the industry for a while, are probably used to seeing charts and graphs produced by different authors that attempt to bring structure to the chaotic hotel tech ecosystem and organize our tech players into clean categories.

One of my favorite ones is the 'Hotel Technology Market Map' produced by Hotel Tech Report, which can be found in their 2020 HotelTechIndex™: Hotel Software Market Leaders Report.[64] I'm attempting to provide the graph below but as you see, due to the amount of players, it becomes hard to read, so you're better off downloading your own via the link referenced in the footnote.

And that's the very issue we're dealing with - so many players that they can no longer fit on one page, which makes it hard to even read.

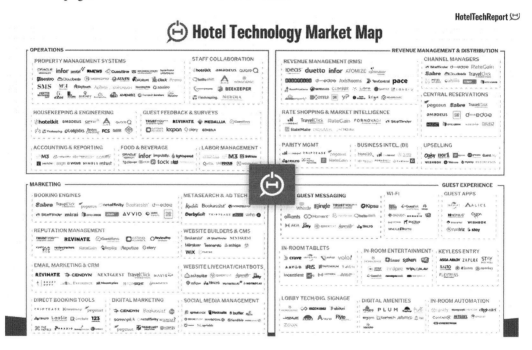

The main categories of players that are normally listed are the following. I'm using the above map as the base, but slightly modifying it to reflect the map that has been built in my head over the last 2 decades.

1. **Operations**

   a. PMS (Property Management System)

   b. Staff Collaboration

   c. Housekeeping and Engineering

   d. Guest Feedback and Surveys

---

[64] Hotel Tech Report: 2020 HotelTechIndex™: Hotel Software Market Leaders Report: https://www.research.hoteltechreport.com/hotel-software-leaders-index-2020/

e. Accounting and Reporting

f. F&B (Food and Beverage)

g. Labor Management

2. **Distribution**

a. Channel Managers

b. BEs (Booking Engines), in my head it belongs to the Distribution category, though I agree that it can be listed under Marketing as well

c. CRSs (Central Reservation Systems)

d. GDSs (Global Distribution Systems)

3. **Revenue Management & Analytics**

a. RMSs (Revenue Management Systems)

b. Business Intel

c. Upselling

4. **Market Intel**

a. Rate Shopping and Market Intelligence

b. Parity Management

5. **Marketing**

a. Metasearch and Ad tech

b. Reputation Management

c. Website Builders and CMSs

d. Email Marketing and CRM

e. Website Live Chat/Chatbots

f. Direct Booking Tools

g. Digital Marketing

h. Social Media Management

6. **Sales**

a. Meetings and Events management

b. Sales CRM

c. Group Sourcing & RFP's

7. **In-house guest experience**

a. Guest Messaging

b. Wi-Fi

c. Guest Apps

d. In-room Tablets

e. In-room Entertainment

f. Keyless Entry

g. Lobby Tech / Digital Signage

h. Digital Amenities

i. In-room Automation

8. **IT & Building Management**

a. Preventative Maintenance Software

b. Energy Management Systems

c. Payment Processing

d. Cyber Security & Fraud Prevention

e. HSIA & Hotel Wi-Fi Solutions

f. Asset Tracking Software

9. **HR & Staffing**

a. HRIS

b. Learning Management Software

c. Applicant Tracking Systems

d. Employee Engagement Software

e. Staffing & Recruiting

f. Payroll

Describing what each category does is outside of the scope of this book. There's a great resource for that - Hotel Tech Report[65] website, where you can find an overview of the categories and main players along with company descriptions and customer reviews.

One of the earlier Skift reports[66] also suggests plotting those categories using the underlying logic of a customer journey. Not a bad idea. I support anything that brings some order to the messy puzzle of hotel tech vendors.

---

[65]Hotel Tech Report: The World's Hotel Software Marketplace: https://hoteltechreport.com/
[66]Skift: The State of the Hotel Tech Stack 2018 (June 2018): https://research.skift.com/report/the-state-of-the-hotel-tech-stack-2018/

As noted in that report, "*The hotel tech stack should be organized and thought of in terms of the hotel's core business strategy: providing an overall seamless experience for the hotel guest. What this means is thinking about what each technology's role is in every step of the customer journey and how that technology should work with other technologies along the way so that the overall experience feels smooth and enjoyable to the hotel guest.*"

Pre Stay	During Stay	Post Stay
Loyalty and Rewards		
Website and Mobile App Builders and Content Management (CMS)	Merchandising and Upselling	Marketing Analytics and Meta Search Management
Customer Relationship Management (CRM) and Email Marketing	Guest Messaging and Concierge Services	Guest Feedback and Reputation Management
Digital Marketing Software and Personalization	Guest Room Entertainment Services	Revenue Management Software (RMS)
Event Planning and Management Software and Services		Hotel Market Analytics and Business Intelligence
Booking Engines	Food, Beverage, and Spa	Meetings and Events Intelligence
Channel Managers	Labor and Task Management	
Central Reservations Systems (CRS)		
Distribution Channels		
Meeting and Events Sales Software		

Property Management Systems (PMS)

Finance, Accounting, and Reporting | Procurement, Inventory, and Room Management | Payroll and HR | Facilities, Engineering, and IT

Now... The bad news is that the above lists are not comprehensive because it's literally impossible to come up with one that will paint the full picture of the tech vendor landscape with clean categories. One reason is that sometimes categories overlap (some tools serve multiple purposes) and another reason is that things in our world change rather quickly. New players emerge that reshape categories, and disruptions happen that constantly mess things up.

As a result, the hospitality tech ecosystem is by no means a fixed entity. It's an organism that is living, breathing and evolving. All we can do is draw snapshots every once in a while to track its evolution (just like parents take pictures of their children on a regular basis, and then Google sends you an AI-generated movie that shows you how much your kid has changed in the last few years).

So what we're discussing in this chapter is the current snapshot, or at least attempting to approximate what this current snapshot may look like.

The two plots I referenced above are my personal favorites because they help bring some order to the complexity of our vendor ecosystem. I always refer to them when I get confused about different players. Yes, after nearly 20 years in the hospitality industry, I still get confused at times. And I can't imagine how newbies or hospitality students feel when they look at this mess. And remember, it changes every year. So, as I mentioned earlier, we need to update our guides constantly because this area is so dynamic.

We also absolutely need to teach this to hospitality students and ensure that our academic syllabus is constantly updated as well. If you are a professor of a hospitality school reading this book, and you'd like me to come talk to your students about hospitality technology - I'll be happy to. Please reach out.

Hierarchy and what is changing

Regardless of what logic is used to group vendors into categories (operational departments or customer journey), one thing that is pretty clear is that historically, PMS has been the center of the tech universe (as we discussed in detail in the 'Integration dependencies' chapter). [67]

The above picture seems to be changing, however. There is a chance that PMSs will be eventually dethroned, and the laurels will be given to RM/BI (Revenue Management and Business Intelligence) solutions. The reason being is that the capabilities and the data needs of an RMS are far, far superior over the data needs and capabilities of a CRS or a PMS.

---

[67]Skift: The State of the Hotel Tech Stack 2018 (June 2018): https://research.skift.com/report/the-state-of-the-hotel-tech-stack-2018/

So when hoteliers make decisions about how they're structuring their tech stack and what they need in order to optimize their commercial capabilities of the future - they will inevitably start looking at RM/BI capabilities first, what they want to achieve in that area, and then work backwards to which PMS connects and integrates best with those capabilities.

Currently, in many cases, hotel owners and operators find themselves in a situation when they make a PMS or a CRS decision only to find out later that those don't support the very advanced functionality that was actually going to drive profit and efficiencies for the properties in their portfolio. So they end up being limited by that decision.

There's a lot to be said for seeing the revenue management (and profit optimization, whenever one is offered) platform as the center of the ecosystem rather than peripheral. It's all about data after all. So most advanced hoteliers now understand that they need to start building their tech stack from the most 'data demanding' piece that plays a key role in their business strategy (that is, RMS/BI platform) and then work backwards to find the right PMS, and not the other way around. Because otherwise, you run the risk of being faced with a lot of disappointment.

And as the distribution landscape continues to evolve, and complexities and costs grow, effective distribution, pricing, and profit optimization strategies are gaining importance, which makes it even more critical to ensure that operators have the right tools to build those strategies in an optimal manner.

If a hotel company already has a PMS that doesn't have the right integration capabilities - I suggest ripping it out. There are nearly 1000 PMSs in the world. As we discussed in one of the previous chapters - who will be there in 5-10 years? Every other industry has gone the consolidation route, and cloud-native solutions with proper API capabilities are clearly winning. Many legacy PM systems, as well as smaller regional players, are not going to survive. Software vendors are not going to build and support integrations with them. We will end up with 10-20 PMSs which will be the leaders, and it will certainly be the ones that are natively built in the cloud, and are open-minded in terms of integrating with other vendors.

So hoteliers need to look at it strategically to avoid a huge pain later.

Mylene Young (Son Hospitality Consulting) agrees with me:

Somebody who is looking for a new PMS, needs to ask themselves: how is it going to affect all other systems that are connected to it and that I want to connect to in the future? All integrations with every vendor that you had before: Channel Manager, Booking Engine, CRS, CRM, RMS, POS, you name it. It becomes very cumbersome because there are myriads of PMS vendors out there. You need to look at different aspects to make the right decisions.

But unfortunately, this is not the case in most situations. Hotel companies tend to just pick a random PMS and start from that. That's why they often end up with technology that then causes a lot of problems.

Indeed, there are so many hotel companies that are struggling with technology and because our hospitality ecosystem is so complex, it makes it very hard for hotel owners and management companies to navigate in this space. I recently provided consulting services for a newly opened resort in Mexico and helped them assemble their tech stack to automate operations based on their needs and their specific use case. I'd like to say that there's no way they would have been able to pick the right list of vendors on their own. It takes a person with years and years of hotel tech experience to assemble the most optimal combination of fully integrated elements into an assembly that works flawlessly. It was a masterpiece when I was done, though.

So I'm hopeful that eventually there will be consolidations, like what we have seen in other sectors and starting to see in ours as well, that will make hoteliers' lives more comfortable and allow them to easily build or upgrade their tech stack without it being a traumatizing experience.

Distribution category, the problem child

I think many would agree that the most complex part of the hospitality tech ecosystem is certainly the Distribution element.

For a very long time, hotel marketing and distribution was rather simple. The majority of hotel bookings came directly from guests either walking through the front door, calling the hotel, or calling the reservation center. But then everything changed.

Mylene Young (Son Hospitality Consulting), who has more years of experience in the distribution space than anyone else I know, provided a summary of how this space has evolved.

In recent years, distribution has come to the fore as a key factor impacting the hotel sector. The internet, followed by the growth of social networking and now the 'sharing economy' has added successive layers of complexity to the marketing and distribution of hospitality services. The technology disruption of the mid- and late 1990s completely flipped the way consumers book hotel rooms. Online travel agencies like Booking.com and Expedia have become one of the primary ways consumers book hotel rooms.

And now that is changing, too. It is likely that the original disruptors (the large OTAs) are themselves going to be increasingly disrupted, notably by the launching of onsite booking by Google, Amazon and Facebook.

The other disruptors of course are the accommodation rental websites led by Airbnb, which are already visibly taking share from the hotel industry – especially in some leisure markets.

The evolution that Mylene described above is what has shaped the hotel software distribution landscape as we see it today.

One of the latest Skift studies[68] provided a map of the Distribution ecosystem. Notice the word "simplified" in the title of the graph. It is there for a reason, for the very same reason that I mentioned above, which gets even worse when we start talking about Distribution. It is impossible to draw a complete picture of the relationships between different players in that space. We would end up with a myriad of scattered elements, with a bunch of lines going from one to another, in all kinds of different directions.

All we can do is approximate, to be able to organize those elements into some major categories, using some underlying logic.

Exhibit 1: A simplified map of hotel distribution tech[69]

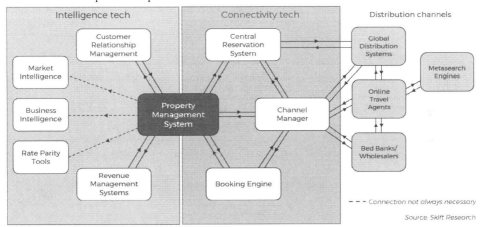

What we're noticing though, is overlapping and merging of categories in the Distribution section, and blurring lines between them. It is the trend that Wouter Geerts of Skift calls "solution blurring".

This is how he describes it: *"As a result of the increasing penetration of technology into hotel distribution, there are more and more systems and tools available, offered by more and more vendors. While many vendors are predominantly known for one or a few tools, we are seeing an increasing focus by distribution tech vendors on offering a host of tools under their brand umbrella. There are still specialist players, like booking engine vendors, but most vendors are increasingly of the belief that particularly owners of small and independent hotels want an end-to-end solution for their distribution needs."*[70]

The graph below (taken from the same Skift Distribution report) paints a picture of how various tech vendors are moving towards offering more comprehensive solutions that cover a number of use cases and thus, penetrate multiple categories at the same time. Notice how many vendors that originally emerged from the distribution category started tapping into other categories like RMS, BI, Market Intel and Marketing.

---

[68] Skift: Hotel Distribution 2020 Part I: The Channel Mix (November 2020): https://research.skift.com/report/hotel-distribution-2020-part-i-the-channel-mix/

[69] Skift: Hotel Distribution 2020 Part II: The Tech Landscape (November 2020): https://research.skift.com/report/hotel-distribution-2020-part-ii-the-tech-landscape/

[70] Skift: Hotel Distribution 2020 Part II: The Tech Landscape (November 2020): https://research.skift.com/report/hotel-distribution-2020-part-ii-the-tech-landscape/

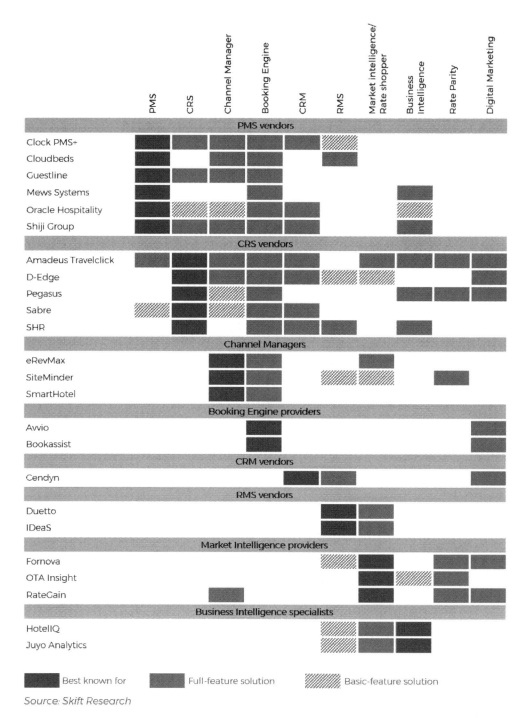

Source: Skift Research

We're seeing this trend not only in the Distribution part of the ecosystem, but also in other segments. As I mentioned earlier, I believe that as a result, our ecosystem will start looking more and more integrated and less cumbersome with more categories consolidating. We will see more companies moving to the cloud, more mergers and acquisitions and more collaboration between departments at properties to work together towards addressing the complete customer experience: from looking to booking to departing and returning.

Until then, we have a gazillion of startups entering the market every minute, filling functionality gaps, solving new business problems, and creating new categories.

Let me share a lifehack with you: my favorite way to measure the evolution of hospitality technology and to keep an eye on new entrants into different categories is to review the vendor list of the annual HITEC[71] conference. You will notice many players who consistently show up year after year, but then there is also a myriad of new startups that try to contribute to the innovations in the industry. Not all of them survive, but many grow to be amazing companies offering wonderful solutions to make the lives of hoteliers easier, more efficient and more profitable.

Let's talk about startups and their role in the development of the industry.

Startup ecosystem

What we're seeing in our industry right now (constant emergence of new entrants in the tech space) is a natural stage of evolution, and cloud computing is mainly to thank for that. Another reason is that consumer (B2C) apps have developed rapidly in the recent decade, so now humans got a feel of what a good piece of software could look like (cloud-based, mobile friendly, intuitive and real-time) and they can no longer tolerate what legacy B2B vendors in the hospitality industry have been offering.

So they started asking for more. And legacy companies can't give them more, because they're big, old and slow. That's where startups come in, filling gaps in legacy functionality or offering better, more optimal solutions to some of the old problems, for less money, and with a sleeker UI.

Since Google and AWS both offer cloud solutions, I asked representatives from both companies about their opinion in regards to the role startups play in our industry. That led to very interesting discussions.

| Ira Vouk

Do you have a lot of startups reaching out to you from the hospitality space?

| Sekhar Mallipeddi (AWS)

Oh yes. I work with them a lot, I'm a startup advisor. I help them refine their go-to-market strategy. Because we see a lot of clear signals from our customers on what they want. And when startups approach us and say, "This is what I want to build," we can say, "Yeah, that's perfect, let's go get it implemented," or we say,

---

[71]HFTP: Hospitality Financial & Technology Professionals website: https://my.hftp.org/

"You know what, that's not exactly what customers are looking for, how about you make a change to this, and that way you can be more successful."

And we give them resources. We give them credits to innovate and then we help them be successful with our customers. Because startups innovate much, much faster than a lot of older companies. They have very agile delivery models and they are willing to experiment a lot more than other established players.

Amazon Web Services has a free program named "Activate"[72] that is specifically designed for startups and early stage entrepreneurs. It provides eligible startups with tools and resources, including AWS credits, and AWS Support credits to help them get started and grow their business. The Activate program is open to bootstrapped, self-funded, and funded startups up to and including Series A. Companies can use their credits for AWS services from infrastructure technologies like compute, storage, and databases - to emerging technologies, such as machine learning and artificial intelligence, data lakes and analytics, and Internet of Things.

Now, let's turn to Google. Here's my conversation with Ravi Simhambhatla, Managing Director/CTO, Digital Transformation - Travel & Transportation at Google Cloud).

Ira Vouk

We all agree that the larger the company, the slower it is to adopt new technology. Large companies in our industry are very slow to adopt new things and to innovate.

What we are seeing in our space is that innovations mostly come from little vendors or startup companies that appear faster than I blink. Due to the evolution of cloud solutions in the last 5 years or so, every year you see a bunch of new vendors who are trying to disrupt the industry.

But they are so tiny and it's hard for them to compete with those larger players who own a very large market share, who are like the Titanic - slooooow. And those little players are like little boats in the ocean trying to make waves. I would love to hear your opinion on this matter.

Ravi Simhambhatla

The startup ecosystem is absolutely necessary. Even though it's not as effective as one would think (there are some statistics that 8 or 9 out of 10 startups fail) but the reason why I think it's essential is because they see the world through a very different lens, from a very different point of view.

But startups have been trying to solve very atomic problems, very finite, very well defined problems. The issue with that is that the world is a far more complex place. There are multiple causes and effects to things. So as a startup, as a small

---

[72]AWS: Activate for Startups, Founders & Entrepreneurs: https://aws.amazon.com/activate/

company, having a very finite view on the problems that you're trying to solve is detrimental. Which is why you end up becoming a really small fish in a big sea and literally one of three things happen: the big fish eats you, the big fish consumes you, or you're just insignificant and inconsequential, you're so small that nobody cares.

Ira Vouk

I think the goal is for the big fish to buy them. That's what normally their target is.

Ravi Simhambhatla

You hit the nail on the head. The problem is that many startups are building products not to actually change businesses but to fill in those gaps that the big companies leave, in the hopes of being bought out. To me, that does not add much value over time. Because in many cases, when these startups get bought out, the more legacy a company is, the more likely that what they bought will just get buried.

The startup is coming in with let's say 40 people who are full of energy and enthusiasm. And boom, they get acquired by a company of 50,000 people. Those 40 people are not going to be able to change those 50,000 people, it's impossible. So they're going to get absorbed. Those big legacy corporations - that's where startups go to die.

So I think startups need to focus on solving slightly more "macro" problems. If you look at a true problem you're trying to solve, it's at the epicenter of your world and then you draw concentric circles around it. That problem that you're trying to solve in itself, is not the entirety of the problem set. It's like a ripple effect in a pond. There are ripples that go out. So you could think you're solving a problem, but if you don't address the macro then you're just noise.

So they need to figure out what the right balance is, how far they should extend out into the outer ripples without going so far that they lose their DNA and their passion and enthusiasm, but also not too shallow.

So the startup ecosystem like I said is very, very important but something has got to change. With all due respect to Silicon Valley, I think running after financial windfalls is very fulfilling. But what have you truly achieved?

Google also invests in startups. One notable example is the acquisition of Deepmind[73] in 2015, a British artificial intelligence and research laboratory founded in September 2010. The company achieved some amazing things in various areas of application through AI-based research and development.

---

[73]Wikipedia: DeepMind: https://en.wikipedia.org/wiki/DeepMind

I myself am a former founder of a hospitality tech startup, a revenue management system (iRates). The company was founded 12 years ago and it was the first RMS in the industry that was running on machine learning algorithms, very compute heavy. And one of the problems... or, rather, the main problem I would say, was that it wasn't built natively in the cloud. It was developed by a team of very talented scientists in Moscow, as a premise-based solution. And then years later, when we realized that the whole world is moving to the cloud, it was very difficult to move our product there, due to the complexity and computing demands of our system.

And only later I realized that if it had been natively built as a cloud solution from the beginning, it would have been a much more successful business that would be easier to scale. And that's a very good example of how much value companies like AWS and Google bring to the hospitality industry and to the entire world, and how these tools have significantly increased the speed of innovations.

Technology investment trends

While discussions with Google and AWS were mostly technically oriented, Jordan Hollander (Co-founder and CEO of Hotel Tech Report) helped me view the evolution of hospitality from a different angle - the financial and investment aspect of it.

We had a very engaging conversation, which I'm sharing with you below.

| Ira Vouk

What has changed in the hospitality industry in the last 10 years in your opinion, and in the technology realm in particular?

| Jordan Hollander

There has been a shift in the openness of private equity and venture capital to invest in the market.

Historically, there was a period that was like the Golden Age of hospitality when Synexis was founded and Micros and Travelclick and all these companies that ended up getting looped into Oracle and Amadeus. And then there was a lull where investors were scared to invest in the hospitality market just because of how challenging it really is to scale.

And now there's an increased aptitude to invest in it again.

| Ira Vouk

Do you see different trends in B2B vs B2C in our space?

| Jordan Hollander

Early to mid-2000s were really about consumer apps, like finding the coolest travel app and activity planning, etc. and there were enough of those that came and went. Now the probability of success to create the next booking.com is very low. And so I think venture capitalists like this idea that there's a much higher probability of success in creating great business software.

I think in general, investors have seen how successful vertical market software could be, and B2B software in general. So the number of tools that companies are now using, and as you know the SMB space (small businesses) didn't even use technology before. Everything was on pen and paper and now that they're all going digital, a ton of these tools popped up.

And I think venture capital naturally has an orientation to look at a market and say, "There's a ton of these small players. What happens if we put it all together and cut out the fat and invest in innovation?" And so I see there's certainly an orientation towards that.

Ira Vouk

And when it comes to B2B, what investment trends are worth noting?

Jordan Hollander

One of the recent big changes is for hospitality tech vendors to go from regional to global. We see many examples of those in the industry now. 10 years ago there were many more localized regional solutions. It sure still exists in many ways today but I think the global companies are taking more and more share. And ultimately, it's great for hotels because those global companies are able to invest in innovation, where a regional player is really just making ends meet and it's more of a cash flow lifestyle business. Whereas larger global companies may have private equity and venture capital come in that allows them to invest more resources in the product, attract better talent, better thought leadership, provide better education.

I think there's just a lot of innovation now and a lot of talent. And that brain drain that occurred with the regionalized lifestyle businesses - that is actually starting to reverse. It's easier to attract capital for great ideas and so I think it's a lot of good signs pointing in the right direction for the industry.

Things have certainly changed for the industry in the last 10 years. Cloud computing, new technologies, new data streams, startups, investments, merging categories, consolidations... It's been fun to watch. But then there's so much more that we can (and should) strive for.

As Ravi Simhambhatla said:

There is this saying "disrupt or die". Now is the time. Disrupt or just become irrelevant.

Amen to that!

Right now, more than ever before, investors and technology vendors have so much potential to drive the industry forward, towards more innovations. The hospitality industry has been stagnant for so many years, and now finally, we're starting to see a lot of improvements in the area of technology adoption. The pandemic made us realize that human resources are very limited and we need to be able to do things differently in a more efficient and optimal manner, and technology is here to help us with that.

It looks like the industry is finally starting to understand that technology is not an enemy, it's our friend. And the cloud is our BFF.

Cloud computing

Cloud revolution

"You've got to think, you've got to try, you've got to experiment..."

Ravi Simhambhatla

We spoke about cloud computing briefly earlier. But this topic definitely warrants a dedicated chapter because this is one of the major driving factors of the tech revolution I'm describing in this book.

There are three main providers of Cloud Computing products on the market right now: AWS, Microsoft Azure and Google Cloud.[74] While Microsoft also has a large market share in the worldwide total spend, the 2 most prominent companies in the Travel space are Amazon and Google, and we will talk about those in more detail later.

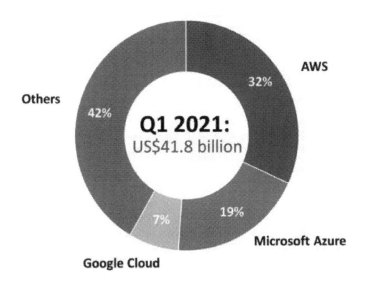

What is Cloud Computing and how has it affected hotel tech? The answer is simple: it is the technology that causes new tech startups to pop up like mushrooms after a rainy day (as we say in Belarus) through accelerated time-to-market, and that allows hospitality companies to adopt these new tools quicker and with less costs.

Here's a simple definition of Cloud Computing from my favorite source: "Cloud computing is the on-demand availability of computer system resources, especially data

---

[74]ParkMyCloud: AWS vs Azure vs Google Cloud Market Share 2021: What the Latest Data Shows (May 2021): https://www.parkmycloud.com/blog/aws-vs-azure-vs-google-cloud-market-share/

storage (cloud storage) and computing power, without direct active management by the user... Cloud computing relies on sharing of resources to achieve coherence and economies of scale, typically using a 'pay-as-you-go' model which can help in reducing capital expenses."[75]

In simple words: if you want to build (or buy) software - you no longer need to buy expensive hardware to run your company from the servers in your garage. You can use someone else's server and connect to it via the Internet. And that "someone else" will take very good care of it, will protect your information and will only charge you for what you use, on a monthly basis. And if you need more resources - they will automatically offer more, you don't even have to ask for it. And if you need less - they will automatically give you less and charge you less. How cool is that?

As a result, the evolution and wide adoption of the "cloud" allowed organizations to significantly lower their capital expenses, which made it much easier (and cheaper) to build and maintain software, which led to introduction and wide adoption of a SaaS model. [76]

SaaS (software as a service) is a software licensing and delivery model in which software is licensed on a subscription basis and is centrally hosted. SaaS is also known as "on-demand software" and Web-based/Web-hosted software.

With SaaS, hoteliers subscribe to the use of the software, as well as data storage in the cloud. The vendor hosts the data and software in the cloud, and there is no need for physical hardware at the property.

SaaS apps are typically accessed by users using a thin client, e.g. via a web browser or a mobile app. SaaS became a common delivery model for many business applications. Wikipedia says, "*It has been incorporated into the strategy of nearly all enterprise software companies...*" The author is clearly not aware of the situation in our industry. Though things are certainly getting better for us and there's definitely the light at the end of the tunnel.

I love how John Burns (President of Hospitality Technology Consulting) phrased it using the hospitality language:

> *At some point people started saying, "We need technology, and Excel spreadsheet is no longer sufficient. We're going to have to have more now." We looked around to see what "more" meant. And until cloud-based systems came along, "more" was really expensive. An enterprise software could cost $125-$150 k to install. And then extra costs, extra costs, extra costs. So there was a financial reluctance that fortunately has been largely removed by SaaS, and now you can pay per room per month.*

---

[75]Wikipedia: Cloud Computing: https://en.wikipedia.org/wiki/Cloud_computing
[76]Wikipedia: Software as a Service: https://en.wikipedia.org/wiki/Software_as_a_service

And this simple model has revolutionized the industry, mainly through 2 things:

1. Removing financial barriers to start a technology company, due to lower startup costs

2. Removing financial barriers for hospitality companies to adopt new technology due to lower activation and subscription costs (via SaaS model)

BIO model and large hospitality organizations

As mentioned earlier, large hospitality organizations are the ones struggling the most with their cloud journey. Michael Blake (CTO of AHLA, former CEO of HTNG) has a lot of experience working with such companies. Here's one of the comments he made:

When you're talking about displacing on-premise tools with cloud solutions, if you capture all the costs, you're going to find that the cloud is always cheaper. I could generally devise an ROI on most of the solutions that we had. So I could tell them, "Look, you can keep doing what you're doing - and you'll be slow, you'll be more expensive and you'll be way behind the times. Or you can be better, faster, cheaper. It's up to you. What do you want to do?"

Unfortunately, not all hospitality companies know the right answer to that question. But they'll all get there eventually. "Disrupt or die" as we talked about in the previous chapter.

My favorite conversations are the ones where I get to learn something new. And when I spoke to Michael Blake, my horizons significantly expanded because every 5 minutes I was introduced to a new concept. One of them is the BIO model (Broker-Integrate-Orchestrate) that describes the more modern approach to building and operating technology.

The conversation pertained to the problem of large hospitality organizations having old, rigid in-house technology that doesn't integrate well with the rest of the ecosystem and the lack of ability for continuous innovation.

Here are some quotes from that conversation.

| Michael Blake

I'd like to take you on a journey with me.

I think there's a spectrum out there of this model where people build technology. And there are folks who utilize technology.

So think of a bank. What is a bank? It's technology at the end of the day. It is all about bits and bytes and what have you. Whereas when you look at restaurants and hotels and others, they're on the other end of that spectrum - technology enables their ability to serve. So on one end of the spectrum, you need the traditional plan-build-run model where people plan technology, and then they go ahead and build it and then they run it.

Well. What I would advocate for what hospitality needs, is more of a broker-integrate-orchestrate (BIO) model. And that model really runs through the whole dynamic of the industry and how technologies are utilized, how it grows, how people are working through it. And I got to tell you that this COVID thing that happened, I think has some pretty deep implications for the BIO model more so than it ever had.

The BIO model approach stems from cloud computing and dates back to 2012[77] It was first described by Mark Settle (Chief Information Officer at BMC Software) in his article referenced in the footnote.

"IT organizations have conventionally operated under an 'own and operate' model in which they buy or build the hardware and software needed to construct essential business systems. The inevitable consequences of the 'own and operate' model are large data centers, 24x7 operations teams and small armies of developers maintaining systems built on a bewildering array of outdated technologies.

Cloud computing – in all its various forms – offers a serious challenge to the conventional 'own and operate' model. Cloud computing provides IT shops with the ability to use hardware and software assets that are owned, developed and maintained by others. Potential benefits include accelerated time-to-market for new business solutions and ready access to up-to-date technologies."

| Michael Blake

That BIO model gets us to a world of creation and it gets us out of this "building stuff" mode where your product is good when you turn it on, and it works but the next day, it's already obsolete. Why? Because the operating systems evolve, something else moves on, and you constantly are in this realm of testing. These days, nothing operates by itself, it all has to be integrated and if you're not integrated within the fabric, then nothing is going to work.

Unfortunately sometimes the senior leadership of large companies don't get that. "I've just bought it, I spent half a million dollars. It should work, right?"

What the BIO model allows me to do is, instead of doing technology myself, I'm riding on other people's innovation curves.

If I start putting their solutions together, I get something better than what I could make on my own. And I think that's generally what I would always subscribe to.

You have to realize how transformational technology can be. And it's not the bits and bytes that we pass behind. It's the ability for people to use it. And if people can use it, they can do better and they'll do better by the company.

---

[77]Forbes: Broker/Integrate/Orchestrate: The New IT Operating Model, Mark Settle (May 2012): https://www.forbes.com/sites/ciocentral/2012/05/14/brokerintegrateorchestrate-the-new-it-operating-model

Very nicely put. Technology enables us to do better and to have better lives. And cloud technology enables us to be modern, agile and innovative. The next section lists all the benefits of cloud technology.

Main benefits of Cloud computing

1. **Costs.** As discussed above: reduced capital expenses, pay-as-you-go model.

2. **Security.** There's still a misconception about how secure cloud services are. I'm referring to larger hotel companies, as well as legacy software players who are having the hardest time catching up with the 21st century. Outsourcing innovation actually ensures security and best practices when it comes to data. Thousands of professionals at a company like AWS or Google know more about security than a few guys in the IT division of a hotel company. The cloud companies will have the latest enterprise software and will take care of our data in a much more secure way than we would.

3. **Handling data.** Another very important aspect is that our internal IT departments will not have the capability to handle increasing amounts of data that the industry is being flooded with. The amount of data is growing on a daily basis and we need proper tools to handle it. And those tools are in the cloud, not in somebody's garage.

4. And last but not least: cloud services ensure **quick software development, deployment and iterations,** which ultimately ensures that if your tech stack is in the cloud, you'll never again find yourself 10 or 20 years behind the curve when it comes to technology.

I'm happy to see that many hospitality companies have been taking advantage of the benefits of cloud computing and the availability of new SaaS software tools. One of the great examples that I really love, which paints a picture of how technology has grown, is STR (Smith Travel Research) and the evolution of their delivery model.

Jan Freitag (National Director, Hospitality Analytics for the CoStar Group, formerly Senior VP at STR) shared during our conversation:

In the 1980s and 1990s we used to, at the month end, print out reports and FedEx them to the headquarters of the publicly traded companies. We don't do that anymore! We used to receive data via fax. We don't do that anymore!

So technology in that sense has made a big difference. Eventually everyone started using emails, so we would email reports to them. And now, as you know, they come to a self-serve portal where the data gets refreshed all the time. They get a ping when new data is ready, then they download it.

So we're paperless. So the big changes have been in that technology part of how we approach data transfer. We get these huge data files now, we don't get faxes. And we used to get letters (don't even remind me of that).

And a view from a software vendor perspective:

Marco Benvenuti (Co-founder of Duetto RMS)

When we started Duetto, we were the first RMS solution built on cloud technology. And there was a lot of reluctance to it. Now, 10 years later, everybody's moving to the cloud. And so what that means is that the ability to connect with data is becoming easier and easier. So, there's going to be a point where the industry will reach an ecosystem, where APIs are going to be pretty much open and that's going to open a whole variety of things.

PMS battlefield

What Marco was referring to above is that the Cloud is also helping us deal with the PMS dependency issue that we discussed in one of the previous chapters, which I would say, has been the biggest barrier for non-PMS hospitality vendors to scale their businesses.

Traditional PMSs were originally built for on-premise infrastructure, which comes with an array of disadvantages. Because those solutions have been around for a while, they have become feature-heavy. And the heavier they are, the harder it is for them to transition from premise to the cloud. Essentially, all these systems need to be rebuilt, and clients expect to not lose any features when migrating. This is one of the major reasons why traditional PMSs have seen some of the slowest migrations to the cloud of hotel IT systems, as illustrated by research from the Hospitality Technology magazine.[78]

Hotel Tech Systems in the Cloud

■ 2017 ■ 2018 2019

	RMS	CRS	CRM	PMS
2017	44%	34%	37%	34%
2018	58%	58%	47%	47%
2019	66%	65%	60%	55%

Source: 2019 Hotel Technology Study by the Hospitality Technology magazine. Respondents include subscribers to the magazine, with direct responsibility of 17,980 hotels.

---

[78]Skift: The Hotel Property Management Systems Landscape 2020 (January 2020): https://research.skift.com/report/the-hotel-property-management-systems-landscape-2020/

As a result of this, we have seen many new cloud-native PMS players emerging that started competing with legacy PMS players. These new systems were born out of slow cloud adoption amongst legacy systems.

From <u>Skift PMS Landscape report</u>, "Hetras was one of the first companies to offer a fully cloud-native system, swiftly followed by players like Clock PMS and StayNTouch. Hetras got acquired by Shiji Group in 2016, as was StayNTouch."[79]

Most newer cloud-native PMS providers support and embrace an open API approach that will ultimately allow all parts of the ecosystem to efficiently communicate with each other, thus removing the barriers for vendors to scale their businesses and for hospitality companies to adopt modern solutions.

Conclusion

I'd like to conclude the 'Cloud computing' section with the vision shared by Michael Blake:

I have this premise in my mind that technology really only works at scale. And when you start thinking about tech hospitality companies who have scale, at the end of the day, no one really does, even Marriott or Hilton or IHG, as big as they are, they still don't have the same number of transactions as we see in large companies in other industries. So they just don't have that same level of processing power, or need for processing power.

So what does that get you to? Well, that gets you to a place where the only way to achieve scale is through the cloud. Because the cloud is the dynamic that gets you to that scale. That's the model where you can start seeing your processing power get there.

So as it should be pretty clear at this point, cloud computing is really a big deal.

And that is what will help the industry evolve in the next 5-10 years to the levels it has never seen before.

Google and AWS are playing a very important role in our industry through the products they offer, and that is why I'm dedicating a separate chapter in this book to each.

---

[79]Skift: The Hotel Property Management Systems Landscape 2020 (January 2020): https://research.skift.com/report/the-hotel-property-management-systems-landscape-2020/

Google

> "No matter where in the travel industry you turn,
>
> one company seems to be on everyone's lips: Google."
>
> *Seth Borko, 'A Deep Dive Into Google's Impact on Travel', Skift 2020*

Google Travel

Because Google owns, and will likely continue to own, the top of the customer acquisition funnel in travel, we have to talk about this giant in detail. In addition to that, Google offers cloud solutions, which we will also discuss further.

Google, the online giant, touches, in one way or another, nearly every stage of the traveler's journey. Skift Research[80] estimates that globally, the travel industry may have spent as much as $16 billion on advertising on Google in 2019. Booking Holdings and Expedia Group are the two largest contributors to that.

Google says, "*Our travel mission is to be the trusted place where travelers go for the most useful information to make fast, effortless decisions, and we view our role in the industry as that of a connector between users and travel companies. This will remain true even as our products evolve.*"

Per Ravi Simhambhatla, Google Travel has 2 macro views.

One is the **consumer.** This is where a consumer goes to Google.com and searches for travel or is imagining an experience. Google Travel, as a division of Google, builds up the capabilities to deliver those experiences on Google.com.

And then Google Travel also has **enterprise** products.

Google Travel was formed as part of an acquisition of a company named ITA Software[81] out of Cambridge Massachusetts in July 2010, and that's how the travel division within Google was born.

Their software powers Google.com for travel searches, and flight searches for several global airlines' direct channels. If you go to the websites or mobile apps of the top three largest global airlines (United, Delta and American) and do a flight search - that is powered by the API that Google Travel has built.

First, let's examine the key Google consumer products and where they sit within the organization.

---

[80]Skift: A Deep Dive Into Google's Impact on Travel 2020 (February 2020): https://research.skift.com/report/a-deep-dive-into-googles-impact-on-travel-2020/

[81]Wikipedia: ITA Software: https://en.wikipedia.org/wiki/ITA_Software

I would like to thank Seth Borko, Senior Research Analyst at Skift, as a significant portion of this chapter is based on the research he conducted in 2020 that was published in his report <u>A Deep Dive Into Google's Impact on Travel</u>.[82] It helped me organize my knowledge about consumer-facing products produced by Google that are related to the travel industry.

First, let's talk about travel-related consumer-facing products. [83]

Map of Google's Advertising Ecosystem

Horizontal Search

Google's First Party Ad Properties are websites owned and controlled by Google that monetize through advertising.

The core of this is the search business on Google.com, where users query the website and receive organized results (screenshot below). Google has a 75% global desktop search share and a 90% mobile search share, according to web statistics tracker, Net MarketShare.

---

[82]Skift: A Deep Dive Into Google's Impact on Travel 2020 (February 2020): https://research.skift.com/report/a-deep-dive-into-googles-impact-on-travel-2020/

[83]Skift: A Deep Dive Into Google's Impact on Travel 2020 (February 2020): https://research.skift.com/report/a-deep-dive-into-googles-impact-on-travel-2020/

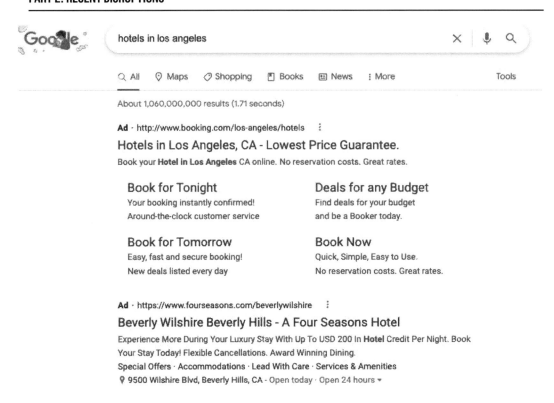

Google can then capture the intent outlined by the user and serve ads around it. This product, called Google Ads (formerly known as Google AdWords), is the bread and butter of Google's business and drives most of its revenue.

The sponsored links (marked with the word "Ad" in the screenshot) are a horizontal search product, meaning that they work in the same way for queries across any industry. The query "trips to Los Angeles" may serve up to four blue ad links, just like a search for "Christmas gifts" would do.

Advertisers bid to have their sites displayed as high as possible in the search results of a given query and only pay Google when a user clicks on one of their links. This is known as a pay-per-click (PPC) or cost-per-click (CPC) bidding method.

Vertical Search

In addition to the classic search described above, which works the same way for everyone regardless of the industry, Google has also built out a number of vertical search tools specific to the travel business and its sub-industries, which dramatically increased its impact on the travel industry.

Rather than the one-size-fits-all blue links and text descriptions that come with horizontal search, the vertical search modules have been customized to display additional relevant search information specific to individual travel segments. The four travel segments Google currently operates in are: flights, hotels, short-term rentals and things to do.

These vertical travel search offerings have grown rapidly in prominence, both as a function of their convenience to travelers and due to strong promotion by the Google algorithm.

146

Below are more details about Google's vertical products.

1. Google Flights

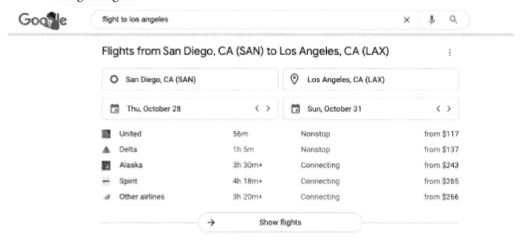

Starting from January 2020, Google stopped charging airline partners for referral links on Google Flights.[84] The results within Google Flights will continue to be ranked by relevance to the user, based on factors like price and convenience.

2. Google Hotels

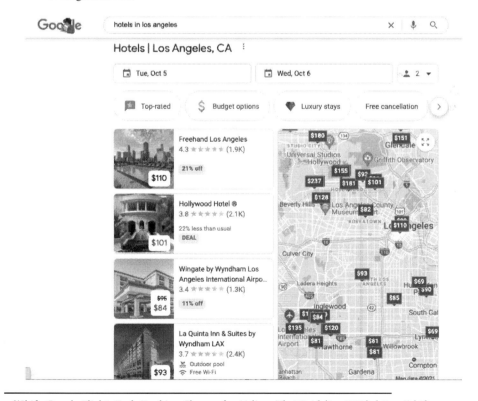

---

[84]Skift: Google Flights Ends Booking Charges for Airlines That Paid (Jan 2020): https://skift.com/2020/01/22/google-flights-ends-booking-charges-for-airlines-that-paid/

According to Skift analysts, the hotels module accounts for the majority of Google's vertical search revenue today, as it is the most profitable of Google's vertical search offerings. The in-line version of the module displays a select few hotels that it believes are relevant to the customer, alongside a location map with prices.

The hotel listings returned within the Google Hotel Ad units are also organic and unpaid. However, when users click into the unit to view more hotels, it takes the browser over to Google's full hotel search site. Here, Google will insert paid sponsored hotel ad listings into the top spot of results (see listings marked with the word "Ad" in the screenshot below).

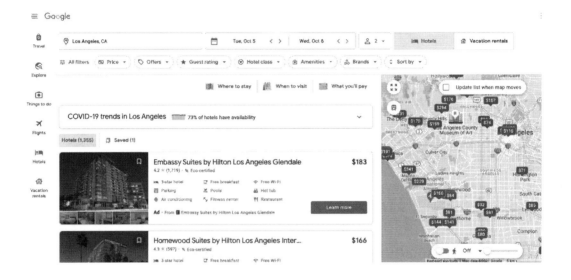

Once you select a specific property to book, Google also monetizes in a classic metasearch style, displaying multiple offers for the same property from across the web.

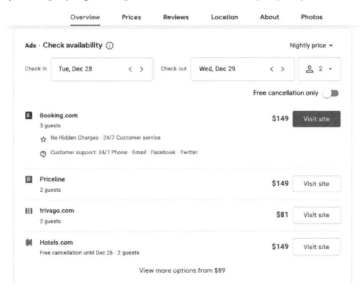

The top section ("Ads") are paid listings where OTAs and brands compete for positioning. Free listings appear under "View more options". As mentioned in one of the earlier chapters, ads are charged using a number of different models.

CPC (cost-per-click), which is most common, where hotels and OTAs bid a per-set amount on specified search terms. The bid amount, together with other factors like the room rate, will determine the ranking order on the results page. Hotels and OTAs only pay if the consumer actually clicks on their link.

CPA (cost-per-acquisition), where a hotel or OTA only pays if a booking is made. All the major metasearch engines offer this alternative.

CPS or PPS (commission-per-stay) is the name and this is where hoteliers and OTAs only pay Google after the stay has actually happened.

There are two major differences between hotels and flights driving better monetization (from Google's perspective) in this channel.

The first is that hotels are much more highly fragmented than airlines. The other issue is the large presence of online travel agencies and metasearch websites in hospitality. The OTAs and metasearch sites rely on Google for a substantial portion of their customer traffic.

Google's dedication to having a completeness of hotel offerings, even if that means including unpaid results, only benefits the hotels that receive free listings. But if the OTAs want to feature prominently, and they do because much more of their profit comes from hotels than airlines, they need to bid on ads. And that leaves the big chains with little option but to respond as well, helping to drive the monetization of this Google product.

3. <u>Google Vacation Rental</u>

One of Google's latest vertical travel search offerings is short-term rentals. The module is very similar to the Hotels user experience.

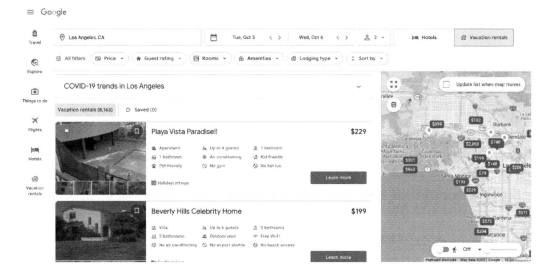

4. Google Things To Do

The newer Things To Do vertical product is aimed to help users discover new and unique things to do in an area and to make it easier for businesses to promote their tours, attractions, and activities and connect with interested consumers. With Things To Do, partners can surface their inventory via free listings and through a dynamic ad format. Google encourages attractions, tour operators, and activity providers to take part.

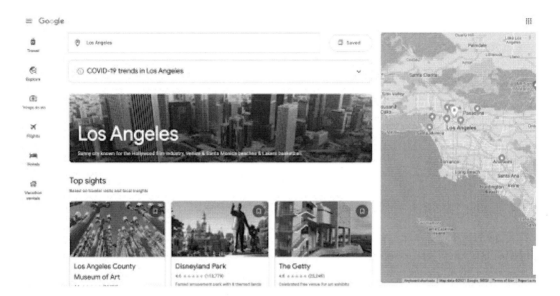

Google monetizes their Things To Do module via ad campaigns.[85] A Things To Do campaign allows businesses to bid for ad placements that appear when a traveler searches for tours, activities, and local attractions on Google Search. The ads appear above the search results and show various details including photos, prices, company's name, and a booking link for the activity.

Google Maps

If you own a restaurant, bar, spa, beauty supply store, tourist attraction, event venue, or hotel, or offer services to any of these sectors, you probably have a Google business listing, which gets you into the Google Maps app for discovery purposes.

Google has monetized its position in maps by building sponsored listings and other forms of advertising into its interface.

---

[85]Google Ads Help: Things to do ads campaign setup: https://support.google.com/google-ads/answer/10723637

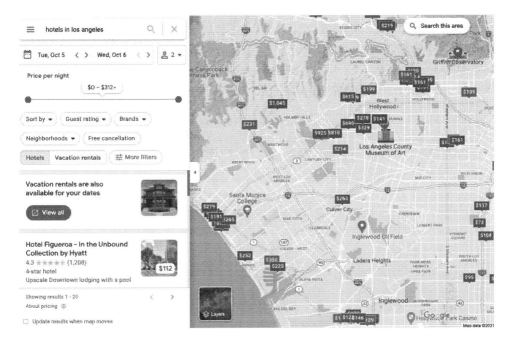

Display Ads: Youtube, Gmail and 3rd party

Parts of the display network are in-house, most notably online video giant YouTube.

YouTube's influence on the travel industry is twofold. First is the wide range of popular content creators and travel vloggers that use the video platform. These influencers are key sources of travel inspiration and reviews for many young customers. Increasingly, we are seeing sponsored relationships between travel brands and these social media stars, but those transactions take place off the Google platform.

Google also offers Gmail ads which are units formatted to look like new messages, complete with subject line and sender, that show up in the promotions and social tabs of a user's inbox. Gmail users can click on the ads which then expand in an email-like way into a more interactive ad.

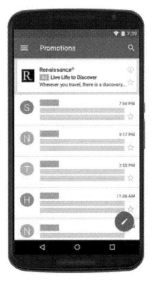

The same highly targeted placement of display ads by user profile, demographics, and behavior as is done on Google's own sites can also be extended to non-Google websites through its 3rd Party Display Network that allows it to connect with customers not just on Google owned sites, but on those customers' favorite sites and apps.

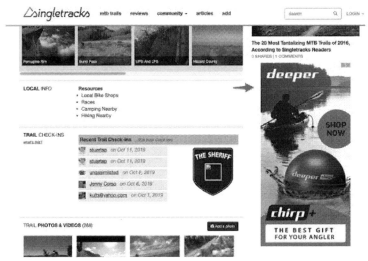

As you can see from the above, Google is one of the very few companies that can reach across the entire customer travel journey, from inspiration through visitation to returning.

Google can tie together data from across the entire travel journey in ways that few other companies can. Not only does it have a deep vertical reach, but it can pull in web browsing behavior from non-travel activities to develop a much more holistic view of the customer. This is a powerful competitive advantage that few can replicate and explains the company's business dominance.

It is becoming increasingly difficult for independent travel metasearch sites to survive in markets where Google has a large presence.

The key tipping point was the launch of industry specific vertical search units described above, which effectively replicate a traditional metasearch comparison shopping screen but places it on or near the top of the Google search results page.

The natural next question is, can Google apply the same pressure it put on metasearch sites, intentionally or not, to the online travel agencies? I believe it already has. As mentioned earlier in the chapter about OTAs, Google is very persistent with building direct connections with hotel companies and Booking Engine providers to display their availability and prices in the vertical search product bypassing OTAs. As more companies get connected to Google via their booking engines, more traffic will be eventually redirected to hotels' direct channels and away from OTAs. And considering that Google is not charging anything for organic listings, it won't be long before the majority of hotels globally get hooked up to the vertical search.

On another note, with the new vertical search products, Google now has their hands on the key top funnel customer data (for 4 major sectors: flights, hotels, VRs and activities and, who knows, maybe they will eventually add car rental vertical as well), which is the **ultimate indicator of forward-looking strength of demand for those industries.** If this data becomes available to travel data aggregators and/or analytical software vendors, it will be the key element that will **revolutionize demand measurement and forecasting for the entire travel industry.**

Google Cloud

Google Cloud Platform[86] (GCP), offered by Google, is a suite of cloud computing services that runs on the same infrastructure that Google uses internally for its end-user products, such as Google Search, Gmail, file storage, and YouTube. Alongside a set of management tools, it provides a series of modular cloud services including computing, data storage, data analytics and machine learning.

Per Ravi Simhambhatla (Managing Director/CTO, Digital Transformation - Travel & Transportation of Google Cloud), they are in the process of building up a travel vertical within Google Cloud (similar to what AWS has), but as Ravi rightly noted, between Google Ads, YouTube and Google Travel, they are already very well embedded in the travel industry - more so than any other company. And he's not wrong.

---

[86]Wikipedia: Google Cloud Platform: https://en.wikipedia.org/wiki/Google_Cloud_Platform

As we discussed earlier, with the growth and wide adoption of cloud computing, many hospitality software providers started building their products natively in the cloud, and many hospitality companies turned to providers of cloud solutions to transition their tech from "premise" to "cloud".

As Ravi Simhambhatla shared, there are really 5 reasons why any corporation would look at a "cloud journey" with Google:

1. Infrastructure modernization

Hospitality corporations are old companies and they want to get rid of the data centers and they want to get their hands on "scale up and scale down" computing. So it's primarily compute, network and storage.

2. Application modernization

Companies also look at application modernization where they have a large application stack that serves the internal business units and/or the external consumers and these stacks have been built over time over the legacy technologies. The problem with legacy technologies is they do not enable agility in the organizations to develop software and products that meet the market demands. And businesses have to react very quickly to change every day. Now, the world has been changing so rapidly in the last year and many of the businesses could not react quickly enough because those legacy technology, infrastructure and application stacks held them back. And they turn to the cloud to address that.

So, the first two pillars are mostly designed for cost arbitrage, when you want to take costs out, in a permanent and sustainable way.

They are also designed to modernize your technology stack, so you become contemporary and because you're on the cloud, you continue to remain contemporary. You will never come to a point where you suddenly find yourself having built a monolith and you become a legacy, because cloud technology is constantly evolving. So you're always contemporary.

With that, what happens is your teams (your technology teams, your product teams, engineering and design teams) also become contemporary. They also become more agile. They become more modern in how they develop products. So, it's not just technology, it's also people enablement. And that creates the right environment to take the company forward, to grow and innovate.

So it's all about cost modernization and being constantly contemporary.

3. Data science and analytics

Companies are also looking at a higher value add that is powered by data science and analytics. Google is data. Google's ethos is data. One of Google's principles is to organize the world's information and to make it universally accessible and usable. So those corporations that start the "cloud journey" with Google want to work with Google to better understand and harness their data, so they can drive more accurate and more timely business decisions and insights.

4. Innovation

These corporations also want access to all the innovation that is happening in all of Google. Their interests go beyond just Google Cloud. For example, Sabre and Google jointly developed two products for the Travel industry: Sabre Travel AI[87] (AI-driven technology that learns continuously from consumer behavior, helping travel businesses redefine their retailing and customer strategies), and then there is Sabre Smart Retail Engine[88] (a machine learning based retail engine for airlines that uses marketplace insights to dynamically price and bundle products in real time).

Per Ravi Simhambhatla, *"Sabre has been around since the mid 60s. So they understand travel very well, they have fantastic business acumen but their technology, as it always happens, was lagging."* So together Sabre and Google Cloud launched these products by bringing Sabre skill sets and Google skill sets together to create an umbrella platform and power it with Google's AI capabilities.

Currently these products only apply to the airline sector but may eventually be replicated for hospitality.

Ravi Simhambhatla:

So with this collaboration between Sabre and Google (Google Cloud and Google Travel), we're doing this to maximize value for the industry and that's what our partnership is driving.

And our ethos is that we're doing this to make the industry better, to raise the bar, to create better customer experiences, to create better B2B and B2C experiences, which will consequently create value back for consumers and travel providers.

So these other two pillars (data sciences and analytics, and then innovation) are designed for economic viability. How can I increase my market share? How can I create more markets? How can I generate more revenue? How can I find more revenue streams? How can I increase my margin and my yield? So it's not just about revenue. It's about better quality revenue. And it's designed to propel companies forward and create new adjacencies.

5. Culture

The fifth foundation is Google's culture of getting stuff done. It's the SRE (or site reliability engineering culture), what they call "the no-fault culture".

| **Ravi Simhambhatla**

It is amazing, you wake up in the morning, you come to your virtual desk with a simple thought, "How can I help people around me be more successful?"

| **Ira Vouk**

---

[87]Sabre Travel AI: https://www.sabre.com/page/sabre-travel-ai/
[88]Sabre Retail Engine: https://www.sabre.com/page/smart-retail-engine/

Sounds like a dream place to work.

| **Ravi Simhambhatla**

It is, for me at least. I can't think of a better place to work, other than maybe a motorcycle repair shop, which may happen one day.

It's a faultless culture. And because it's a faultless culture, consequently, more good things come out of it. There are always things that are happening that may not necessarily be in line with the values of the company, but eventually good things get done, which is very different in the rest of the world that I've experienced.

So these are the five pillars, with the culture being the foundational pillar. How do you behave and how do you treat people? It's so simple, but it's so lost in today's corporate world.

Side note, Google has been carbon neutral since 2007. The company spends an incredible amount of capital on its own data centers globally and their data center engineers used to spend a lot of time optimizing the usage of power. They came to a point where the human could not optimize it any further. And so, they started using their own machine learning algorithms to do the optimizations and that yielded 40% more reduction in energy usage.

Google is constantly reinvesting back into technology to make things better for the world. Ravi Simhambhatla shared that using this environmental technology that Google has developed for the data centers, he wants to apply the same concept to airports. He has a dream of making a smart airport with smart sensors, where he can tell the footfalls and use video AI to look at where people are going and create the right environment for them, and wherever people are not going - change the environment to conserve energy.

Ravi Simhambhatla:

Imagine if we could take that paradigm and apply it to airports, hotels, offices. It will be beautiful.

And it's not just Google, there are other companies too that are actively contributing back to society.

Sustainability to me is very important because we have our kids, and they'll have their own kids, and the circle of life will keep going. And hopefully we leave this world without too many problems. But what kind of a world do we leave for them?

Being environmentally friendly and doing the right thing for society should be any company's ultimate goal.

Amazon Web Services

Amazon Web Services is another company that is very prominent in our space, for 2 reasons:

- It's the largest player in the cloud computing realm
- It has a dedicated Travel & Hospitality division that allows the company to directly target hospitality organizations and hold their hand when taking them on the "cloud journey"

Amazon Web Services, Inc. (AWS[89]) is a subsidiary of Amazon, providing on-demand cloud computing platforms and APIs to individuals, companies, and governments, on a metered, pay-as-you-go basis. These cloud computing web services offer a range of basic, abstract, technical infrastructure, as well as distributed computing building blocks and tools. AWS's virtual computers emulate most of the attributes of a real computer.

The AWS technology is implemented on server farms throughout the world, and maintained by the Amazon subsidiary. Fees are based on a combination of usage (known as a "Pay-as-you-go" model), hardware, operating systems, software, or networking features chosen by the subscriber's required availability, redundancy, security, and service options. Amazon markets AWS to subscribers as a way of **obtaining large-scale computing capacity more quickly and cheaply than building an actual physical server farm. All services are billed based on usage**, but each service measures usage in varying ways.

I met with Sekhar Mallipeddi (at the time of the interview, Global Travel & Hospitality Technology Leader at AWS). He provided valuable insights into how the company operates and what products it offers.

Sekhar Mallipeddi:

At Amazon Web Services, we do not have any hotel-specific solutions that we offer. In fact, I would actually almost go as far as to say that our job is not to provide hospitality or hotel solutions to our customers. Our job is to provide AWS services to build data lakes, lake house architectures, a really fast and cheap way of building serverless architectures, machine learning models, and IoT. So that you can take these capabilities and build a solution.

But I work on a daily basis with a lot of startups and system integrators to build solutions for hospitality companies, hotels, casinos, cruise companies, etc. We enable partners (startups, independent software vendors and service providers) to innovate.

Even though these AWS solutions are not built specifically for hospitality, the company is doing a huge favor to the industry by the mere fact that they actually have a

---

[89]Wikipedia: Amazon Web Services: https://en.wikipedia.org/wiki/Amazon_Web_Services

"Travel and Hospitality" division. They go after legacy hospitality companies, drag them into the 21st century by their ears and help them modernize their technology after they've been holding onto their legacy for decades.

Sekhar described their approach to working with hospitality organizations:

We solve custom problems at the end of the day. We ask companies, "What is the problem you currently have?" They'll say, for example, "I want to innovate my digital channels." Then we go and look at what the current challenges are, and how we use AWS services to go about solving that problem. We come back with a blueprint and a reference architecture on how to go about doing it.

If you want to, let's say, improve the way your digital channels are personalizing the customer experience, giving them relevant offers and interacting with them in a really personalized way, we have a blueprint on how to do it using Amazon Web Services. Or if someone wants to change the way their call center agents interact with their customers and make those interactions more personalized and more importantly, timely - we have an idea on how to go about doing it and we have a blueprint for that. And then customers go and do this themselves. That's one way to solve it.

And the second way to solve it is where we work with partners, startups that have solutions they build on AWS that they can actually go and deliver to the customers directly. So those companies can provide capabilities, for example, for master data management, or customer data platforms that actually can solve a lot of customer data problems for our hospitality companies. [Remember the BIO model we discussed earlier? This is exactly what Sekhar is referring to.]

If you go to AWS' website and go to AWS Architecture Center,[90] you will find 50 or more different assets that they publish on how a customer can modernize or innovate on AWS.

For example, they have a blueprint for revenue management for hotels that describes how you would build an RMS if you wanted to start from scratch. It talks about data from Travelclick and other sources, and how to pull it all together with your PMS data, with your CRS data, with your shopping data, and you can actually create a revenue management solution using that blueprint.

AWS has blueprints for data platforms, for personalization, for customer engagement, for contact centers - a lot of different ideas where a company could look and understand how they would use AWS services.

So again, to clarify, AWS doesn't offer hospitality solutions. They have blueprints, architectures and instructions on how to go about building them if you choose to do so.

---

[90]AWS: AWS Architecture Center: https://aws.amazon.com/architecture/

They also have travel and hospitality competency partnerships (technology providers). They vet their partners and make sure that they understand travel and hospitality, understand this business and have solutions that can solve business problems for hospitality organizations. AWS curates these technology providers. So that if a travel and hospitality customer is interested in a specific technology or product, AWS can direct them to a partner/vendor that already has a solution.

One of the most important use cases that AWS targets in our industry (just like essentially any other cloud computing provider), is helping hospitality companies enable cloud capabilities for some part of their tech stack, or their entire tech stack. How it happens is, for example, a hotel group or a legacy hospitality software provider has technology that resides on physical computers as a premise-based system. They come to AWS and say, "Let's move to the cloud because we are in the 21st century."

And then, as Sekhar Mallipeddi explains, there are multiple ways of doing it:

1. Re-hosting

If it's a COT solution (common off-the-shelf software) that runs "on premise", what can be done is "re-hosting" it in AWS instead of having physical servers. That's where you move it to the cloud but you don't change anything about that application. So that actually is really the simplest way to think about moving something from premise to the cloud. So technically, you just move everything to a different place but it still has the same deficiencies. It has the same software. Nothing changes, though you still save a little bit of money. Per Sekhar, generally speaking, with re-hosting, you can save 20% on your TCO (total cost of ownership). But you don't change anything about it: you keep the same software, you keep the same licenses.

2. Re-platforming

If we're talking about a custom solution, it can also be re-hosted doing exactly the same thing as described above. Or, the next level of progression is what they call "re-platforming" where you'll make some changes, but won't change the whole thing. You can upgrade to more efficient databases, more efficient data stores, you can use more efficient APIs and hosting. You're re-platforming it, making some small changes, but keeping the whole as is, just using more efficient techniques for data.

The suggestion on what approach to take, comes from AWS in the form of options to improve costs (TCO). The AWS team is providing their recommendations to show how companies can be more efficient. For example, re-hosting saves 20% of TCO, while re-platforming can save up to 40% because you can get off some database licenses or some solution licenses, and go to a full cloud solution for those pieces. But you're keeping everything else intact.

3. Re-architecting

The last option is what they call "re-architecting", which saves anywhere from 60% to 80% TCO. This essentially means taking the guts out and modernizing the whole thing.

Further, Sekhar explained how the hand-holding happens at AWS when they work with customers from our industry.

Ira Vouk

So I'm a software vendor or a hotel brand, and I have a solution that I have built and it currently sits on-premise. I don't have enough brain power to understand what exactly needs to be done, but I think that I can definitely be more efficient if I run this thing on AWS. So then I come to you. Do you have a team of people who work with me and help me understand how exactly it needs to be re-architected or do I have to have my own team of experts to figure this out?

Sekhar Mallipeddi

It's a combination of both. We provide guidance, but the actual work itself of re-hosting, re-platforming or re-architecting needs to be a collaboration. So it's not a one-time event because you still need to support and maintain it and manage it. And we do actually have professional services that can help you with it. But the expectation is that either you or a system integrator that you work with have to basically go and do that work.

From my conversation with Sekhar, I discovered that there's a difference between the role a COT (common off-the-shelf) vendor plays and what a customer himself (like a hotel brand) could do.

A COT vendor could be a tech company that has a software solution and sells it to whomever. So it runs on premise, or it runs in different places. If, for example, Wyndham uses a premise-based PMS solution provided by Oracle and wants to re-host it, they can do so without even contacting the vendor. But if they want to re-platform it, or re-architect it, then the vendor has to do it and provide a version that runs on AWS.

But if it's a custom solution, then the customer (in this case, a hotel company or a casino, or a cruise company) has to take their custom solution that runs on premise, and decide whether to re-host, re-platform or re-architecture it. An example of this could be a custom solution offered by a vendor to a hotel chain, like EzLITE RMS that Infor customized for Wyndham Hotel Group.

So during that process, there would be three players working together to make sure it's successful: the AWS account team, the customer and the software vendor.

AWS has partner success teams that work with software vendors that target hospitality industry customers. They also have customer success teams that work with customers. And in the case described above, an ideal scenario would be for the partner success team, the customer success team, and then the partner and the customer - to all work together.

| Ira Vouk

So based on my understanding, we're kind of relying on the players in the hotel space themselves to understand that there is a need for them to do all those wonderful things to improve their tech stack, right?

| Sekhar Mallipeddi

Yes.

| Ira Vouk

The good news is that you have a business development team within AWS that does some promoting of your services in the travel and hospitality space. So there's some initiative coming from your side, which is great, otherwise I don't think there would be enough progress among those legacy companies to revamp their systems.

| Sekhar Mallipeddi

Absolutely. But at the end of the day, the customer has to decide what is in their best interest: saving up to 20%, or saving more and re-architecting for the future. Because when you re-architect, you can really leverage the full potential of the cloud. You achieve much greater cost-savings and efficiencies. But it involves work, it involves resources to do it. So we have to figure out what is right for the customer, on a case-by-case basis.

| Ira Vouk

So, as far as I'm aware, a large hotel chain right now is signing up with a large RMS provider for... a gazillion hotels. Are you guys in the picture?

| Sekhar Mallipeddi

Yes. We have an account team. But we also actually have partners that work with the hotel chain. We also have ISVs (independent software vendors) that implement things for them.

So what we can derive from my conversation with Sekhar, is that these are the main categories of target customers that AWS works with, when it comes to our industry:

1. **Software vendors** who are built on AWS and target hospitality companies as their customers.

2. **Hotel companies** who want to upgrade their tech stack by building their own in-house solutions in the cloud, moving their existing premise solutions to the cloud, or utilizing existing cloud-based solutions built by software vendors (BIO model).

3. **System integrators.** AWS works with companies like Accenture, Deloitte, PwC as partners; their job is to provide the scale and resources that can help their

customers build a custom solution or implement a software package. For example, instead of a hotel group implementing something on their own (for example, building an in-house RMS), Accenture would be implementing that solution for them.

4. **Startups.** Those are vendors, technically. They're just building stuff from scratch. We discussed those in the previous chapter.

And a bit more from my conversation with Sekhar Mallipeddi on their plans in the travel industry and the barriers they face when working with hospitality companies.

| Ira Vouk

Do you think AWS or maybe Amazon in general, will ever decide to move deeper into the hospitality and travel space, in addition to just cloud solutions? To provide targeted tools for the industry or even become an OTA?

| Sekhar Mallipeddi

At this point, we have no plans for that.

Our idea here is to provide services that will help our customers innovate. But we do not have any hospitality-specific solutions at this point.

We have a couple of things like industry kits, for example, to do a hotel search or to store customer reviews or to do small things like that, but those are all basically code that is available for people to take and use, but not actually products that we sell.

So no, not yet. We have no plans to do that. We enable that through our partners, whether they are tech partners, independent software vendors, system integrators or startups - that is really how we scale. But at this point, we have no plans for products.

| Ira Vouk

Thanks for sharing. So in regards to scaling, what are the main barriers that you're seeing when you deal with the hospitality industry players, in terms of promoting AWS solutions among those companies? I assume, like any other business, you would like to sell more subscriptions. So what are the barriers in our industry that prevent you from selling more of those?

| Sekhar Mallipeddi

That's a good question and the answer really depends upon what the customers want to do. For us, our goal is not to sell more services. Our charter is to help our customers innovate and meet business needs. We don't sell services. We enable solutions that solve business problems. At the end of the day, whatever we do has to have a business value. We don't do things for the sake of doing.

If the business value is a reduction in cost - that makes sense for us. It is about empowering businesses to innovate, empowering them to have full access to data, so they can personalize, they can provide a better customer experience, or improve operations. Those are all the goals that we go after.

So it really depends on the customer and what's important for them and where we can help them through our personal services or help them through our system integrators or through our tech partners.

To wrap up this section of the book, I'd like to say that there's so much that cloud computing capabilities allow us to do. There's just so much above and beyond what legacy hospitality companies have been able to achieve using old technology. And this is why I'm very excited that companies like AWS and Google are here to help drag us out of the Stone Age. These companies are playing an important role in our industry. They are the players that could really help disrupt things and teach the industry how to get to a whole different level in terms of technology adoption, innovation and data management.

Artificial Intelligence/Machine Learning

There's a lot of marketing buzz around Artificial Intelligence and Machine Learning in hospitality. And in many cases, they are used very liberally and not always accurately. There's a clear lack of understanding among many of us regarding what those terms really mean and how we can apply them in our industry.

And because we don't understand it, we reject it.

I recently participated in a HospitalityNet panel discussion <u>AI-based Technology for Revenue Optimization - Friend or Foe?</u>[91] The fact that we're still asking ourselves whether AI is good or bad for us, confirmed my perception of where we are as an industry in the adoption lifecycle. We shouldn't be asking whether technology (and AI/ML in particular) is good or not. We should be asking why we are so far behind other sectors when it comes to the adoption of automated tools, and especially machine learning, in our decision-making process.

We interact with AI everywhere in our daily lives: Facebook shows you targeted ads based on vast amounts of information digested by their ML algorithms, your smartphone uses AI-based face recognition software to unlock, Netflix offers you a suggested list of movies to watch using your previous viewing history, Alexa and Google control nearly everything in your house... and yet, we can still count the number of AI-based hospitality tech solutions on the fingers of our 2 hands (and maybe one or two toes of the left foot).

Here is the list of factors that I have outlined so far that are affecting this trend. I will attempt to address all of them in this chapter.

- Lack of understanding of what AI and ML really mean (this is the major one).
- Unwillingness to lose control over one's strategy by handing the reins over to technology.
- Leadership unaware of what is happening on the property level and what issues they're working to resolve (i.e. too much time is spent on manual tasks in day-to-day operations as well as on forecasting and optimization decisions).
- Lack of awareness about the benefits of AI-based technological solutions (vendors failing to clearly communicate those benefits to the audience, possibly caused by lack of optimal and reliable communication channels in the hospitality marketplace).
- And last but not least: we, as an industry, haven't come up with a standardized way of measuring ROI from automated tools and assessing their performance.

---

[91]HospitalityNet Panel: The Revenue Manager: https://www.hospitalitynet.org/panel/125000123.html

Let's address the "lack of understanding" problem first.

Here's an excerpt from my conversation with professor Parsa (University of Denver, Daniels College of Business, Hospitality Management) to illustrate our current situation.

H. G. Parsa

Industry is actually afraid of artificial intelligence. They don't know what that is. If I ask you tomorrow, "Ira, somebody wants to take you to space for free." Would you go?

Ira Vouk

I would, actually. I'm the kind of person who would totally say yes.

H. G. Parsa

You know, but I can't. I have my wife, my kids and my family. It's not an easy decision because it's an unknown destination. So, the point is - people are afraid of the unknown. They're afraid of AI. They don't know what it is.

Or, would you like to go to Uganda? My department head just went for two weeks. Some people don't even want to go to Alabama! That's just how we are. The industry is afraid of anything that is not familiar to them.

Now that I'm thinking about it... I wouldn't mind going to Uganda either. Right after that space trip.

And more wisdom from John Burns (Hospitality Technology Consulting):

In the hotel business, we don't know what AI is. I'm working with a couple of companies that are doing sophisticated AI and it is a very slow process to integrate it into the hotel processes and then to explain to hoteliers what it's all about. It is going to happen. It is going to change the world. But it is going to take time.

So for those who are advocating for the adoption of artificial intelligence by hospitality, the big task right now is educating the industry about what AI and ML can do and how we can benefit from it.

In this chapter, I would like to shed some light on these 2 terms with a goal to make it as clear as possible for the non-technical part of my audience what those things really mean and how they can be applied to take the hospitality industry to a new level.

Definitions

So what is AI and what is ML?

In most simple terms, **artificial intelligence (AI)** is intelligence demonstrated by machines, as opposed to the natural intelligence displayed by humans or animals. Leading AI textbooks define the field as the study of "intelligent agents": any system that perceives its environment and takes actions that maximize its chance of achieving its goals.[92]

So, essentially, it's a system (non-human) that has an ability to digest some data and then use it for decision making and taking actions to reach a certain goal.

Machine learning is actually a form of AI. Machine learning is the study of computer algorithms that can improve automatically through experience and by the use of data. It is seen as a part of artificial intelligence. Machine learning algorithms build a model based on sample data, known as "training data", in order to make predictions or decisions without being explicitly programmed to do so. These algorithms are used in a wide variety of applications.[93]

Here's a simplified version of the relationship between AI, ML and DL (deep learning,[94] you don't need to worry about this one) illustrated using a Venn diagram:

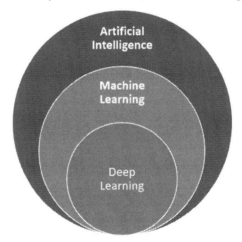

Figure 1: artificial intelligence, machine leaning and deep learning Source: Nadia BERCHANE (M2 IESCI, 2018)

Recently, I have been watching youtube podcasts by neuroscientist Andrew Huberman.

In the summer of 2021, he invited Lex Fridman (a computer scientist, a researcher from MIT that studies AI, autonomous vehicles, human-robot interactions and ML) to talk about machines and artificial intelligence. When these two masterminds meet - the

---

[92]Wikipedia: Artificial Intelligence: https://en.wikipedia.org/wiki/Artificial_intelligence
[93]Wikipedia: Machine Learning: https://en.wikipedia.org/wiki/Machine_learning
[94]Wikipedia: Deep Learning: https://en.wikipedia.org/wiki/Deep_learning

combined intelligence of the world population jumps to a whole new level. It was the most fascinating conversation that started with a short and the most easy-to-understand definition of AI, ML, deep learning, supervised learning and unsupervised learning.

I'm providing an excerpt from that podcast episode "as is" because I find it fascinating, informative and very clear. After the next few pages, you will have a much better understanding of what those mysterious words ("artificial intelligence" and "machine learning") actually mean, on a large scale and in simple terms.

Lex Fridman and Andrew Huberman on the topic of Artificial Intelligence and Machine Learning. Podcast by Andrew Huberman (#hubermanlab), episode #29 from Jul 19, 2021.

I'm also referencing the link[95] to that podcast in the footnote.

***

What is **artificial intelligence**? And how is it different from things like machine learning and robotics?

That question is as complicated and as fascinating as the question of "what is intelligence?" At the big philosophical level, it's our longing to create other intelligence systems, perhaps systems that are more powerful than us. At the more narrow level, it's also a set of computational mathematical tools to automate different tasks. And then also it's our attempt to understand our own mind, so we build systems that exhibit some intelligent behavior in order to understand what intelligence is in our own selves. So, all those things are true.

In the community of researchers and engineers, AI is a set of tools, a set of computational techniques that allow you to solve various problems.

There's a long history that approaches that problem from different perspectives. One of those communities goes under the flag of **machine learning** which is emphasizing in the AI space the task of learning: how do you make a machine that knows very little in the beginning, follow some kind of process and learn to become better and better in a particular test?

What's been most effective in the recent 15 years, is a set of techniques that fall under the flag of "**deep learning**" that utilize **neural networks**. What neural networks are - those fascinating things inspired by the structure of the human brain. They have a network of these little basic computational units called neurons, artificial neurons. They have these architectures, where there's an input and an output, they know nothing in the beginning and their task is to learn something interesting. That "something interesting" usually involves a particular task.

---

[95]YouTube: Dr. Lex Fridman: Machines, Creativity & Love | Huberman Lab Podcast #29 (July 2021): https://youtu.be/VRvn3Oj5r3E

There's a lot of ways to talk about this and break this down. One of them is how much human supervision is required to teach this thing. So "**supervised learning**" is a broad category where the neural network knows nothing in the beginning and then it's given a bunch of examples, a large database of examples. The neural network is able to learn by example, that's called supervised learning.

And there's another contrasting set of ideas, their attention is what's used to be called "**unsupervised learning**" and what's commonly now called "**self-supervised learning**", which is trying to get less and less human supervision into the task. It's been very successful in the domain of language models, natural language processing and computer vision tasks. The idea there is to let the machine just consume the data and try to learn something generalizable about the ideas it's analyzing. We humans have this giant base of knowledge that we call common sense (for example, what's the difference between a cat and a dog), on top of which we build more sophisticated knowledge. So the idea of unsupervised learning is for the machine to build this common sense knowledge about something that it's learning about, without ever having human supervision.

What's exciting is not the theory - it's the application. One of the most exciting applications of artificial intelligence, specifically neural networks and machine learning, is Tesla autopilot. So these are systems that are working in the real world, this isn't an academic exercise. These are semi-autonomous vehicles. They are currently not fully autonomous, meaning human supervision is required.

So there is another space of human robot interaction when AI systems and humans work together to accomplish tasks. **The world is going to be full of problems where humans and robots have to interact because I think robots will always be flawed. Just like humans are flawed. And that's what makes life beautiful. But they're flawed, that's where learning happens - at the edge of your capabilities. So you always have to figure out how flawed robots and flawed humans can interact together, such that the sum is bigger than the whole, as opposed to focusing on just building the perfect robot.**

Semi-autonomous driving is a really good example of machine learning because those systems are constantly learning. There's a process, where you build a system that's pretty good at doing stuff, you send it out into the real world, it starts doing the stuff and it runs into what are called edge cases, like failure cases, where it screws up. There are just weird situations that you did not expect. So the data engine process is: you collect those edge cases and then you go back to the drawing board and learn from them. It's another important concept where that piece of data goes back to the mothership for the retraining of the system to then send out an updated version. And through this data engine process, it keeps improving and getting better and better.

***

I don't know about you, but the above few paragraphs opened up my horizons and changed my perspective on how we perceive AI and robotics. I hope this information also helps you achieve a deeper level of understanding of the fascinating achievements of humanity (artificial intelligence in all its shapes and forms) and what it can truly do for us.

The possibilities are infinite. In the hotel industry, we're just starting to learn about those things, taking baby steps to become comfortable with these concepts, and slowly adapting them in our decision making.

In my opinion, the ability to capture data, from which hoteliers can generate actionable insights for improving business processes and driving innovations that further enhance the guest experience and operational efficiency, is the top benefit of an AI technology initiative.

When it comes to areas of applications of AI in hotel businesses, they can be bulked into 2 main categories: customer-facing applications and back office applications. Let's take a look at both.

Customer-facing AI (enhancing guest experience)

More and more hotels are using AI-powered customer service and data analytics in hopes of redefining the current industry standards for a personalized guest experience.

The guest journey is the record of every interaction and transaction, both digital and in-person, that a guest has with the hotel throughout the entire course of their trip (including planning). With its ability to learn guest behaviors and preferences, the potential of artificial intelligence is immeasurable.

In most cases, humans and machines work together in a way that is complementary and benefits both hotel staff and hotel guests.

AI also improves employee satisfaction. It does this by handling mundane tasks, such as answering frequently asked questions, freeing employees to focus on higher value, high-touch tasks, and by enhancing their knowledge and performance.

As stated in the guidebook 'How artificial intelligence has enhanced the guest experience' recently published by Hotel Management, an online magazine,[96] "*By being able to respond to guest inquiries far faster than the human service rep counterparts, and by being able to field any number of inquiries simultaneously, with virtually no capacity constraints, AI devices are shortening guest wait times in very significant ways while providing immediate access to information and services.*"

Hotel guests are becoming more and more comfortable with using technologies. These days, even guests who normally like to interact with hotel staff are often happy to augment those interactions with technology options.

Here are a few examples of successful implementation of guest-facing AI in the industry:

---

[96]Hotel Management: [Guidebook] How artificial intelligence has enhanced the guest experience: https://pages.questexnetwork.com/SpectrumEnterprise-Guidebook-061521.html

1. AI-enabled devices for in-person customer service

They are available in a variety of different forms - the most visible are the robotic butlers, concierges and luggage handlers.

The most fascinating example of this so far has been an AI robot called 'Connie',[97] adopted by Hilton. The robot is able to provide tourist information to customers who interact with it. Most impressively, it is able to learn from human speech and adapt to individuals. Ultimately, this means the more customers speak to it, the better it will get.

2. Mobile and voice-activated assistants

Think Google Home devices or Alexa by Amazon. This is a huge opportunity for hoteliers where AI will play an increasingly important role. Hotel guests are already accustomed to receiving information and recommendations from digital platforms in their homes, which helps make the transition to the hotel room easy.

3. Chatbots and messaging

AI technology has been shown to be extremely effective when it comes to direct messaging and online chat services, responding to simple questions or requests.

For example, AI chatbots have been utilized on social media platforms, allowing customers to ask questions and get almost instantaneous responses, 24 hours a day, 7 days a week. This is invaluable to hotels, because it provides the type of response times that are almost impossible to maintain with human-to-human interaction.

4. Frictionless booking process

Site bookings are one of the friction points for the hospitality sector. Many people use aggregator sites or OTAs to search and book. When they want to make a direct booking from the hotel website, isolating preferred dates and check-in details can be time-consuming and complex. The opportunities to communicate with hotel staff are limited, and no one wants to call and wait for a response in an era of online messaging.

AI-based functionality introduced into the hotel's website can reduce this friction, maximize the sales potential, and provide a booking experience tailored to the customers' choices. AI algorithms can cross-check the preferences of travelers and then fine-tune the results based on the user information. In addition, the introduction of virtual travel assistants for search and booking will allow hotel owners to increase their reach without any effort.

The next generation of search and booking will be using natural language to book your next trip - to actually be able to speak out where you want to go and what you want to do. That may happen one day and that day will be exciting for the industry.

---

[97]Skift: The Tiny Hilton Robot Concierge That Hints at IBM's Ambitious Plans for Travel (March 2016): https://skift.com/2016/03/09/the-tiny-hilton-robot-concierge-that-hints-at-ibms-ambitious-plans-for-travel/

5. Experience shopping

"Experience shopping" is the next big thing, that is something that the alternative accommodations sector has been (successfully) experimenting with in the last few years. And ML is the best tool to be able to put the right set of experiences and choices in front of a consumer. This is where deep learning comes into play (being able to understand vast amounts of rows of data in real time) for the purpose of understanding the consumer's needs and displaying the right options for them as they enter the website.

6. Targeted Ad campaigns

AI can help serve consumers more relevant, targeted ads. As the algorithms keep advancing and richer consumer data becomes available, AI will continue to learn purchasing behaviors and deliver more relevant content for potential guests in the form of advertising.

Clearly, artificial intelligence is here to stay, and the evolution of related technologies will progressively improve the overall guest experience.

But the road to collecting that data isn't always easy. We will talk more about it in one of the subsequent chapters.

As Tim Webb (University of Delaware, Hospitality Business Management) explained:

AI and ML tools really derive their value from data, without "big data" the predictive advantages of these techniques are rather limited. As firms begin to capture more consumer data points that span all areas of the purchase process (initial search, to final booking, and all the clicks in between), the value of AI and ML tools will increase. They will be able to anticipate when customers prefer to book and hone in on their preferences and willingness to pay.

So now let's talk about data-oriented back office applications of AI in our industry.

Back office AI (operating efficiency and profit maximization)

Another way in which AI is being utilized more and more widely within the hotel industry is in data analysis. In this capacity, the technology can be used to quickly sort through large amounts of data and draw important conclusions for optimal decision making.

Here are different ways of applying artificial intelligence in our back office functions.

1. Analysis of customer reviews

Machine Learning can help analyze the large pool of information across a broad range of online sources and provide valuable insights into customer sentiments. The ML algorithms and techniques allow for deep analysis of all reviews in real time, determining positive and negative phrases. This data can help adjust hotel offers & services to meet customers' needs.

2. Automation and efficiency of operations

Robust hotel software systems with AI at the core can automate all repetitive operations like check-ins and check-outs, housekeeping deliveries, room assignments, and the like. In combination with the chatbots mentioned above and powerful analytics tools, hotels will be able to minimize response times, reduce costs, and ultimately increase revenue through the use of AI.

3. Revenue management and profit maximization

In my opinion, this is the item that yields the highest ROI for hotel owners and operators, if implemented properly through modern AI/ML algorithms.

When it comes to revenue and profit management, AI and ML make the most sense when applied for the purpose of forecasting (mainly demand forecasting but really anything you want to predict) and optimization (dynamic pricing and other decisions that influence revenue and bottom-line profit).

As Marco Benvenuti (Co-founder of Duetto RMS) noted:

The algorithms that you use are never fully done. They're living and breathing things and they always need to get better. And so AI and machine learning will make these algorithms better and better.

Remember that all the pricing mathematics that we use today were actually invented in the 1950s. Now is the time for AI and machine learning to take over a little bit more. And then maybe in the future there's going to be something else that will make these algorithms better and smarter and more reliable and more precise.

And one very important note (have I mentioned this before?) - it's all about data.

2020 was the breaking point for the industry in many ways, and one of them - coming to an understanding that we can no longer use only historic internal hotel data for the purpose of demand forecasting and pricing optimization.

More and more data sources are becoming available to us (like forward-looking market data) that will allow analysts and, more importantly, analytical tools to build better forecasts and make more optimal decisions that maximize profits for hotel owners. More and more companies are starting to incorporate new data into their traditional models, or rebuilding those models altogether. And we can't do it successfully using our old mathematics, this is where the value of AI and ML is maximized.

I love how Mylene Young (Son Hospitality Consulting) phrased it:

Artificial intelligence and machine learning are becoming extremely important in our new reality because we went from dealing with only OTB (rooms on-the-books) and historical data from the PMS into a range of "big data": all the external market data, flights data, destination demand information, the product perception value, OTA page rank, online reputation, events, competitors' prices, search volumes, etc.

So if you use all of that, there's no doubt that you cannot only work with your old linear regression models, because that would not be sufficient to really understand how those things relate to each other and to understand what that data really tells you.

So I think that's where machine learning is becoming extremely important. We have absolutely no choice but to embrace it.

Predictive analytics today is extremely important. We live in a very volatile period of time. Some markets have rebounded, for some it will take years to rebound, but if you don't have a proper way of forecasting and optimizing through machine learning, I think it will be very difficult to gather that data and make sense of it.

We are in an age of data. Full stop. *Not just in the hospitality industry. The data is dirty and not always consistent, and that's another story, but if you identify the right data that you think is valuable for your hotel and your destination and apply the right algorithms to analyze it - that's going to tell you a lot about the future.*

And it pertains to other areas outside of revenue management - really anything that has to do with decision making in hotel operations: marketing, sales, cost management, customer communication, the list goes on.

Adoption rates are still very minimal when it comes to utilizing true AI in those areas of application.

Amanda Belarmino (University of Las Vegas, William F. Harrah College of Hospitality) pointed at that issue during our conversation:

I think that there's a learning gap with some of that within the industry. Key players need to understand the effectiveness of AI and ML. Machine learning does a much better job with forecasting, in many ways than what we're getting from more traditional types of forecasting. It can be much more sophisticated, especially in times like these, with a high level of uncertainty. 2021 doesn't look like 2020 and it doesn't even look like 2019.

So I think it's about understanding what it does and having some patience with it. Understanding where you want it, what you want it to do, where you want the human interaction and what the human is supposed to do.

So there are going to be times where machine learning and AI are going to complete tasks that your manager shouldn't necessarily be spending their time on, because the humans need to look at the more complex situations and spend their time making better decisions for more strategic things. That's where I think it's going to go, but I think it's just going to take a little bit of learning from some advocates of it to make it accepted in the industry.

A reasonable question that many (including me) have been asking is how do we truly understand the benefits of AI? And that all comes back to the ultimate question of how we measure performance of our algorithms (any algorithm or essentially, any new solution we're introducing). This is a problem that the industry hasn't been able to solve yet due to lack of ability to run A/B testing in real life. I would love to participate in any initiative that attempts to address the problem of ROI measurement from automated tools that target any aspect of hotel operations. If you're working on such a project (or planning one) and need another perspective on how to possibly solve this problem from a person with a diverse industry knowledge - please reach out, I'll be happy to participate.

I spoke about it with all the hospitality professors I interacted with in the last year or so. And they were unanimous in seeing this the same way I see it: a complex problem that can potentially be solved mathematically but hasn't yet been addressed properly.

Regardless of the fact that exact ROI is technically impossible to measure, it doesn't mean we can't see improvements in our operational efficiencies and profit metrics from the implementation of new technologies and AI-based tools in particular.

Amanda Belarmino believes that our lack of trust in these new technologies in many cases leads to giving up on them instead of continuously improving them through a collaborative effort:

*I think that the tendency in the industry too often is to say, "Alright, I did a test and the human did better. So now the human is going to continue to do it." Well, no, how do you fix the technology? The human did something that the technology didn't know how to do. **It isn't a competition.** It should be a "let's train the system" approach.*

Let's make this work so that, for example, your revenue manager is not spending six hours of their day looking at prices for the next six months trying to decide where they need to increase or decrease them. That's what the machine should be doing. And humans should be looking at things like: Who do I need to partner with to fill a gap in occupancy on this day? What do I need to do to understand how I'm going to maximize this? How should I be working with my OTAs?

Let's look at making decisions based on profitability and let machine learning make those small, day-to-day decisions. For example, a revenue manager shouldn't be a person with a spreadsheet and a ruler looking at each day's pickup. That's not what we should be doing now. In 2022, we should do better.

And yet again, I'd like to conclude this section with a quote from Ravi Simhambhatla (Managing Director/CTO, Digital Transformation - Travel & Transportation at Google). The way he talks really inspires me and makes me believe in the future of our industry, and the ability of humans and machines to work together effectively.

Ravi Simhambhatla:

Machine learning even a few years ago was a thing, but it was a thing that was relegated to high performance computing companies like Google or to very deep research by NASA, etc. But now it's mainstream, it is real. So I think that's the power.

When an airline or a hotel chain hires brilliant data scientists and revenue management analysts, the biggest problem they have is that these brilliant people spend most of their time correcting the errors of the models that are generating this data. That's not why they got educated. That's the most boring thing for them to do. They want to create new opportunities.

*So how about we build demand forecasting systems and revenue management systems that decrease your forecasting accuracy error down to 2%? Think about that. So as an analyst, all you have to do is figure out how to optimize the remaining 2% of opportunity. And then the rest of the time, you spend on creating value for your company. And I think that is magical, it is very real. I'm very excited about it because it's not that companies did not want to invest. It's not that people are not smart. It's none of that. It's just that **these tools have only now become mainstream, these tools are now finally available for everyone to access, use, and exploit them.***

There is no doubt Artificial Intelligence will reach wide adoption in our industry in the near future, and especially in the area of data analysis. There's no way to stop that trend. And those companies that ignore that trend, will fall behind.

#disruptordie

Conclusion

Leif Jägerbrand (Founder of Atomize) describes his vision of the future the same way I see it:

I would say that proliferation of AI, and machine learning in particular, in our industry is inevitable. And that is because older types of solutions cannot properly adapt to quick changes in complex environments. But AI is much quicker to adapt to new and uncertain situations. Just look at the pandemic that recently hit the world. Traditional systems do not work well in such an environment because it hasn't happened before. But AI systems are quick to adapt and find profitable patterns. And that is our future.

I'm very excited to see where this takes us and how this will affect the industry in the next 5-10 years. There is no doubt AI and ML applications will result in conceptually new ways of solving the industry's problems, they will take us to a whole new level, just like the invention of the Internet did some time ago.

My desire to be part of this movement led me to join HTNG's "AI for Hospitality"[98] workgroup (the most nerdy group you can think of, and that's the way I like it). We talk about areas of AI application in the industry and work on putting together use cases for AI/ML adoption.

We need more success stories from the industry describing what different companies achieved through AI-based technologies so that others can learn from these examples and become more comfortable in adopting them for their own use cases.

AI is one of the technologies that drives the digital transformation of hospitality businesses, making them more efficient and more profitable, and at the same time, improving the guest experience across the whole travel lifecycle. ML & AI are making everything more efficient from top to bottom, bringing a new level of responsiveness and personalization. With the technology curve, hospitality businesses of all sizes can benefit from AI-powered software, and I firmly believe that it will become mainstream very soon. And we can either continue resisting it, or start embracing it and let it help us.

Let's learn from other industries and start catching up. Let's come to some agreement on the basic concepts of ROI measurements. Let's provide clear guidance for the end users about the benefits of AI-based technology. Let's invite AWS and Google to our discussions more frequently and stop relying on legacy companies to dictate tech trends for the industry. Let's get investors excited about our industry to drive innovation.

Let's not be afraid of technology. We live in the 21st century after all.

---

[98]HTNG: List of Workgroups: https://www.htng.org/page/ListofWorkgroups

EVOLUTION OF THE ALTERNATIVE ACCOMMODATIONS SECTOR

Another major disruptive force (along with the evolution of technology) that has been reshaping the hospitality industry in the last decade or so, is the emergence and rapid growth of the alternative accommodations sector.

As John Burns phrased it, *"Alternative accommodations is no longer alternative, it's mainstream, it's huge."* Jordan Hollander (Hotel Tech Report) referred to the rapid growth of that sector as a "seismic shock" for the industry.

The sharing economy has certainly become a prominent phenomenon over the past several years. Airbnb is the market leader as it relates to the vacation rental industry. Its presence in key markets all over the world has been growing at a rapid pace.

Have you noticed that I've just used 3 different terms to define the sector? Alternative accommodations, vacation rentals, temporary accommodation... It's because we still don't know what to call it, and one of the reasons is that the sector is evolving so fast that it's hard to catch up.

Here's what Scott Shatford of AirDNA thinks about it:

| Ira Vouk

So "alternative accommodations" probably wouldn't be the right term anymore, "vacation rentals" is probably not the best fit either. What should we be using to identify that sector nowadays?

| Scott Shatford

I think we've been struggling to figure out the right word for this for a long time. I don't like any of them. "Private accommodations" maybe. "Short-term rental" seems like what everybody's landed on.

But even that is no longer relevant as Sonder is making inroads into the long-term stay segment and more bookings are made on Airbnb for LOS of 28+. Maybe a better term would be the "anything-but-hotel" sector.

So what we have to ourselves is an "animal unknown to science", just like the famous Soviet cartoon character Cheburashka[99] aka the Great Russian Che (do look it up!).

Let's examine it in detail, so we know how to deal with this new phenomenon.

---

[99]Russiapedia: Cheburashka: https://russiapedia.rt.com/of-russian-origin/cheburashka/index.html

Are hotels sharing demand with the shared accommodations sector?

I asked many industry experts about whether this new "animal" is negatively affecting the hotel sector, and I ended up with alternative views on the effect of alternative accommodations on our industry (sorry I can't stop playing with the terms).

1. Some believe that the time has come for the hotel industry to bleed to death unless we do something drastic about it.

One of my favorite industry consultants John Burns always uses the most vivid analogies:

We in the hotel business look as though we've been hit by a car and our arm is sheared off and we keep going around saying, "Oh, nothing's wrong, nothing's wrong. I'm bleeding to death but nothing's wrong."

We are like ostriches with our heads buried in the sand, ignoring this every time you see press releases from Airbnb with their performance numbers.

They are a huge force and they're getting bigger. They are very good at e-commerce and CRM, in many respects better than we are.

Sure, they've got a problem and it is supply. So they're desperately looking for additional hosts. And if you have a pop-up tent in your backyard, they want to fill it.

So we run from the reality of very successful Airbnb and their peers - shame on us.

| **Ira Vouk**

Why do you think hoteliers are trying to ignore it and pretend that nothing is happening and not admitting that there is a monster in the room?

| **John Burns**

In part, because we don't know how to respond. In part, because our owners (often private equity and publicly held companies) cannot be told negative information. So you can't have the new president of Marriott going out and saying, "We're in serious trouble, we really have to get a whole lot better if we're going to compete with Airbnb," because that sends the stock price down and threatens his job. So we all sit in the lifeboat, as we watch the Titanic sinking and say, "Oh I wonder when the bar is going to open."

2. And there's an opinion on the other side of the spectrum that there's enough market for everyone and there's nothing to fear.

Jordan Hollander (Co-founder and CEO of Hotel Tech Report):

There are segments of travelers who want kitchens, who want bigger spaces, who want higher capacity, who may be a bachelor party who want some privacy - they prefer vacation rentals. There are just different market segments that VR served before COVID, even before Airbnb. They serve different use cases than hotels do. And I think that will continue.

Many don't want to go somewhere and be alone and with no action and not have any people-watching. And if something goes wrong, there's no one to talk to. And I think that's why business travel at hotels will continue to be resilient.

I definitely agree that the people-watching factor is a good reason to go back to hotels where you can sit at the bar and do just that. That, and eating in bed while watching a movie.

Bob Gilbert (President and CEO of HSMAI) has a similar opinion:

I think it's really just a different type of lodging that gives consumers more options.

There are many markets which can be targeted and captured. But I think this segment of lodging captures much of what's called VFR (visiting friends and relatives), which previously used to stay with families at home. I think there will always be crossover among some of the major market segments, but usually in very small amounts. So I think it's over-hyped, if you will, in terms of its direct impact on the industry.

3. And then there's an opinion in the middle.

Scott Shatford (Founder and CEO of AirDNA):

Whether VRs are stealing hotels' market share has been a big question for as long as I've been around here.

And I'm sure I'm not going to say anything new. There's becoming a much clearer divide on what is a hotel trip and what is a vacation rental trip. You're going with your family of five for a week somewhere - you're probably not going to be looking at hotels first, right? Unless you're a loyalty member and you got thousands of points. But most people are selecting a four-bedroom house for privacy and cost effectiveness, and the location.

I think it's just become very clear that those people are going to be looking at Airbnb first. But if you're going for one night on a business trip, you're not going to deal with the hassle of booking that thing.

So I think we're just going to see much clearer divides on the length of stay, the size of your group, the type of destination. You're going to be either a hotel kind of customer or a vacation rental customer.

There will still be a battle for those 3-4 night stays between hotels and VRs. Hotels

179

should ask themselves how to stay relevant for a little bit longer stays and bigger groups. For example, how to handle the adjoining rooms. Or what amenities they need to add to their rooms. All those things that people want and love about vacation rentals.

So the views on that issue definitely differ across the industry.

Let's ask the numbers person. Because we all now understand that all the answers are in the data.

Jan Freitag (*National Director, Hospitality Analytics for the CoStar Group, formerly Senior Vice President at STR*)

Airbnb shared with us their data once in 2016 and I co-wrote an article with some other people and talked about the impact of Airbnb on the US lodging industry. And at that time, the data seemed to suggest that there was not a lot of room demand being moved into alternative accommodations.

When you look at 2019 - that was the strongest year that the industry ever had: most rooms available, most rooms sold, most revenue generated, highest ADR, occupancy and RevPAR.

So, what's the impact of Airbnb in 2019? It's hard to say. Could we have sold more rooms? Maybe. But we were already pretty full, running the highest occupancy ever.

But RevPAR growth that year was 1%. So that's interesting. So we're running at the highest occupancy ever but that doesn't seem to be translated in our pricing power. Why is that? Well, maybe the pricing power that we saw in the prior years 2012-2014 came a lot from compression nights.

Top 25 largest lodging markets saw citywide convention occupancies go way up. And then the last available room that goes to the corporate transient traveler suddenly is sold at a very significant premium. And isn't it possible that the impact of alternative accommodations is that when they know that a large event is going to take place - alternative accommodations providers are saying, "Yeah, for that I'll put my unit on the market." And then the delta on the compression nights' ADR decreases because travelers are certainly saying, "Wow, I can get a hotel room for $750 or I can get a condo for $400-500. Let me do that instead."

And then suddenly we see that in compression nights, the ADR delta compared to an average night is not as robust as it used to be.

But on the demand side, I know that there are a lot of opinions out there. And some say that alternative accommodations really hurt the hotel industry. From a national perspective, I have a hard time putting those things together.

Is it true that on a Saturday night in Nashville, a lot of bachelorette parties rent a house rather than getting 3 rooms in a hotel? Yes, of course. But wasn't that always the case?

You know, alternative accommodations aren't new. Airbnb just built a better mousetrap or built a better app. Is there a crossover? Are there some people staying in alternative accommodations who used to stay in hotels? Yes, of course. But is it really that impactful? Because I, as a corporate frequent traveler, what do I care about? The location. I want to be close to wherever I need to go and I like my loyalty points. I really do. Because then I can take my wife or my family for that one really, really nice vacation to that 5-star resort I don't have to pay for because I have those points. So the alternative accommodations' lack of loyalty programs, which they could certainly overcome, but they haven't today, is really helping branded properties to maintain the corporate transient travel and the corporate group travel.

| **Ira Vouk**

Very interesting. So the next thing that Airbnb is going to do is come up with a loyalty membership program.

| **Jan Freitag**

They should have done that five years ago.

To conclude this section: regardless of which camp is more accurate in their estimation of the current situation, what we know is that the VR segment (or whatever name we come up with to define it) is not going anywhere.

And whether the truth is that "the hotel industry is going to bleed to death", or "there are enough segments for everyone", or somewhere in the middle - we certainly can't ignore this disruptive force because there is a lot the hotel industry can (and should) learn from this phenomenon. We'll talk about what exactly those lessons are towards the end of this chapter, but first, let's take a look at a few major players in the market that are worth discussing.

Airbnb

Brian Chesky was the only person who I couldn't get to participate in the interviews. Well, he and Elon.

I tortured their PR department for a long period of time, but they didn't give in. So the content of this section is mostly based on the most recent (at the time of writing) earnings call and the shareholder letter.

Airbnb[100] was born in 2007 when two hosts welcomed three guests to their San Francisco home. It has since grown to 4 million hosts who have welcomed more than 900 million guest arrivals across over 220 countries and regions.

From Aibnb's 2021 Q2 earnings call: "*In Q2, we had the highest number of gross nights booked of any quarter in our history. And we just had the biggest night on Airbnb since the pandemic began. Last Saturday night [August 7, 2021], more than 4 million guests from around the world were staying in an Airbnb. That is more people than the entire population of Los Angeles...*"

On December 10, 2020, at a $100 billion valuation, the company went public[101] via an initial public offering, raising $3.5 billion.

Airbnb charges their hosts about 15% per transaction on average, and according to the leadership, there are no plans for that to change in either direction.

As Airbnb says, "*Every day, hosts offer unique stays and one-of-a-kind activities that make it possible for guests to experience the world in a more authentic, connected way.*"

Brian Chesky (*Co-founder and CEO*) said on the earnings call:

We have more than 4 million hosts. 90% of them are individuals and most of them couldn't have hosted, if not for the tools we provide.

People are traveling to many more destinations than before. And when they travel, they stay longer.

We ended Q2 with the largest number of active listings in Airbnb's history. Now, there are a couple of reasons for this. First, our demand is driving supply. This is what's so powerful about our model. For example, in Q2, our highest supply growth was actually in high-demand destinations. And second, our marketing and product initiatives have been really accelerating to support host recruitment and they're working.

To do this, we've been perfecting the end-to-end experience of our core service. And this includes four themes: first, educating the world about hosting; second, recruiting more hosts; third, simplifying the guest journey; and finally, delivering world-class service.

Dave Stephenson (*Chief Financial Officer*)

And what we need to do is have the right listing for the right guest at the right time. And as people continue to get more flexible on when and where they travel,

---

[100]Wikipedia: Airbnb: https://en.wikipedia.org/wiki/Airbnb

[101]NPR: Airbnb Now A $100 Billion Company After Stock Market Debut Sees Stock Price Double (December 2020): https://www.npr.org/2020/12/10/944931270/airbnb-defying-pandemic-fears-takes-its-company-public-in-ipo

as we get better at focusing those hosts on the flexible locations and dates that they have in mind, we're going to get better at utilizing the supply we have all around the world.

In terms of TAM (total addressable market) for alternatives versus hotels, if you really think about Airbnb, it's not just a travel company. It's all about travel and living, and really, any kind of stay, any kind of accommodation.

Not many people are aware that even a full-year lease can be accommodated in Airbnb. And that's reflected in a strong growth in stays of 28 days or longer, which was 19% of nights booked on Airbnb in Q2 of 2021! One fifth of all bookings are long-term stays. Okay, let's now officially agree that we can no longer call it a "short-term rental" sector.

The shareholder letter also highlights the fact that 50% of the nights booked were 7 nights or longer. The leadership of Airbnb argues that those are not typical hotel guests because hotels' average length of stay is much lower. With Airbnb, the average is 4+. As Dave Stephenson stated, *"Clearly, during this time period, we have taken share from traditional accommodations."*

Dave Stephenson *(CFO)*

The increased flexibility of how people are traveling and living, increases the overall TAM of what Airbnb is able to address because if you're going to be staying longer, if you're going to have more flexibility, you're much more likely to want to stay in a hosted Airbnb with the amenities that you have in Airbnb versus being in a hotel room.

Brian Chesky *(CEO)*

In addition to long-term stays, which is essentially an entirely new category that is not even really traveling, it's living, which has, I think, been significantly expanded by COVID, you have a number of other dynamics happening. People are traveling to many more locations. And oftentimes, people are now traveling to places that don't even have hotels.

So that would explain some expansion of TAM there. There's also a general shift from business travel to leisure travel because we think that as fewer people travel for business in their home, they're going to have a greater desire to travel for leisure. And again, over the course of the pandemic, many people, millions of people, in fact, have tried Airbnb for the first time.

Zoom is here to stay. And if we believe that Zoom is here to stay, we believe that flexibility in remote living is here to stay. And therefore, it's pretty obvious that what would happen is that we are going to continue to see more and more longer-term stays. And I think this is going to help us smooth out our seasonality over the coming years.

Latest product developments

Airbnb is all about flexibility these days (#agile). As stated in the Airbnb Q2 2021 Shareholder letter,[102] the company's product innovation supports the new ways people travel. *"Many people now have greater freedom around where and when they travel, and we've improved our product to better meet their needs."*

Airbnb announced new product innovations to allow for more flexibility when searching for a place to stay, along with improvements that make the entire guest flow simpler and easier to use.

Flexibility is at the heart of their improved guest experience and includes three new ways to search on Airbnb:

- First, **Flexible Dates search** supports guests with more flexibility for when they travel. Instead of having to narrow down exact dates for their trip, guests are now able to search for a weekend getaway, a week-long vacation, or even a month-long stay "sometime in the next few months". They're already seeing an increase in guest bookings using Flexible Dates.

- Second, **Flexible Destinations** offers guests a new way to plan trips when they don't have a specific destination in mind. Guests can easily discover properties and simultaneously help hosts with unique listings get more bookings.

- Finally, they're rolling out a new feature called **Flexible Matching**. It increases the number of search results by showing options that are just outside the criteria entered by the guest. For example, if a guest searches for listings under $300 per night, it will show listings that fit all other criteria, but are priced slightly outside of that range. These features offer guests the flexibility they want and allow them to drive bookings to more hosts in more parts of the world.

Beyond improving the guest booking flow, they've also taken their product innovations further, to meet the changing needs of guests while they travel.

From the shareholder letter: *"As the flexibility to work and live from anywhere continues, knowing a listing's wifi speed before booking is essential; wifi has been one of the top searched amenities over the past year.* [Now, how would they know this if they didn't have easy access to their data in the cloud? #itsallaboutdata] *We now provide an easy and efficient way for Hosts to measure and post their listing's wifi speed using the Airbnb app. We've rolled out this feature globally."*

In addition, their new arrival guide improves the on-trip guest experience. The arrival guide displays essential on-trip information, such as directions, door codes and wifi details. It has contributed to an overall increase in five-star ratings.

---

[102]Airbnb Shareholder Letter Q2 2021: https://s26.q4cdn.com/656283129/files/doc_financials/2021/q2/Airbnb_Q2-2021-Shareholder-Letter_Final.pdf

Airbnb also recently launched a redesigned help center, more than tripled their supported languages (from 11 to 42), and updated their safety resources, including localized emergency information for fire, police and EMT services.

Outlook

The Airbnb leadership team states that their success is driven by both their ability to adapt, as well as their focus on innovation to support new ways of traveling.

| **Brain Chesky** *(CEO)*

Our model is inherently adaptable. We can adapt to the changing use cases of guests and that's because we have hosted nearly every community offering nearly any type of space at every price point.

And number two, we're continuing to focus on product innovation. We're going to continue to build new products. And these two things, I think, have demonstrated that this pandemic, as hard as it's been for us and as hard as it's been for everyone all around the world, it's made us a stronger, a more efficient and a better company. And we are prepared for what's to come and for the future of travel and the future of living.

The opportunity for our core business is probably greater than anyone ever really imagined before the pandemic. And part of this is just because more people are traveling to more locations, many of which don't even have hotels, millions of people have been introduced to Airbnb.

Number two, as we said, long-term stays are a huge boon to our business. This is an entire category of travel that didn't really exist when Joe, Nate and I started this company more than 13 years ago. But I think there's this entire new category of travel where travel and living is blurring.

Three, experiences. We thought last year could be a breakout year for experiences. Obviously, the opposite happened. We had to put the product on pause. But I think that people are going to be yearning for experiences.

And then finally, number four, I think there's a huge number of opportunities to unlock more hosting. And we're going to take guidance from the creativity of our community.

To conclude, I believe that Airbnb will remain the major player in the alternative accommodations sector for years to come, mainly thanks to the flexibility of their model and continuous investments in technology and product innovation... and obviously, the amount of money they now have in their hands.

Sonder

Another big player that is definitely worth noting is Sonder. This San Francisco short-term rental startup raised $225 mln in 2019 at a valuation north of $1 bln.[103] In April 2021, Skift wrote about Sonder's plans to go Public at $2.2 Billion Valuation.[104]

I was very fortunate to catch Co-founder and CEO of Sonder, Francis Davidson between meetings and ask him a few questions about the company and future plans.

Francis shared their story. I found it very fascinating so I would like to share our conversation with you "as is".

| Ira Vouk

What inspired you to start the company? What was in your head when you made that decision?

| Francis Davidson

I wasn't actually even expecting to start the business that we have today. I was just trying to solve this problem that I encountered as a student. I live in San Francisco now, but I'm from Quebec and went to university there and actually incorporated the business during my first year in college.

I had no expectation that that would ever happen in my life. I wasn't planning to be a business person. I wasn't thinking that hospitality was the thing I was going to spend the next decade contributing to. I was really just noticing that my apartment would be empty during the summer. I was going back to my hometown just a couple hours away and I thought, "Hey, maybe I can find some travelers to stay in it."

And it turned out there were a bunch of other people that were in similar situations. So one thing led to the next, and my co-founder and I managed something like 80 apartments for students during the summer and we realized, "Wait a minute. There's no brand that does this. Why is there no standard high-quality consistency, the same kind of value proposition that large hotels bring? Why does that not exist in the alternative accommodations space?"

So we set out to build that business and a couple years later, we realized that actually, the opportunity was a little bit deeper than that. The hospitality industry itself could be improved upon. And so now, the business has evolved towards becoming a hospitality brand challenger so to speak, that is more tech-driven, that is more focused on design. And half of what we do today is hotels. So we

---

[103]Tech Crunch: Hospitality business Sonder confirms new investment, $1B+ valuation (July 2019): https://techcrunch.com/2019/07/11/airbnb-competitor-sonder-confirms-new-investment-1b-valuation/

[104]Skift: Sonder to Go Public at $2.2 Billion Valuation as Short-Term Rental Sector Stays Hot (April 2021): https://skift.com/2021/04/30/sonder-to-go-public-at-2-2-billion-valuation-as-short-term-rental-sector-stays-hot/

started as an alternative accommodations business but then realized that there was actually an opportunity that was quite broad.

| Ira Vouk

Do you think that the alternative accommodations sector has evolved significantly since you started the company?

| Francis Davidson

It started as kind of a niche thing, especially for urban travel. I think, for the longest time, people have been renting cottages and villas and finding ways to do that. There have been a lot of property management companies that had those offerings, but the idea of urban travel and staying in anything but a hotel is quite recent. And now it's just something that's, especially for millennials and gen Z, is as common as staying in a hotel.

So I think that's probably the biggest change. It's in the popular consciousness.

I think a lot of other changes relate to how cities are responding. So initially it's a small thing, it doesn't really matter and then it captures attention as it scales. And now we're in a situation where in nearly all urban markets, there are quite clearly spelled out regulations and they prohibit people from using housing to offer short-term accommodations. And that's actually a really crucial evolution in our business model as well to go towards full buildings and partner with developers that would actually build properties.

And in many ways, what we've evolved toward is more of an extended stay kind of offering where we manage the entire building and it's in the right zone, we file our taxes, etc. So I'd say that the regulatory environment has shifted a lot over the last two years and from my perspective honestly, quite for the better. Now there are much clearer rules to play by, that are on even playing field with the rest of the hospitality industry.

| Ira Vouk

In the beginning, when the company was growing, what were the main obstacles to scale it?

| Francis Davidson

The biggest challenge has always been for us to scale the organization. On the one hand - there's a ton of supply, on the other hand - there's quite a lot of demand.

We've grown so rapidly. For example, leading up to the pandemic in 2019, we started the year with 400 employees and we ended the year with 1200 employees. We launched several countries, and it's just the difficulty of scaling at that speed is insane.

Building an executive team, the culture, rethinking a process that worked six months ago and that doesn't work now because the company is too large. That was definitely challenging.

And dealing with competition as well. This idea that we're pursuing is one that a lot of other companies have been pursuing. I think many of us probably between 2012 and 2015 thought about it because it didn't exist. There were a lot of these companies, over a dozen venture backed companies in that space. And so ensuring that we can achieve breakout growth before these other players become too substantial, was a really important theme for us.

When we saw the rise of Oyo rooms backed by SoftBank, we realized, "Wow, they are really aggressive and expanding extremely rapidly all over the world." So all these things motivated us to have to grow and seize the market opportunity. And then we faced all those challenges of scaling our organization. That's probably what was most difficult.

Ira Vouk

What do you think was your main competitive advantage that allowed you to become the leader in the market? What is the secret sauce?

Francis Davidson

I think that our commitment to extremely rapid growth to scale really substantially is what allowed us to then win more deals with property owners and developers. So there's kind of a flywheel that exists in our business: the larger you are, the lower your cost structure is, the more you can afford to invest in technology, which differentiates the guest experience and again, the operating cost structure.

The larger we are, the better our credit worthiness is, it allows us to raise more capital and look more impressive to developers. And so if we give an offer and a competitor gives the same offer - they're going to choose us, almost always, because we're larger, and that allows us to compound our advantage over time.

So we saw pretty early on that the biggest player would have a lot of advantages and so we just engineered our business so that we could grow rapidly.

Another one of the ingredients to make that happen is just focus on unit economics because it is a complicated business. There are some operations involved. This isn't like the software 90% gross margin kind of company and so it could be really easy to lose sight of just financial discipline. And for us, it's been embedded in our core right from the start and we're very, very thoughtful in the way we underwrite deals.

And one of the metrics we cared the most about that I think was foregone by other companies, was the payback period, the speed at which we could recycle our capital.

So, we managed to get developers to hand over really exceptional buildings to us without us having to contribute meaningful security deposits. Now, almost all of the properties and contracts that we signed with owners are what's called "capital light" for us. So, we don't even contribute any of the money to improve the asset, to furnish it, to decor it to our standards. They fund that. So that allows us to basically take our dollar really far. And we've modeled all this for our approach versus our competitors' approach. And we saw that with say 100 million dollars that we raised by 2018, every dollar that we invested would yield substantially more units and then that would count on our advantage over time.

So when the pandemic hit, we were just so clearly almost an order of magnitude larger than the second player and I think that gave us the capacity to get through the crisis.

| Ira Vouk

Do you think the alternative accommodations sector has changed significantly how hotels should look at their businesses? How has the hotel sector been affected by this? Are there things that they should do differently now?

| Francis Davidson

Definitely. Guest experience and operations.

I think one of the biggest shockers to the hospitality industry was how the hell can an industry that has no 24/7 front desk or security on site, no concierge service, no key cards (sometimes you have to go through some sort of a labyrinth to figure out how to get in) - how the hell can they succeed? It just violates every assumption of the hospitality industry.

*And I think the wake-up call in my view should be that **the next generation traveler is very different, and they're much more savvy.** Their perception of great service isn't a bunch of stuff available at the ring of a bell. It's not white glove. It's not like, "Mr. Davidson this, Mr. Davidson that, let me hold your luggage for you." It's more of, "Well, where are all the cool places around here and are you a real human when you interact with me or not? Do you have something cool in your space? Do you have good recommendations for things to do?"*

People now travel with supercomputers in their pockets. They can do a lot of stuff, they don't need room service, they could just order food on their phone. They can figure it out even if they're traveling internationally. It takes about two seconds to figure out what company delivers food in Barcelona and you download the app and you order from a local restaurant, and it shows up at your door. It's the simplest thing.

The hospitality industry has these massive operations to deliver services that are just not needed in 2021. So I think that's the main thing. I think that's what the hotel industry has to learn from the rise of alternative accommodations.

Essentially you can take limited service to its logical extreme and say, "There's going to be almost no service. But what I'm going to give you is a really awesome place and a great location."

It has to be really well designed and not feel like a cookie cutter. There is a lot of demand for that, and people are willing to pay a pretty price for that specific guest experience that the hotel industry is not providing today to these travelers.

| Ira Vouk

So we are a generation of introverts who are seeking experiences? I guess that's the target audience that you're pursuing?

| Francis Davidson

Not necessarily introverts. Some gen Z person will routinely hang out with their friends in this virtual non-physical space. They'll have a group chat, or they'll be on Snapchat or they'll post videos on Tiktok with their friends. And so, as a hospitality company we're saying, "Hey, instead of having a check-in where I'm going to describe to you in great detail the amenities of the property, why don't I just send you a short giphy with a couple of snappy sentences with no capital letters and some emojis." That will feel warmer and more native to that audience.

| Ira Vouk

Do you think consistency is something that the new generation of travelers is looking for? Or are they expecting a different experience in every new location?

| Francis Davidson

That's right. It's an interesting paradox. I think there's something that you want to be consistent and there are other things that you want to be different.

Things that you want to be consistent are: comfort, the bed must be comfortable, you also want to be able to set the temperature that you want in the room, and there shouldn't be crazy noise between the rooms, etc. Things like that.

So I'd say the base standards of the quality of the experience ought to be extremely consistent and then other things you want to be very different and surprising. For example, the lobbies can be a little bit more creative, partnerships that occur on the property with local businesses as well as the accommodation types.

So, we started with apartments, but now we have hotels, we have a couple of resorts and over time, we want to add more accommodation categories, we want to have a plethora of choices. So I think that variability is welcome, but not the variability of "If I call, will someone pick up?" You want that to be very consistent. The answer must be, "Yes, there must be someone to help me 24/7 within seconds."

Ira Vouk

Has the pandemic changed significantly the way you approach things, the way you plan your business, or your financial situation? How has it changed your perception of your business overall and the future path?

Francis Davidson

In the short term, we did a lot of things to ensure that we could generate really strong performance through the pandemic. Our revenue versus comp properties has been really extraordinary, upwards of two times greater than our comp properties during the pandemic and that's mostly due to our efforts on extended stay. So that helped quite a bit.

In the long run, we're just focused on building a great hospitality company based on great design, great technology, lower operating cost, with modern service. That still holds true.

I think there's one thing that the pandemic has accelerated is the rise of the Digital Nomad. We've surveyed a lot of our guests and also just the general population (young adults in the US in particular) and realized that they are really, really curious to try this out. I've myself done it in the last 12 months. My girlfriend and I have been on the road for over 9 months, just hopping from Sonder City to Sonder City. I'm actually in one right now, we're spending two weeks in Montreal. I can work very productively here.

And that's a really interesting demand stream for us. And I think we're really in a unique position to meet the needs of those Digital Nomads: our price points make sense, consistency in the quality, the reliability of the Wi-Fi, the selection of locations, all of that is attractive for them.

Ira Vouk

Absolutely, I'm one of them as well. I love traveling, I work from home, a coffee shop, or from under a bridge, wherever it is. And I love this opportunity to be able to just take off and go.

Francis Davidson

There is still some uncertainty about the size of the Digital Nomads community. Everyone recognizes that this trend is going to be more important than it was prior to the pandemic, but how big is it going to be? That's still a question mark. There's a question mark around the future workforce, how much flexibility will employers provide? My view is that it's going to be quite a lot and that means quite a lot of opportunity for folks to just spend a month in Mexico City and two months in Spain and still keep working through it. And then the other question is on business

191

transient, and especially that trip that could be replaced by a video call.

There's another thing that is not often mentioned but is another component of demand that we will see as a result of remote work, it is company offsites. For example, we hire a lot of remote workers and our folks are in various cities. So it's rare that a team at Sonder is all in the same city. But in order to keep the team cohesion really high, every three months or so we're going to have all of our team members go to one of our cities and spend three or four nights there and just bond and do quarterly planning and other creative work together. So I think the rise of remote work will also mean that companies will have a slice of the budget to do these offsites frequently.

I'm very happy that I got to meet with Francis as I found this discussion very educational. I personally learned a lot and so I believe there is so much that the hotel industry can learn from that, too. I will summarize those things, from all my conversations, in the last section of this chapter.

AirDNA

In my attempt to dig deeper into the world of the alternative accommodations sector, I turned to the main data-generating player on the market.

AirDNA is a great example of a data supplier that helps our industry evolve (the hospitality industry in general). They currently mainly operate in the short-term rental sector, but I'm sure soon we'll see them better represented in the hotel space as well. Because remember... data is the key to successful decision making.

I sat down with Scott Shatfort (Founder and CEO of AirDNA) to hear his story. Well, "sat down" wouldn't be exactly accurate... We met via Zoom and I was standing at my desk. I asked Scott about his journey in the hospitality space. He was very kind to answer my questions and share his vision on the evolution and the future of the sector.

| Ira Vouk

What inspired you to start the company?

| Scott Shatford

As an Airbnb entrepreneur, operator, host (whatever you want to call it) I think there was just this general curiosity that I had about this crazy new thing, called Airbnb. I thought, "I'm making pretty good money with this side hustle, I have 5 one-bedroom properties, and why should I work so hard in my corporate career for 10 years?" I could make more money just spinning up a couple properties and playing a lot more beach volleyball. And so that was the initial idea behind founding the company.

I thought, "There's something here and I've got a data & analytics background." My curiosity was the driving factor, it was such a new market.

I was getting super geeky about it. So it started off really like an eBook. I left the corporate world and wrote a book, which is like the Airbnb expert's playbook. It has been downloaded almost a million times now, in the last seven years.

I was really trying to figure out how I put more data behind the debate and really have some concrete answers on: What's the best way to operate? Where's the best place to buy? What is the best price for your Saturday, versus your Tuesday? And so on.

I saw that the marketplace was growing like crazy, 300% every year and I saw an opportunity in building a data source for this industry.

Ira Vouk

Interesting story. I'd say that even in the mature hotel industry, a lot of decisions are still made based on gut feeling, not based on real data. But it's a different discussion.

Can you provide a brief description of your company, the main products and the purpose of those products in the industry?

Scott Shatford

We are a data provider for the short-term rental industry. We are the largest aggregator of data for about 10 million plus properties around the world.

We have a few products. One of them is called MarketMinder and that is our consumer or prosumer product, which is built for vacation operators, real estate investors, mostly for smaller independent managers that are really trying to figure out how to dial in on their Airbnb or Vrbo portfolio, how to do revenue management better, how to analyze the competition, how to benchmark the performance. A lot of these stats have been available to hotels for decades. But in our space, this wasn't available before we got started. So we're really trying to help people become more data-driven in the short-term market.

On the enterprise side of the business, we also have an offering where this data can be delivered via API, plus other reports that may be more relevant to a travel agency or a hotel. The data can also be spun up to really help support other companies that are being impacted by short term rentals, like companies in real estate business, etc. So there are many other ways to use our data.

Ira Vouk

Out of all these various types of users, what is your primary target audience?

Scott Shatford

Since day one, it's really been built as a product to help support Airbnb operators, real estate investors, and small entrepreneurs in their decision making. That's our primary audience. There are about 2 million of them in the world that are making their full-time living on Airbnb. And their main objective is to try to maximize profitability from the properties they have and the ones that they want to acquire. So everything we build is really trying to help these people elevate their game, and start to become more data-driven. You've got one property, you've got one opportunity, either get it right or wrong.

| **Ira Vouk**

Do you have any customers that are from the hotel revenue management space, maybe Revenue Management Systems? Somebody who'd want to source this data from you on a regular basis, to help hotels identify the strength of demand for future days, to see how many units have been sold at what price, how many are available, etc?

| **Scott Shatford**

We sure should and we've talked to every single one. But I think there's this attitude, "If my competitors are not doing it, then I don't need to as well."

I think it's hard for those companies to get it on the roadmap because nobody has really analyzed the potential from this opportunity to use this data to really prove its value.

We've had lots of good conversations and everybody is interested in having a comprehensive view of the lodging landscape. So I think it's just a matter of time before we figure out the mechanics of these partnerships and data sharing that will result in this win-win for both worlds.

| **Ira Vouk**

I personally believe that this is the elephant in the room that we can't ignore because it does ultimately affect the demand and the availability in the market and we, hoteliers, have to pay attention to it when we make our pricing or forecasting decisions. I think it's definitely a very valuable piece of data.

| **Scott Shatford**

Certainly. We release a report with the latest trends regularly, there's a ton of good data in the industry report section of our website.

| **Ira Vouk**

So, going back to the evolution of AirDNA. Has it been relatively easy to scale the company or have you encountered a lot of obstacles in your journey?

| **Scott Shatford**

I feel pretty fortunate. I haven't had a lot of the good war stories that a lot of people have had and I think one of the reasons is being laser focused on what our mission and objective is.

COVID of course gave everybody a few wounds, but other than that, it's been pretty clear.

I took a couple gambles, which was that Airbnb was going to be dominant and disruptive and was going to beat Vrbo and booking.com in this space.

Another bet that I placed early on is that this wasn't going to get professionalized, meaning this wasn't all going to be managed by people with 10,000 properties, that the individual host would be very successful in the world, that people were looking for unique experiences, unique properties and that would win at the end of the day.

Those are the bets I placed and so I focused on Airbnb and the small host on those platforms. We of course had lots of bumps on the road, all over the place, but nothing that felt like it was "game over" at any point.

| Ira Vouk

Do you think the alternative accommodations sector has significantly changed since the time you started the company 6 years ago? How has it evolved?

| Scott Shatford

It was alternative six years ago and it's not really alternative anymore, in my opinion. There was a novelty factor when people would book my properties when I was a host back then. Some people were saying, "I can't believe this exists. And I can't believe this is your house and I'm staying in it." So there was a novelty there but very little expectations in regards to what it was, or what the quality should be. It was all sort of like the Wil Wild West and people's expectations were low and they were pretty happy.

That has changed over time. People are expecting an easier check-in process, they're expecting the same cleaning as they experience at hotels, etc.

| Ira Vouk

So I shouldn't be asking whether that sector is here to stay or not, right? You look pretty confident that it's not just a temporary glitch in the lodging domain?

| Scott Shatford

A more interesting question is not whether it's going to exist, but in what form and how many different models there are going to be and how many different types of properties and ownership models we will see. We already have so many now, all these models for co-ownership of properties, etc.

| Ira Vouk

So you think that the government regulations aren't going to destroy the sector?

Scott Shatford

It's a tough one. It's hard to forecast what the government's going to do. There's a chance we'll see more regulations in the next 20 years. But it's tough to say what exactly will be regulated.

I could say that COVID was probably a positive thing for short-term rental business from that standpoint. It resulted in extra income for hosts, more jobs, more economic activity.

So this old argument that the affordable housing issue was the reason to get rid of Airbnb before, I think this correlation-causation of Airbnb and housing prices - it has been broken in the pandemic.

At some point, nobody was traveling on Airbnb, but home prices across the US went up by an ungodly amount. I think that the thing that does scare me is that housing is going to get really expensive. There's always going to be a scapegoat as to why it's expensive and it's a complicated issue so hotels can still use that power and convince uneducated City Council members to take those regulatory actions.

But I think what's interesting is that hotels are also getting into the short-term rental space, companies like Marriott, so many of them don't want to finance those regulations anymore. That allows them to have a competitive advantage over other big brands. So I feel optimistic about the future of the short-term industry.

Ira Vouk

So, it also leads to my next question. When you look at the data and you compare different parameters and data points, and trends between the hotels and their patterns and the alternative accommodations patterns, do you see significant differences in those patterns?

Scott Shatford

For sure. Average length of stay is longer in our world, it's closer to four days for vacation rentals. Now we're starting to see longer stays. The midterm stays, the extended stays - that's really picking up. It's like "live anywhere, work anywhere", bouncing from Airbnb to Airbnb, one month at-a-time. I think that is a realistic future where a significant portion of revenues will be coming from. Sort of "live on the platform".

Ira Vouk

Digital Nomads, right.

Scott Shatford

Yes. I think that's super interesting in terms of the trend, and it is what we see happening.

Another difference is the DOW pattern. With many hotels, Sunday, Monday, Tuesday, Wednesday, Thursday are booked and weekends are slow. And it is sort of the opposite with vacation rentals.

Think about the business traveler vs leisure traveler. Airbnb demand is nearly 200% higher on Fridays and Saturdays than other days. And so there's obviously just a different customer type, the demand is really mostly leisure weekend. So yes, when I chart DOW patterns for short-term rentals and compare with those of hotels - they're inverted.

Ira Vouk

And how about booking windows? I assume they're wider in your world?

Scott Shatford

Absolutely. They're also different for every single market and time of year but generally, 60 days. COVID has made things weird where it became 15 days at some point in time. But previously, 60 was normal, and during peak season it could go up to 6 months even.

It's a huge luxury for VR managers.

Ira Vouk

Let's talk about whether the VR sector is competing with hotels or not. My understanding is that in many situations, these units that are on Airbnb are not really concentrated in the same area (submarket) where hotel rooms would normally be concentrated, for various reasons, for examples regulations by the city. Is that what you're seeing in your data as well? Does it mean they're not really competing because they're not really always in the same sub-market?

Scott Shatford

That's right. I think the other part is that these investors are smart enough not to put their property right next door to a Four Seasons. You don't really want your property to be right next to where there are 3,000 hotel rooms. You want to be a half mile away where there's zero hotel rooms.

We know there are 2 main reasons people are picking vacation rentals: value and location. So you want to sort of fill a void on the map where there's not a ton of lodging options. Because people want to stay right next to their Mom or the graduation, whatever the event may be. And so typically, hosts are looking not to compete directly with the hotel next door. They want to be filling in the voids on the map.

Ira Vouk

And this is where they can use your product to figure out what the potential is, right? To see where the market is saturated.

Scott Shatford

Absolutely. Our product is helping those people make that decision. We help people find markets in cities where we think real estate is going to go absolutely insane, where homes are going to appreciate. But that's half the battle, that's where the journey begins.

Then there are questions like "what type of accommodation is the best", "what submarket", etc.

And that's where the data is fun to look at, how to dissect individual cities to understand what's trending up, where the supply is, where the opportunities are, etc.

Ira Vouk

Interesting. So what do you see happening in that sector in the next 5-10 years?

Scott Shatford

In the short-term rental space, there are so many different issues that everybody is trying to solve independently, and possibly what we'll be seeing soon is consolidation into some sort of an operating system for vacation rentals that will solve those problems for the hosts.

They don't have a revenue management department, they don't have a team of front desk people, so they really need something that automates everything: communication, revenue management, distribution, check-in/check-out, etc.

What you see is that the majority of hosts are not early tech adopters, they don't want to have to pull together 5 different solutions to solve 5 different problems to run their couple VRs. They need a Plug-and-Play solution that is intuitive and comprehensive to be able to do everything in one place and monitor all their properties.

Airbnb owned all their supply and then Vrbo had their own supply channel and then connectivity became more and more complicated for hosts to manage their calendars, their rates and their check-ins/check-outs.

There have always been solutions for big operators with hundreds of properties to be able to do this in a PMS and get charged a ton of money for it. But I hope what we're going to see is similar solutions emerging for smaller operators.

We have seen three steps in the evolution of data in the short-term rental space.

First is when nobody had any data, you gave them a chart and then they could figure out what to do with that information.

The next step was generating recommendations for the users based on that data. Now, we have good data and we have your data and we can figure out what you're doing wrong and how you can improve.

198

The next step in that evolution is what we call automation, which is: okay, we figured out these recommendations are good, so now you're going to go on autopilot and we're going to change your picture layout, your copy, your pricing automatically for you to improve your performance.

So from my perspective, that's what's interesting, that's what real AI machine learning will enable us to do. We will be able to connect into your property, change things dynamically while you sit back and check the results.

| Ira Vouk

I totally see this coming eventually in the VR space. So do you imagine a big player stepping in and maybe pulling different parts of the ecosystem together or just building a solution from scratch that would address all of these different kinds of aspects of the operations for those hosts? How do you see that happening?

| Scott Shatford

It's a good question. It may happen in a few different ways. I think right now the industry is trying to address this through partnerships of these different solutions. But I think what you really want is a native solution that has it all built together. So I think it's going to happen through consolidations, mergers and acquisitions. Like five companies being rolled up by a private equity company.

| Ira Vouk

We already see some of the players attempting to address this (Cloudbeds being the most prominent one). But from what I'm seeing, it's so much harder to sell to those individual unit owners. That's why these companies naturally try to steer more towards larger operators and chains. It's much more beneficial for them to sell to one customer with 30 buildings, which equates to 3000 rooms, for example, than to a thousand different individual owners.

So in order for us to get to what you describe, I think we have to first make our technology so intuitive and make it based on a true self-service type of model with easy subscription on the website without any human interaction involved in the process. I don't know if the industry is there yet from the technology standpoint.

| Scott Shatford

Yes. Acquisition of those customers is hard, they're all over the place. How do you get these people at a cost that makes sense?

And we love that problem. That's what we do well. We just get people really early in the journey. So that right after a dinner party, where one of their friends mentions that they have a short-term rental property, what do they do next? They put in the address of their mom's second home to see if it's worth anything, to see how much they would be making if it was listed on Airbnb. We get people right there, when they're sort of exploring this new concept.

And so, we capture people very early at that stage. And then, when they're ready to list their property - they come to us first to think about how to set that property up.

So that's what we like about this. It's that we get people super early and then we can figure out how to monetize them later in the process when they're ready for more nerdy solutions like accounting tools or revenue management tools, whatever it might be.

It looks to me that AirDNA is very well positioned to be that medium that could open up the doors for hotel tech solutions to the alternative accommodations sector so that someday the individual hosts will be able to easily subscribe to a comprehensive end-to-end solution that will allow them to manage all aspects of their operations. One day that will happen... right after we solve that same problem for the hotel sector.

COVID recovery of the shared economy sector

As Scott Shatford put it, "COVID gave everybody a few wounds," and the whole hospitality industry (all sectors) definitely experienced a crisis for some period of time. However, what we're seeing is that different sectors (as well as different segments within those sectors) have been recovering at a different pace.

In July 2020, Cloudbeds hosted a webinar and then published an article[105] where they compared recovery trends between the hotel sector and the VR sector. Cloudbeds enlisted the help of leading benchmarking and data insights providers, STR (on the hotel side) and AirDNA (on the VR side). According to the author, *"The data shows a clear shift in demand across geographies, price points, and property types."*

The analysis included data from 2019 to June 27th 2020 in 27 markets globally, including 12 regional destination markets and 15 urban markets. The data showed a pretty drastic difference in performance between the 2 sectors.

As COVID-19 took hold around the globe in March of 2020, traditional hotels saw the most severe year-over-year decline in occupancy, down about 77% across the 27 markets, compared to rentals that were down only about 45%.

And then, if we look at the recovery trends, as a result of the global crisis, VRs started leading in terms of occupancy levels, thus turning the pre-pandemic trend on its head.

Clearly, traveling as a family or in small groups and booking a vacation rental home

---

[105]Cloudbeds: Hotel vs. Vacation Rental Recovery: What the Market Data Shows (July 2020): https://www.cloudbeds.com/articles/hotel-vs-vacation-rental-recovery-what-the-market-data-shows/

as opposed to multiple hotel rooms, especially for longer stays, became more common at the height of the outbreak and restrictions.

Short-term rental occupancy outperforming hotels

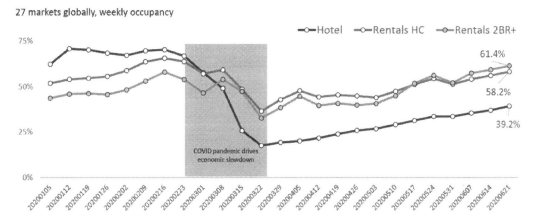

Rentals HC = "Hotel Comparable" (Studio & 1BR short-term rentals that are comparable to traditional hotel rooms)

Regarding ADR, the analysis found that rates have held steady or even gone up slightly for short-term rentals since the start of the year 2020, whereas for hotels the average daily rate has dropped from more than $150 in January of 2020 to about $104 at the end of June of 2020.

You can find more recent VR-related COVID stats in AirDNA's "COVID Data Center"[106] and most recent hotel-related COVID stats on STR's page "COVID Hotel Industry Data". [107]

So all in all, what we see is that the pandemic affected the two sectors in a very different manner.

STR says it has to do with the fundamental difference in the normal type of demand that goes to these property types. Hotels are much more business and group orientated, and we know that type of business still hasn't come back in terms of demand for accommodation (in 2021 and even in 2022). So it's no surprise that hotels would fall further and wouldn't have recovered as fast. VRs have the advantage of being more leisure oriented, as well as having a higher proportion of long-term stays.

Scott Shatford (CEO of AirDNA) said that longer-term stays and vacation rentals' ability to accommodate leisure travelers seeking longer stays have helped give them the advantage for now. But also, the types of amenities that they offer also play a part, mostly in terms of properties with a kitchen, larger spaces, and laundry facilities. He describes

---

[106]AirDNA: COVID-19 Short-Term Rental Data: https://www.airdna.co/COVID-19-data-center

[107]STR: COVID-19: Hotel Industry Impact and Recovery: https://str.com/data-insights-blog/coronavirus-hotel-industry-data-news

the ideal property type in this COVID era as "that drive-to, single-family, standalone, control-the-access" property where you don't have to interact with people and can feel safe isolating in an environment that's controllable.

Here's more from my conversation with Scott:

There is just so much going on that we saw in that comparison. Short-term rental owners got very lucky. They had this inherent advantage of not trying to cram a bunch of people into a small space and allow people from small spaces to move into larger spaces, bigger yards and bigger properties. There was also that unfair advantage with a lot of people wanting to go to more rural places with more space and a pool. Hotels just couldn't offer that. So that segment recovered super quickly while hotels are still struggling to get to pre-pandemic levels.

What we've seen is that the pandemic forced many people to form these new habits of going to a four-bedroom place in Nantucket for the first time. Many people were amazed to see how good and affordable that experience was. And so what we're seeing is that it's getting harder to lure them back to the hotels after they have had some of these great experiences with VRs.

There is this mental barrier for people to make that first VR trip. But after they've tried it, most actually make a second and third trip. And so, I think there has been that shift for those people that were the laggards. They had to say, "Hey, let's give it a try." And that has been the biggest advantage for the short-term rental industry that resulted from the pandemic.

Now, who knows where we're going to be in 6 months or a year. People might become tired of being isolated in their four-bedroom apartment and their own pool. They might want to go back to the hotel and be at the bar and in the lobby. We don't know how people are looking to travel quite yet.

So it's definitely an interesting phenomenon that we can't ignore. COVID gave many people that push towards trying out VRs for the first time. Previously, there was that mental barrier to entry for them, but now that they've tried it, they're hooked, they're now "users" because for many, staying in an Airbnb is so much more exciting and in many ways better than staying in a traditional hotel. And it's normally more affordable, especially if you're splitting the bill with a few other people.

During our conversation, Jan Freitag (National Director, Hospitality Analytics for the CoStar Group, formerly Senior Vice President of STR) further explained the reasons behind the drastic difference in the recovery trends:

In the US Hotel industry, the room demand is a three-legged stool: it's leisure, corporate transient, and corporate group. I'm combining the leisure group and transient together for ease of conversation.

Those are the three things that matter the most and we've clearly seen the recovery of leisure travel. Weekend occupancies are basically where they were in 2019 and weekend ADR is above where it was in 2019.

What we're missing is the midweek traveler, you and me, people who work for a fortune 1000 company. We're not traveling right now [this conversation was taking place in August 2021] *and we're certainly not going to large group events.*

So the recovery on the hotel side is leisure driven and that has also helped the alternative accommodations providers.

But we hope we will see some more sustained corporate demand midweek and some corporate group demand as well.

So the million dollar question is: as the alternative accommodations sector clearly benefited from the pandemic while taking advantage of the (temporary?) disproportionately skewed customer needs, which resulted in VRs leading position compared to hotels when it comes to occupancy levels - will this continue to be the case as we go back to "normal" modus operandi or will the lines on the above graph reverse to pre-pandemic placement with hotels occupying stronger position in the market?

I don't believe anyone can answer that question. I'm writing this paragraph on October 16, 2021 and we still haven't fully come out of the pandemic and there's no clear end in sight in terms of full recovery. What is also unknown is whether the industry is ever going to be the same as it was in 2019 or whether we will have to get used to a new "normal".

While nobody truly has the answer, I'm referencing opinions of a few people who are way smarter than I am. Two of them are unbiased and the third one - not so much, but still worth mentioning.

| Jan Freitag *(CoStar / STR)*

COVID has shown a much higher acceptance (at least in the US) of the VR segment. The American traveler is much more comfortable going into somebody else's home or apartment.

Back in April of 2020 I said, "VRs are going to have a hard time, because who in their right mind wants to go to a house of somebody you don't know?" You don't know if it's clean. You don't know if Jan who rented it out is a certified cleaner or a slob. Are you willing to bet your life on it?

And I had it completely wrong. I made the completely wrong call because it turns out what people feared more were elevators and lobbies, and what they wanted was to wipe down their own living space, three times a day if they wanted to. They wanted to have complete control of their 'bubble'. And that is what alternative accommodations providers offered.

And I think during the summer of 2020, providers made huge strides in consumer awareness that it's safe, it's easy. And so, VRBO, Airbnb and other providers are running out of owners. They're desperately looking for more inventory, which is super interesting.

So what have we learned in the last five years? I think because of COVID, consumer acceptance is much higher. What is the impact on the hotel space? Way too early to tell because the data from 2020 is very distorted.

So let's talk about the summer of 2023. People who drove 18 hours because they didn't want to fly and stayed in an Airbnb because they didn't want to stay in a hotel - are those people going to say no to the hotel again? Unlikely. I've had two shots plus two weeks. I'm going to fly and plus, I don't want to cook, I don't want to make my own bed. I want a hotel stay. This will be interesting to observe. But the demand seems to indicate that hotels are doing well with the leisure consumer.

So will this pendulum swing back to something that is "normal", which is the trend between 2017 and 2019 where there were always alternative accommodations users, but they were definitely always leisure hotel users? That's the question. I can't answer that today. Ask me in three years for your next book.

Ira Vouk

I'll make sure to give you a call when I start working on the Hospitality 3.0 manuscript.

Jordan Hollander *(Hotel Tech Report)*

The vacation rental sector got lucky during COVID. The markets saturated with VRs is where everyone wanted to go during COVID to be out in nature and so there are naturally more of those units in those markets. So they disproportionately benefited.

I think that those are more of short-term blimps and in my opinion, COVID has made us want to be around people more. This isn't to say there's no value in vacation rentals. It's only to say that in my mind, the value proposition of that sector will stay the same as it was before the pandemic.

I think COVID has made us all much more likely to spend at a higher level, and enjoy our lives and prioritize balance and prioritize having those great experiences. And so I think we will be more willing to spend on hotels than ever. People want to be together and people want to be around other people.

Dave Stephenson *(Chief Financial Officer of Airbnb)*

Zoom is here to stay. And if we can take a one-hour Zoom call on a Thursday, you're likely to be able to do a longer weekend with the family where maybe historically you've been stuck in the office. And so we believe that all of these trends will just continue to accrue to Airbnb and be tailwinds to our business going forward.

So let's check back again in a few years and see how those trends look.

What is clear though, is that the alternative accommodations sector is huge, it's evolving, it's here to stay and we can't ignore it. It has its target consumer segments. There will always be people who will prefer to stay in hotels and people who prefer to book on Airbnb, at least for some of their trips. And for some segments, the two sectors will have to compete. And if hotels can learn how to improve their value proposition, then they will be able to compete better.

So what's the verdict? What should hotels learn from this?

I believe we all agree that the alternative accommodations sector is definitely a disruptor.

And regardless of whether we can call it direct competition, it's essentially shaping up the expectations of consumers. So what are the conclusions that we should draw from the VR boom, and what are the things that we, hoteliers, should modify in our behavior in the future?

Here are the key takeaways, with quotes from various industry leaders to support each of the items.

1. Learn to differentiate and improve your value proposition

John Burns (Hospitality Technology Consulting):

VRs are legitimate competitors and in many respects, more important competitors than Marriott or anybody else. So we have to understand that they are really good at formulating and communicating their value proposition. And we have to be equally good in the hotel sector. You don't have much floor space. What do you have? You have security, you have consistency. You have someone immediately available to fix things, etc. You have daily housekeeping.

They've been very smart in using technology but out of the gate they said, "We're different. We're going to capitalize on what's different. So on our website, we're going to have a booking engine." But rather than saying, "What Marriott do you want to go to?" it's, "So, what do you want to do? Where do you want to go? What do you enjoy?" It's a conversation, they've taken the basic interest in travel and completely reoriented it in a much more traveler-friendly, exciting way.

So we're selling a night of real estate at a Marriott and they're saying, "What's your passion?"

Bob Gilbert (HSMAI):

What should hotels learn from this trend? I'd say they need to learn to differentiate. They've always had to differentiate, whether it's with product, or service, or price. If you think about alternative accommodations, what's the first thing a reservation agent asks you for? "Why are you in town? And what can I do to help you with that? Here are the local restaurants," and so forth. And hotels need to learn that level of customer service. If that's what our customers want, then ask that question right up front, so you know when you can customize the experience and increase your customer satisfaction rates.

So I think it's all going to be what the customer wants, and the customer deserves to have a choice.

2. Improve operational efficiencies to stay competitive

Jordan Hollander (Hotel Tech Report):

Hoteliers are realizing that they need to get leaner because of how competition affects business in aggregate: if you have substitutes with a higher profit margin and lower expense base, they're going to start reinvesting in customer acquisition at a heavier rate because they have more money to invest. They're going to outcompete you over the long term.

Historically, hotels have been competing with each other, but now they are competing with different substitutes. It's not a one-to-one competition because there are some customer types that will never book an Airbnb but in aggregate, you have new entrants in the market. Those entrants have a lower cost basis and higher profit margins and so hotels need to think about how they can achieve those profit margins to the best of their abilities, with the infrastructure that they have and the value proposition they have for consumers.

3. Rethink services and amenities

Jan Freitag (CoStar / STR):

I think what Airbnb and other alternative accommodations providers have done is put into the consumers' mind that concept of "stay like a local". Be in the thick of things, near the local restaurants and so forth. And so some hoteliers are already reacting to that and they're saying, "Hey, our restaurant is the place to be, our rooftop bar is the place to be, that's where the locals hang out. So why don't you stay with us?"

So I think as the hotel industry, we're taking a page from the marketing playbook of the alternative accommodations providers. And I think we've seen that already in the way that we design and "activate" lobbies, restaurants, rooftop pools, what have you. So that's what's changed and that's a very positive trend.

Another piece is that the alternative accommodations sector has shown that there is a need for multiple connected bedrooms with social space. And so a brand like Element is saying, "Okay, we can do that, too." So then your prototype is exactly that: a social space with connected bedrooms. And I think a lot of hotel designers and architects are thinking about connecting rooms, which before was maybe a bit of an afterthought.

Scott Shatford (AirDNA):

There will still be a battle for those 3-4 night stays between hotels and VRs. Hotels should ask themselves how to stay relevant for a little bit longer stays and bigger groups. For example, how to handle the adjoining rooms. Or what amenities they need to add to their rooms, all those things that people want and love about vacation rentals.

4. Don't ignore the VR competitive data in your revenue management strategy

John Burns (Hospitality Technology Consulting):

At some point, we have to be able to put Airbnb data into revenue management. I know that there's talk about that. They're our competitors. Forget Hilton - they've got one hotel or a handful of hotels in a city. Airbnb's got 10,000 units in the city. Let's look at them. We've got to understand them.

But we in the hotel business would rather ignore than confront our competition. This is a disaster waiting to happen. They are already good and are just getting better. So we should be looking strategically at our sales and marketing and thinking about how we compete successfully with them. And then on a tactical level, in areas like revenue management, we have to be able to consider them competition and think about how they fit when we're talking about competitor rates.

Jan Freitag (CoStar / STR):

I think you need to look at AirDNA or other providers like that. I think on the pricing side though, you just have to be very careful about what you're comparing yourself to. But yeah, is it helpful? I think so. More data is good. And when in doubt, I want more data. Even if the results of that analysis is that I don't have direct competition with those unit owners. Maybe that data will show me that multi-generational travel goes there but the individual transient traveler on a Wednesday night wants their loyalty points and stays with me. All that is data and it's also helpful.

I've always had this idea of being able to run a detailed analysis between vacation rental data and hotel performance.

So if I'm a brand, or a franchisor with multiple brands and properties in my portfolio, in different locations, it would be great if we were able to run correlations between different Airbnb data points and the performance of my properties, for different types of properties, in different locations, or maybe even individual room types. That would allow us to see whether there is a strong correlation between VR data and some individual "pieces" of my portfolio: specific room types, specific property types, or specific locations, etc. Then we only use that data for those properties where the correlation is found, because that will allow us to know what data has a predictive value, and what part of it is going to help us make better decisions (forecasting, pricing, optimization, marketing campaigns, targeted customer offers, etc.).

That's the kind of approach that I'm hoping our revenue management solutions will adopt going forward, because I believe that this data is very valuable.

5. Lean on technology to help with all of the above

Jordan Hollander (Hotel Tech Report):

Technology can help hotels compete. Because what else can you really do? You're not going to rebuild your hotel. You have regulations around staffing and security, etc. So ultimately, the only lever you could pull is to invest in technology to make your company more efficient, to restructure operations, to acquire customers more profitably, to optimize pricing. So those are the levers that hotels can pull because the asset is relatively fixed and it's very expensive to renovate or upgrade or alter. So ultimately, it's all about processes and process improvements, and I think technology hits on every type of process improvement you could possibly want to do.

John Burns (Hospitality Technology Consulting):

The VR sector uses technology brilliantly to support the basic sales message.

We could be doing that, too. We could have the same technology but we're just old and tired. We still have the same booking engine that looks the same way it did 20 years ago, shame on us.

Marco Benvenuti (Duetto):

When the hotel industry decided to split the management side, versus the brand side, versus the real estate side - it really put a disincentive on investing in technology. Because if you invest in technology, you need to look a little bit more on the longer term. If you're looking at just flipping a hotel, you're better off just replacing the carpet as they say. And so putting all these players on the same agenda when you're selling technology to them is hard. So that made it hard for new technology to come in as well.

But now we are seeing this paradigm starting to break. Airbnb comes in and blows everything out. So when disruptions like these happen, then you start moving fast. So we'll see how things go.

And the last message in this chapter from yours, truly.

As the alternative accommodations sector has evolved and become not-so-alternative and not-only-vacation and not-so-short-term, what we now have to ourselves is the "hotel sector" competing with the "everything else" sector.

It's not clear who is winning but does it have to be a battle?

Maybe, just maybe, sometime in the future, the line between the two will blur and we will become one big happy family. *insert heart emoji*

COVID PANDEMIC, THE ELEPHANT IN THE ROOM

"It's not the strongest of the species that survives,

it's the one that is the most adaptable to change."

~~Charles Darwin~~ COVID-19

We would all agree that COVID has taught businesses that it's not enough to just recognize changes in the environment, it's necessary to be able to adapt to those changes in order to survive. And as history shows, as always, most innovative and adaptive businesses will recover much quicker and thrive, leaving everyone else behind. Look at the examples of Airbnb and Sonder described in the previous chapter. Hotels have so much to learn from their ability to adapt and re-adapt, mainly through the use of modern technology and continuous innovation.

In 2020, the hotel industry suffered the worst decline in history. The resulting business failures were in the news everyday, and most industry experts agree that it will be several years until the industry returns to anywhere near the health it had in 2019.

Some illustrative statistics from the industry's favorite data supplier Smith Travel Research:

2020 - worst year in the history of the hotel industry
Occupancy actuals, Full Year 2020 compared to Full Year 2019

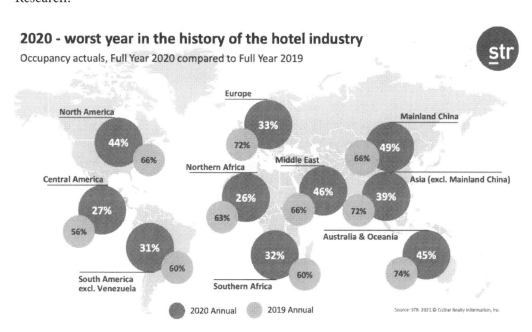

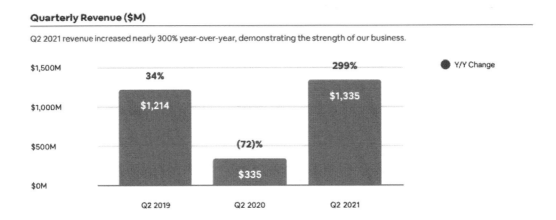

Quarterly Revenue ($M)

Q2 2021 revenue increased nearly 300% year-over-year, demonstrating the strength of our business.

It's not clear whether we will ever get back to how things were in 2019 because many aspects of travel may have changed forever and they'll never be the same. We'll have to get used to the "new normal" and it's inevitable. That means we will all have to adjust the way we run our businesses.

Booking patterns are now different than before: booking windows have changed, LOS is all over the place, segmentation has been messed up, competitive sets have become irrelevant in many cases and need to be revised, the list goes on.

So if you're one of those hotel companies that is still working with the exact same set of tools you had pre-pandemic (same technology, same strategies, same policies, same services and amenities, same segments, same compsets, same promotions and marketing campaigns, same distribution strategy or lack thereof) - you will soon become obsolete.

COVID and technology adoption

According to the Global Travel Staffing Barometer,[108] due to the pandemic, travel companies around the world laid off or furloughed over half a million people, and many of them are not coming back because they have actually left the industry. And I don't blame them, everyone needs stability, and the travel industry hasn't been able to offer that to their employees lately.

As John Burns (Hospitality Technology Consulting) pointed out:

We are at a point where we are questioning everything. That's not a bad idea, but we're even questioning revenue managers and we're losing them to other places. Revenue managers did good things for us, they were important. Other industries are recognizing the value of our experts and taking these people.

---

[108]Phocuswire: More than 530,000 Travel and Tourism Industry Workers Laid off or Furloughed (April 2020): https://www.phocuswire.com/videc-global-travel-staffing-barometer

The same is true for other roles that are affecting the activities of many departments.

So as a result, many many hotels are struggling and will continue to be struggling to run their operations with minimized human resources. And this will be our reality for a while, so we better come up with a new way to run our businesses.

How? Three words: automation, automation, automation. And here you thought a revenue management expert would know how to count...

More from John Burns:

I think there's an inflection point here and some big changes are happening.

So, we have been very timid and really have not looked to hire technology professionals to the extent that we should. We don't have the technology visionaries, we don't embrace them. It's still a supporting service as opposed to a strategic service. But that is changing. New people, new sense of urgency.

So one of the good things that came out of the global crisis of 2020 is the push for automation.

The travel industry has been hit hard. But what's nice to see is that travel technology companies did relatively well in the recent 18 months and most are still floating (except for the ones that were relying on hotel transaction fees in their business model). "Do more with less" became every single hotel's motto in 2020, which definitely helped raise awareness about the importance of technology in our business strategy.

John Burns:

The pandemic has changed the industry significantly. The pandemic took us through five years of normal evolution in 12 months. So I believe that we have to force ourselves away from conventional thinking, because a lot of things have changed and we don't know the extent or impact yet.

What we do know is that suddenly, we've got a lot more technology on property (contactless technology, primarily). We know that we've got fewer staff. So we're going to need more technology. We know that a lot of the people who set the slow pace for technology adoption are gone. So there's a new generation of executives that comes with a savviness for technology and more of a sense of urgency.

"Thanks" to the pandemic, our conservative industry is finally starting to realize that technology is a friend, not a foe, so tech adoption rates are gradually climbing. And what is also worth noting is that it could also be the catalyst for a more data-driven approach to hotel management (#itsallaboutdata). So the future seems to be looking brighter for the industry in terms of both tech adoption and embracing new ways of mining, analyzing and using data in our decision-making process.

Jordan Hollander (Hotel Tech Report) supports this point of view:

It's an old-school industry. The last generation didn't view technology as a necessity. They were able to get by because everything was going well for a while. You look at global travel trends and you look at ADR and RevPAR growth over the last 30 years - in most places everything was going up.

And so it's moments like COVID where you have a shock and say, "Oh wait, we may need tools to help us pivot our business." So that 30-year rising tide of travel was obviously beautiful and it gave hotels more and more money, but it also means that historically, it was pretty easy to just open a hotel and succeed because there was this constantly growing demand.

And so I think, for the first time, during COVID there was really this existential threat, kind of like a seismic shock that made hotel leaders think, "Wait a second, it isn't just going to always go up, we need to think about how to be more dynamic in our businesses."

And that is very true. Hospitality is one of the world's oldest industries and it's predicated around two things: experiences and guest-centricity. And because of that, for the longest time we were able to find reasons why new technology was not good for us and why it wasn't going to work. It takes a level shift event like COVID to get it to convince us to become more tech savvy and innovative.

So what lessons can we learn?

While there are many, many things that the industry learned from the recent events, the undermentioned three items are the key takeaways for hoteliers I would highlight.

1. Be flexible, adapt to new types of travelers and new customer expectations.

   #agile

Revise your segments, your policies, your compsets, your pricing strategy, your promotions, your online content. Question everything you've been doing for the last 2 decades. Are you doing it out of a habit or does it actually generate revenue/profit and help you be more efficient or provide better customer service?

There's a lot we can learn from the successful examples in the alternative accommodations sector. From Airbnb Q2 2021 Shareholder letter:[109]

For the past year, we've benefited from the adaptability of our business model, and we've focused on driving product innovations to meet the changing needs of our guests.

Since early in the crisis, our model has proven to be inherently adaptable.

---

[109]Airbnb Shareholder Letter Q2 2021: https://s26.q4cdn.com/656283129/files/doc_financials/2021/q2/Airbnb_Q2-2021-Shareholder-Letter_Final.pdf

Even with ongoing uncertainty around the pandemic, we've shown that as the world changes, our model is able to adapt.

We've also led through our continued product innovation. In the first half of 2021, we improved nearly every aspect of the Airbnb service, from our website and app to our community support and policies. We unveiled new product features that allow us to meet the changing needs of guests and make it easier for anyone to become a Host.

If hoteliers don't do the same, companies like Airbnb and Sonder will keep tapping into more and more of our market share. They're creative, they're agile and they're hungry for more customer segments.

2. **Use data, not the shape of the moon, to make strategic business decisions.**

#itsallaboutdata

Data is key. There will be a full chapter on it further (perhaps, the key chapter in the entire book). For now, a quick summary of why data is important and how it can help us deal with the wounds from the pandemic and navigate the recovery.

- Demand hasn't come back for everyone. Some regions, submarkets or specific locations (especially urban, business-oriented) are struggling and will continue to do so for some time.

  That's why it's very important to be able to use the right data to accurately measure and forecast demand levels in your area by utilizing forward-looking market insights instead of only concentrating on the internal booking data.

- For those areas or properties that are seeing increased demand levels, they will also notice (if they're paying attention) that booking patterns have significantly changed. Booking window is shorter than before. Channel mix is different. DOW patterns are no longer the same either. Mostly, this is driven by the fact that not all types of demand are coming back at the same pace. Leisure is. Corporate/biz and groups are not (yet).

  That's why it's important to dig into deeper layers of data analysis, past just future daily house-level data, so you can actually understand who is coming, from where, how they're booking, how far in advance, how long they stay and what they actually need from the services/amenities standpoint.

- That also means that your sales/marketing strategies should be aligned with the above. If your marketing messages, packages and promotions are targeting the wrong audience - they need to be revised.

  That's why it's important that all departments (marketing, sales, operations, finance, etc.) are aligned with the revenue management analysis and strategy to ensure that all operate in sync, and are pursuing common goals.

- And finally, make sure to maximize the right metrics. It's not just about the top-line room revenue. It has never been, but now, thanks to the pandemic, we clearly see how important it is to target the actual profit (for all departments). Make sure to optimize the right portion of your P&L report. The one that is directly correlated to the bottom-line total performance of the property, and not just RevPAR.

Again, all the answers are in the data.

3. Embrace technology

#disruptordie

Last but not least, and the most obvious one. We shouldn't be afraid of technology. We should embrace it and then we should try to be open-minded instead of sticking to our conservative framework that we have been functioning in for the last three decades or so.

It's all about data and it's all about the right tools (technology).

Let's end our pandemic conversation on a positive note.

Here's a quote from my conversation with Leif Jägerbrand, Founder of Atomize:

When we come out on the other side, it will be a very good industry for all players.

I think the pandemic has sped up the whole process of moving forward. Just look, now pretty much everyone can work from home. It's accepted at every other company, and that wasn't the case 18 months ago. It truly was a challenge for the whole world, but in the end, there will be many positive things coming out of it as well.

There definitely have been a number of lessons from this pandemic. And I think one of the general lessons is that we tend to appreciate things more when they're taken away from us. And being able to travel was one of those things that people seemed to miss the most. So most likely, we haven't even tapped into the pent-up demand yet because, obviously, not everyone has been able to travel yet.

So hopefully we will continue seeing more and more positive numbers as we follow the recovery path. And with increased tech adoption levels, new tools in our arsenal, enhanced strategies and improved value proposition, I believe the industry has a very good chance of coming out of this alive, reborn and more evolved.

When we fully come out of this, we will be on a whole new level of evolution.

PART 3: **THE FUTURE IS HERE**

Hospitality 2.0

Now, the most exciting part of the book. I had to take you on the 200-page journey first, before introducing you to it. Because it is crucial to first understand the past and the present, before you can start seeing the future.

As the COVID dust is settling, we're finally able to look around and see what our new reality is. As John Burns says, *"We'll see patterns."* And if we're agile and innovative enough to detect and act on those patterns, we can be successful.

The questions are: What will we be doing with the old tools we had? What new systems will we be using? And who will be there to use them?

According to the description in the previous part of the book of the three major forces that disrupted the hospitality industry in the last decade and altered it forever, the reality is that we cannot carry on doing things the same old way. It is very clear that the world has changed and we have to adapt.

Here's a high level view of how exactly the hospitality world has changed and what we now have to ourselves.

A key transformational element from the operations standpoint is definitely steering away from only looking at top-line room revenue towards **a bottom-line, profit-oriented approach.**

As a result of establishing this profit-oriented culture throughout the organization, another area of transformation naturally emerges - **departments collaborating closely with each other** (e.g., revenue, marketing, sales, operations, finance). This way, you can ensure that all "body parts" are aligned and are working together towards the same profit-seeking goal as one living organism, versus doing a bunch of one-offs that may benefit a department or address a specific objective, but overall not boosting the entire profit picture.

The **revenue management discipline (and RMS tools in particular) play a crucial role in achieving this,** tying all key stakeholders together, like a glue, a core that feeds everything else with data, insights, forecasting, optimization decisions, strategy, etc.

Popularization of cloud platforms like AWS (Amazon Web Services) and GCP (Google Cloud Platform) has resulted in the rapid growth and development of technology in all sectors due to the following trends:

- Affordability: the cost to start a software business or adopt new technology has significantly declined.
- De-wireization: more and more things are becoming wireless, and legacy promise-based systems are being replaced by younger-generation, cloud-based solutions that are safer, more user friendly, mobile-friendly and less costly.

Rapid growth of the alternative accommodations sector **changed consumer expectations** and reshaped segments.

COVID has resulted in **increased technology adoption rates**, rethinking the way we run our businesses and rethinking our operations.

As I see it, momentum is definitely building around the hospitality tech industry, especially after the COVID pandemic's "kick in the butt" that all of us felt very strongly. It served as a rude awakening and it still hurts but we all understand how many positive things came out of it. The industry has evolved to a whole new level and will never be the same again.

Still, by far the largest **barrier for growth for tech vendors today is the complexity of the hospitality ecosystem,** in combination with the **lack of data standardization**. The latter has become a major issue preventing us from truly utilizing the data we have on hand. And the amount of data is accumulating every day. It's accumulating and just sitting there, piling up. Many companies are sitting on pots of gold without even realizing it. Cloud technology, as well as AI/ML will help us address this.

As a result of the above, **data analysis and workflow optimization** will be an interesting growth market going forward. Because these markets are still immature at this point, companies that are able to become central market players will have a very attractive position.

The last trend to be mentioned is **end-to-end solutions providers**. Being able to take the complexity of solution design and become a comprehensive one-stop shop is definitely an attractive proposition. However, it's still hard to achieve, considering the complex world of use cases in the hotel operations, and the number of those use cases is growing daily (from chat bots, to labor management and scheduling, to campaign management, to payment processing, the list goes on) so is the number of tech vendors addressing them. So some hospitality tech companies resort to providing the key elements in their stack while allowing other vendors targeting less critical use cases via **open API connections.** App stores will become a regular way to source and buy technology, with a "try-before-you-buy" mindset of delivery and enabling sales.

As this happens, and a complex network of vendors continues to grow, most consumers are not going to want to know what's going on behind the scenes. They won't care how those tools are connected, they will just want to know that they're working as expected and covering the necessary use cases and that the technology is constantly advancing.

Connection, setup, and implementation should be a user-friendly quick process that doesn't require a lot of customer engagement. **A clean self-service model** should be everyone's goal as that's what customers are going to increasingly expect from software providers.

As soon as the APIs from a few of the main PMS vendors are good enough, we will **stop seeing new entrants into the PMS market. All new entrants will start being non-essential types of vendors (applications)** that are complementary to the PMS core product. The new vendors will ride on top of the existing PMS/CRS products, which in turn, will compete in a race for the market share. Over time, all but a handful of those will fall off. This is what happened in other industries, and there's a very good chance our industry will be going through very similar cycles and patterns.

What do we do with the old dinosaur legacy systems? Each time new applications or new technologies face the old ones, there's a need to compromise by integrating them, looking for the lowest common denominator. This is not helping technology evolve. Soon everything will be in the cloud, people are just not going to use systems that are running on a bad piece of software that is sitting on a bad piece of hardware. **Traditional systems that are not able to handle this change - will be left behind.**

So if you're a tech startup founder, or a tech executive - when looking for that integration partner, don't look at legacy systems, look at younger promising companies because they are the future. Design your software in a way that doesn't include compromises for the previous generation. Do it the new way, the right way.

So what does the new world look like? The following chapters describe our new reality and attempt to explain how to better navigate in it in order to become successful, efficient, and modern. Further we will talk about the reimagined hospitality industry from different aspects: data, technology and operations.

Data as the new currency

There is so much data... We are being flooded with data, and for the most part, hospitality companies don't know what to do with it (yet). As it has become very clear, data analysis, cloud computing, and machine learning capabilities are going to be very important and meaningful in the future of the hospitality industry. And I hope the industry starts realizing this sooner rather than later, and that the right investments happen in the right areas.

Here is what professor H. G. Parsa (University of Denver) says about the role of data in the development of the industry:

In the future, the whole hotel industry will be driven by data scientists, similar to what is happening in healthcare. Now healthcare is dominated by data scientists who now make more money than some of the doctors. A good example is Epic[110] - a data driven healthcare management company located in Wisconsin. An incredible amount of data is coming in. So, data analytics is the future. It helps answer the questions like, "Where do the customers come from?","What do they want?" etc. etc.

Data analytics is the future. Remember that hotel management was dominated by economists and human resource people for a long time. Hotel management comes from Human Resources management. But we are not in the hotel management business, we're in the hotel business. There's a big difference between the two. We don't manage hotels. We manage hotel businesses. People are part of it but technology is dominating it. And technology needs data - that is the input, just like gas for a car.

And more from another industry mastermind.

Ravi Simhambhatla (Google Cloud):

I believe that there is a real "arms race" going on and this time, the weapon is insights being driven from data in real time. And you feed those insights into the models that are learning continuously, and then you augment that through artificial intelligence to now start making business decisions automatically.

Everything revolves around data. *Retail, hospitality, aviation technology, social - how do you integrate these experiences? At the very crux of all is data.*

And how do you harness that? There are only 12% of companies who have

---

[110]Epic Systems: https://www.epic.com/

actually driven any value from ML and AI, the rest are just experimenting and they're probably not doing much in terms of machine learning. That is where the opportunity is.

So let's look closer at the world of hospitality data.

The data kingdom and who is at the top

Data is the new currency. And the king in the hospitality data kingdom has always been a hotel **reservation** (or the queen, rather).

A hotel reservation has had a central role in the hospitality world and everything has revolved around it for ages. A hotel reservation is nothing but an aggregation of data points. And as the industry evolves - the number of data points that a reservation carries, grows.

There's also "stay" data that is normally perceived as a different type of data as it has a different format but it's still all linked to a reservation - it's all attached to a particular *individual* booking a reservation and staying at the property.

"Reservation", as an entity, resembles bitcoin. Due to the amount of data that it carries, its value keeps growing as days pass, as the hotel tech stack evolves, and as humans and machines develop more ways to utilize this information in more sophisticated ways. And this trend is likely to continue for years ahead. Different systems that consume reservation and stay data, use different elements of it for all kinds of different purposes.

For example, take the concept of personalized pricing, one of the recent buzzwords in the revenue management space. This can be achieved using rich customer data that is carried by a reservation, then captured through CRM tools at the time of booking, pre-arrival, during the guest's stay, and is also enriched by pulling in external sources of data. This valuable information allows an analytical tool to build logic around pricing strategies, ultimately targeting each individual in the most optimal way, through the most optimal price point, with the most relevant room type and package.

While reservation has been the center of the hospitality universe for many decades, the most recent trend in data consumption by RMS systems (and others) is the shift away from using purely internal hotel reservation data collected by the CRS/PMS towards pulling in more external data sources. With that said, the ultimate end goal with that external data consumption is still, obtaining a reservation... - that is, the right amount of heads in beds, at the right time, with the optimal price that leads to higher operating efficiencies and maximized profitability.

The royal position of the reservation in the hospitality data kingdom doesn't eliminate the fact that it's only one of the gazillion data elements that are available out there. That is not the end of our data flood by any means.

Think of a complete **traveler journey** and all the data that one human generates at each step, and all the data that can be gathered, analyzed and used for our decision-making. Customer profiles, their interests, demographics, past booking history, search history, social media accounts, booking details, other travel details... Are they flying in first-class or economy? Are they also renting a car? How many people are traveling together? Did they book multiple rooms? What channel did they use for booking? What time did they arrive? How much did they pay for their reservation? etc. etc. etc.

Then think of the **usage data that can be generated during their stay.** What temperature do they like in their room? Did they use the TV? Did they stream media from their devices? Did they even spend any time in their room or were they mostly out and about? Did they book any experiences from the concierge or from the hotel app? Did they complain about the service? How was the complaint handled? Did they check into your property on Facebook and Instagram? Did they share pictures from their experience during their stay? How many people reacted? Did they fill out a post-stay survey? Did they book with you again? Did any of their friends book your property because of the social media exposure? etc. etc. etc.

That was just customer data.

Then, there's **ARI data** (availability, rates and inventory) that flows from one system to another, and another, and another...

Then, there are all kinds of **other aspects of data** that are available, data that is generated by a myriad of **tools used at the property:** data related to staff collaboration, housekeeping and engineering, accounting and reporting, labor management, property performance, financials, etc. etc. etc.

Then, there is **external market data** that can be gathered from all kinds of sources outside of the hotel and used in the forecasting and optimization algorithms: events, online search volumes, all aspects of competitive intelligence including alternative accommodations stats, macroeconomic data, global trends data, cross-sector data (air traffic, car rental booking volumes), etc. etc. etc...

How could the human brain possibly grasp that? Good news: it doesn't have to.

The more technology we use, the more data is generated, the more technology we need to consume and analyze it, the better and more optimal our business decisions will be.

Data-oriented companies worth mentioning

Recently I participated in a roundtable discussion organized by Cornell's Center for Hospitality Research where I had the pleasure of kicking off a "Technology" portion of the conversation.

During our meeting, I witnessed a passionate discussion among participants related to the potential of technology to make the right decisions for hospitality businesses and how it can utilize data for that decision-making process.

This was an example used. During COVID, an RMS (Revenue Management System) forecasting algorithm was unaware of recent government restrictions in a country. This drove the need for the user (a human), to go in and enter additional information, or tweak the algorithm, or simply override the forecast or the price optimization decision using that knowledge.

One side argued that there is an absolute need for a human to interfere in such a situation because there's no way the machine would be aware of the new piece of information (travel restrictions).

Another side (me included) was wondering why the machine doesn't know what humans know. Humans get their data from a particular source (internet in most cases). Why can't machines get that same data from the same source, and use it as an input into the decision-making algorithm?

Good news: yes, they can. The technology is already there (for example, semantic analysis of natural language using AI[111]) and a lot of that data is already available (in many cases, publicly available, online, free of charge).

The problem is though, that very often companies that develop decision-making tools are not the best at gathering and aggregating data. Building API's to source data and scraping websites is a whole different business model, which requires a lot of resources to maintain it. On top of it, scraping and gathering is not enough, the next step is to aggregate, clean and analyze it to make it useful and relevant.

This is where **Data Brokers and Data Suppliers** come into play. They are companies that specialize in all things data, and I predict that they will become more and more relevant players in our new world in the very near future.

Data suppliers that provide UI (user interface) are targeting humans. There's definitely still demand for those products because humans still perform most decision-making tasks. A human needs to look at a heatmap or a graph and decide what action to take. But as technology adoption increases, and algorithms replace humans in non-strategic decision making (for example, our favorite "How should I price the Single Queen for next Saturday?" that we haven't fully solved yet), non-UI API-only data suppliers will start playing a more crucial role than those that sell products with a User Interface for humans to use.

One example of such a company is Aggregate Intelligence (coincidentally abbreviated as my favorite two letters: AI) who I had a pleasure partnering with in one of my former roles.

I deeply respect the company, their team and their product. They're developing more and more travel-related data solutions to be fed into decision-making systems to help the industry build better and more optimal strategies. They have a footprint in the hotel industry, airline space and car rental.

---

[111]Expert AI: Natural Language Processing Semantic Analysis: A Definition (March 2020): https://www.expert.ai/blog/natural-language-process-semantic-analysis-definition/

While they do have products that have a User Interface, many of their solutions revolve around data flowing through a pipe from one machine to another.

Aggregate Intelligence

Aggregate Intelligence Inc (AI) is a data-as-a-service company specializing in collecting, cleaning and delivering data to businesses to help them make better decisions. They specialize in what they call 'high 3V' data:

- High Velocity: data that changes often and dynamically
- High Variety: data that is in many different forms or in many different places
- High Volume: otherwise known as 'big data'

They identify a need in a market for data that is in the 3V spectrum (and therefore difficult to get) and then build processes to identify, aggregate, normalize/classify and deliver that data in a way that is useful for their customers.

Currently focused on two main market sectors, travel and real estate, AI started in self-storage. They have the leading data intelligence brand in the self-storage industry worldwide, with over 200 subscribers and over 50% of the top 200 companies as customers.

I met with John Tilly, founder and CEO of Aggregate Intelligence, to ask some questions about their products and future plans. Here is our conversation.

| Ira Vouk

What inspired you to start the company?

| John Tilly

AI was founded in 2016. I had previously built a data company called 365 Media that specialized in providing business data services to publishing companies (such as LexisNexis, Dunn & Bradstreet etc). From this we developed and built technology to cope with faster moving and larger datasets, and then identified the need in business for services that specialized in fast-moving data.

| Ira Vouk

What is the company's main target market/customer?

| John Tilly

We identify three types of direct users within a target market and develop products and services for each user group:

- *Enterprise/large companies: these companies have the in-house sophistication to digest data directly to feed their internal data-driven decision systems. For this group we provide API and data feed services.*

- *Mid-market companies: these are companies who typically make manual decisions or partially-automated decisions. We develop dashboard products for this part of the market with visualizations and interactive tools to enable users to view, interrogate and extract data as needed.*

- *Small companies: these are relatively unsophisticated and very price sensitive companies who want to have competitive or market intelligence, but need it in an easily digestible and low-cost way. We provide low-cost report services and integrate with standard BI tools such as Google Data Studio for this part of the market.*

We also work with technology partners who need data as an ingredient for their own products, and provide API or data feed services to these partners.

| Ira Vouk

What is your footprint in hospitality?

| John Tilly

In hospitality we have had most success with tech partners, and have not pursued a direct approach to the market. We have 25+ tech partners across the world serving roughly 40,000 customers.

| Ira Vouk

What other sectors do you have a footprint in?

| John Tilly

We address two other sectors within travel: air and rental cars. In the airline industry, we provide enterprise-level data services to many of the world's largest airlines and have a mid-market product called FareTrack.[112] In the rental car market, we serve most of the larger rental car providers and deliver billions of data points each month.

| Ira Vouk

What are you seeing in other segments (in terms of data needs, data usage, etc.) that is different from the hospitality industry?

| John Tilly

The airline industry has two differences to the hospitality industry:

1. *Pricing is more dynamic and faster-moving, and therefore the need for high-velocity data services is greater than in hospitality.*

---

[112]Faretrack AI: price benchmarking for airlines: www.faretrack.ai

2. *Airline price distribution is more dispersed as there are low-cost-carriers (LCCs) such as Southwest and Spirit who bypass traditional price distribution methods and sometimes only feature prices on their own brand websites. This means that there is less emphasis on sourcing data from GDS or OTAs and finding a way to source from a broader variety of public sources.*

Ira Vouk

Are there plans for expansion into more segments within hospitality or other sectors?

John Tilly

One of our most recent developments is to track airbnb/vrbo pricing to identify occupancy and price, and we are working on a matching algorithm to compare various products within hospitality (e.g. what product in airbnb compares in value to what product from a 4-star hotel).

We have also expanded the development of our global events database as we move towards building a data suite for the travel industry mixing pricing and other data from all sectors to get a local demand trend indication.

Outside of travel, our main expansion plans as a company are in real estate development.

Ira Vouk

Have you seen increased demand in your services from the travel industry lately?

John Tilly

We anticipate delivering roughly 3-times the volume of data to our travel customers this year as compared to 2020.

Ira Vouk

What data are you offering for the hospitality players today?

John Tilly

- *"Low velocity":*

We track roughly 1.2M hotel properties worldwide and track hotel features (amenities, room counts and types, ownership/management, booking engine etc.).

- *"High velocity":*

This is typically fast-changing data and includes pricing, rank, parity across sources, events etc.

I was excited to hear that Aggregate Intelligence is working on a product that will use data from alternative accommodations to compare various products within hospitality. But my personal favorite is one of their newest offerings - a feed of events in the market with an assessment of their impact on demand for a given hotel (using multiple variables as inputs, including the hotel's specific location).

So if we take that and feed it data from IATA's Timatic[113] (the latest version of which has information on the majority of travel restrictions worldwide) and then incorporate this information into existing RMS algorithms to adjust forecasting and optimizing decisions - that provides a solution for the very problem that was so passionately discussed during Cornell's CHR roundtable that I described in the beginning of this section.

That is just to illustrate that technology already exists for many of our use cases. Data also exists and is growing daily. Data Brokers/Suppliers, as a category, are playing a more relevant role in this picture. It's just a matter of the industry recognizing and embracing this new trend, putting it all together and incorporating it into our decision-making processes.

Smith Travel Research

Now, if we're talking about data, we can't not mention STR (Smith Travel Research), one of the industry's oldest and well-known data providers. Arguably, there is probably not a single hospitality professional who hasn't heard that name.

Unlike Aggregate Intelligence, STR's main target audience is the human (human eyes and brain) thus their main products revolve around generating reports, mainly for the purpose of benchmarking. This is not surprising, because the company was founded when everything was manual and machines were not as widely adopted for our decision making. Clearly, there has been a lot of demand for this data as they built a huge business around it.

In 2019, Costar Group (provider of commercial real estate information, analytics and online marketplaces) acquired[114] STR for $450M.[115]

Over the last 35 years, the company has done a great service to the hospitality industry.

Below is my conversation with the person many of you are very familiar with as you have seen him present at numerous round tables and webinars, most of which lately have been devoted to how the industry is coping with the pandemic.

Jan Freitag, National Director, Hospitality Analytics for the CoStar Group, formerly Senior Vice President of STR.

---

[113]Wikipedia: Timatic: https://en.wikipedia.org/wiki/Timatic
[114]STR: CoStar Group to acquire STR (October 2019): https://str.com/press-release/costar-group-acquire-str
[115]Hotel Management: CoStar Group to acquire STR for $450M (October 2019): https://www. hotelmanagement.net/transactions/costar-group-to-acquire-str-for-450m

I hope you will enjoy reading this as much as I enjoyed talking to Jan. The conversation was as informative as it was entertaining. I loved every minute of it.

Ira Vouk

In your own words, how would you describe what STR does? How do you serve the market and what is your target customer?

Jan Freitag

STR was founded in 1985 by Randy and Carolyn Smith in Hendersonville Tennessee, which is still where our headquarters is, where I'm sitting right now. We started here because there's good fishing here. Randy Smith is a bass fisherman, he now can devote a lot of time to that, after he sold the company to Costar.

Randy used to always joke about the name of the company. STR used to be called Smith Travel Research which is really a wrong name because we don't do travel - we do hotels, and we don't do research - we do benchmarking. Smith is true, but everything else is not quite correct.

So STR's business is benchmarking. STR is the premier benchmarking provider to the global hotel industry. Every Wednesday morning, basically every branded hotel around the world has a meeting between the general manager, the revenue manager, the head of sales and the head of marketing to talk about the STAR report (Smith Travel Accommodations Report) that came out from Hendersonville to them that shows how the subject property compared to what's called a competitive set. Compset is a self-selected set of between 4 and 10 or so hotels that the revenue manager, the marketing manager, or the brand sometimes selects to identify their competition.

STR collects data from individual properties around the globe. Initially, when Randy Smith started, we only collected 3 numbers and then we made 3 numbers. That's the beauty of the simplicity of the business model. We asked how many rooms you have available, how many rooms you sold, how much room revenue you generated, by day. And then STR processes out of that 3 numbers, which most are familiar with: ADR, Occupancy and RevPAR.

And more importantly, STR provides the year-over-year percentage change. As you know, in the hotel industry, we don't look at things sequentially (for example March compared to February) because of the seasonality of our business. So we look at year-over-year numbers (for example, March compared to March last year). That in a nutshell is what STR does - benchmarking of these 3 KPIs that drive the industry.

Then, of course, STR added many other products over time. So it started out monthly - now STR does it weekly or daily. It started out with just room revenue - now STR is measuring room revenue coming from groups or room revenue coming from transient, something called segmentation. STR used to say, "We know nothing about tomorrow and everything about yesterday," because the STAR report is backward looking - now it launched Forward STAR where it collects what's on the books 365 days forward. STR used to just count existing hotels, then they added a pipeline product. So now there is an understanding of the whole life cycle of the hotel from inception: from "I have a dream, I have a piece of land, and I'm going to talk to a brand" to breaking ground, to opening, to eventually then, closing.

And with the CoStar acquisition, now there is suddenly a whole host of information that wasn't available before: we can overlay performance data of downtown office space, versus upper upscale hotels. We can look at areas around the airport and see where there's a lot of retail development that hotels follow and so forth.

And this is a global product. We do this globally, STR's main offices are here in Nashville, the main global offices are in London and Singapore. And then STR has 10-15 other sales offices, so it is everywhere, wherever our clients are because our clients don't sleep. We don't sleep. So we're open 24/7, 365.

STR also has a couple of other business lines. It owns Hotel News Now, which is now part of CoStar News, because there was always the thought that there was value in not just providing the data but also providing the commentary. So HNN is that outlet.

Over 10 years ago, STR started the Hotel Data Conference (HDC), which happens in mid January in Nashville every year, the attendees are mostly revenue managers. And then there is the SHARE Center, which is how STR supports hospitality education. The SHARE Center has started something amazing: CHIA certification, which is a certificate in hospitality industry analytics that has become the most widely distributed certificate in the hotel industry ever. Just under 40,000 people are CHIA certified globally. At many universities, for example, my alma mater, the Cornell Hotel School, the freshman class has to be CHIA certified, which is a great thing to put on your freshman resume.

Ira Vouk

This is an awesome company description, thanks for sharing.

So branded hotels are very well represented in your customer base, while we can't say that about independent properties. However, they comprise a very significant portion of the worldwide market. Can you speak about the main reasons why it is so hard to gather data from these independent operators? Is it technology, is it the mindset, is it just the lack of awareness of products that you sell? What do you think the main barriers to scale in that segment are for your company?

Jan Freitag

Based on our data, in the United States, 7 out of 10 rooms are branded, 30% are independent. Globally, that number is different: so it's about 50% branded and

50% independent. We have a very, very strong footprint in the branded market. In the United States, when it comes to independents, if it's a high end property - they participate likely because the GM of an independent luxury resort used to be a GM of a high end branded resort. We frequently see situations where a formerly branded GM comes to an independent property and asks, "Where's my STAR report?"

So in the US, we feel very comfortable. For the properties that don't participate - we have a sophisticated mechanism to estimate their performance.

When it comes to properties outside of the US, it's a very different picture. We think, by price point we're very well represented on the upper end luxury, upper upscale, because they're competing with other brand properties. But with the lower end of the market, it's a little bit harder. Why is that? I think mindset, number one. STR sales associates ask, "Please share your data." And the reaction is sometimes, "Whoa, that's pretty personal, what are you asking me here?" And we say, "No, it's really nothing too personal. We're just asking how many rooms you sold." But for some owners, that is about as personal as it gets. People take their data very, very seriously. So we have to convince them that the data that they give to us is always-always-always-always... always confidential. And that takes some time.

What we have found works really well, is if our salesperson goes to General Managers in the market who are participating and they host a lunch, and then those GMs and directors of sales say, "You should participate because we trust them, you should trust them, too." So that's been helpful. It's really the good old fashioned one-on-one sales effort, but letting new participants know that their data stays confidential is very critical.

| Ira Vouk

And how about from a technology standpoint? It's easier for a branded hotel to share this data because it's centralized. So the franchise normally collects the data and sends it to you in one batch, but for individual independent properties, what would be the process? I mean, you can't connect to all of those small PMSs, right?

| Jan Freitag

We connect to large and small PMSs, but some data comes to us via the website, because it's only three numbers. It can be done through the night audit process. But yes, it's hard. It's a lot easier to say, "We connected into a system and transferred it", versus saying, "Hey, have your night auditor type it in."

More wisdom from this conversation can be found throughout the book in corresponding chapters where I reference Jan.

Google

We spoke a lot about Google and Amazon in the previous parts of the book, but we will touch on these again because, as Wouter Geerts (Skift) mentioned in one of his reports,[116] *"You cannot talk about data, and not mention the giants Google, Amazon, and Facebook.... These companies are native to data, they have a ton of it and know how to use it."*

We have enough Facebook in our daily lives, so we will leave that one out.

Let's turn to Google and see how the company can help our industry solve our data problems.

Ravi Simhambhatla (Managing Director/CTO, Digital Transformation - Travel & Transportation at Google Cloud):

In the hospitality industry, there are extreme volumes of production of data. The issue really is that while they produce data really well, they don't have the tool sets and the capabilities to consume that unstructured and structured data in time frames that are reasonable to drive business value. There's no point in gathering insights from data that's a month late. The opportunity has come and gone.

So that is why you need the massive scale and the capabilities that the tool sets [like Google Cloud products] bring today, that will allow you to mash up structured and unstructured data from a variety of signals. It doesn't matter where it's coming from, it's like a constant stream. But imagine if you had an engine that would just bring these streams together and use your company's machine learning algorithms to constantly improve the fidelity of the outcomes, and then use AI on top of that, to not only make predictions, but to do automated decisioning. That's magical.

Perhaps the only people who may find that magical are geeks like Ravi and myself. But those are the people who will ultimately drive us forward in the next decade. Though it doesn't just take geeks to make a change, it takes passionate and driven geeks. I met quite a few of those as I was doing my research for this book, so I believe the industry is in good hands.

Ravi Simhambhatla:

You've got to have a passion. You've got to have people such as yourself. People just don't get up and say, "I want to write a book about this." This is where your heart is. And so you need passionate people to come together to make a real move to take things to the next step, create the building blocks that will get us to the next step and keep us open enough to accept new things that come into our world.

Being passionate about the travel industry, Ravi also offers an inspiring proposition to remove barriers for data sharing between different sectors of the industry in order to

---

[116]Skift: The Hotel Revenue Management Landscape 2019 (April 2019): https://research.skift.com/report/the-hotel-revenue-management-landscape-2019/

solve the end-to-end traveler experience problem. He also explains how Google fits into the picture.

> *The travel ecosystem consists of different players: ground transportation, hotels, air travel, OTAs and everything else in the middle. So the end consumer's journey from the time they're envisioning travel, to the time they've actually engaged in travel, to the time they've finished their trip, and including the post-stay interactions - all that has always been somewhat disjointed because the players in the ecosystem don't really work well with each other. Collaboration is not there.*

> *Breaking through those barriers is going to be very important. That exchange of data can really open up a door for far greater collaboration.*

> *It's all about data.*

> *The reason why end-to-end consumer travel experience is currently poor, is because the right data isn't available at the right time for the right purpose.*

> *Google has access to a lot of data within the Google ecosystem. There are a lot of incredible demand signals data out there. Bringing those insights in real time and combining them with data that's available to travel tech providers to inform decision making is something that is one of Google's ambitions.* [117]

So, yes. **It's all about data and it's about building the right capabilities to utilize it.** Imagine the world of data being shared among different sectors of the travel industry, and then on top of it ingesting events data, demographic data, foursquare data, etc. etc. We could do so many interesting things with it including coming up with **a very powerful real-time indicator of the macroeconomy,** but nobody has done it at scale yet in our industry.

AWS

Sekhar Mallipeddi explains how AWS helps our industry become more data driven. We also talked about the painful topic of data cleanliness and data consistency. I found this discussion very educational.

| Sekhar Mallipeddi

> *Data is at the heart of everything for us. And we have some very compelling Amazon services that actually help customers ingest, manage, curate and use data. But not only that. We also make it very feasible and scalable. That allows our customers to not only use data for analytics, but also use data for machine learning, building machine learning models and all the things that go with it. So we have several services that make it easy to deal with data.*

---

[117] GDG Cloud Southlake #1 Ravi Simhambhatla: Google Cloud (May 2021): https://gdg.community.dev/events/details/google-gdg-cloud-southlake-presents-gdg-cloud-southlake-1-ravi-simhambhatla-google-cloud-in-aviation/

So we do have these capabilities and we have reference architectures that we've published that say what is the right way to do it. We have some of these concepts that actually talk about how to use data lakes and lake house architectures.

So essentially, it's data architecture that allows data to be "democratized" within an enterprise. That includes democratization of data to business users, power users of data, consumers of data, for example to make this data available to data scientists and lastly to make the data available to developers that actually can build solutions on top of it.

We have a whole set of architectures that enable these capabilities to democratize data in an enterprise. And we have specific architectures that we published for lodging companies: how to create this in such a way that actually can be scalable, but also cheaper, better and faster.

What that means is that somebody has to actually go learn these tools and use those tools and services.

Ira Vouk

And when you're helping those companies build their solutions or improve their solutions and upgrade their tech stack, do you often run into the problem of data consistency or data cleanliness or lack of standardization that would prevent them from building those solutions in a more efficient manner? It seems like it's a big mess right now when it comes to data cleanliness in our industry.

Sekhar Mallipeddi

So it's a very interesting thing. Here's what I have learned and this is my point of view having worked with data for over 25 years. The data quality issues and data challenges are there not because the systems of record are producing bad data. It's because somebody along the way modified it or tried to take data that was actually really good and through a set of processes or ETL jobs or loading jobs destroyed the quality of the data.

So for example, a CRS or a PMS will always give me good clean stays or reservations. A loyalty system would always give me good clean loyalty data. The address might not be nicely cleansed and standardized or the phone number might not be really accurate because somebody forgot to put a plus one for US numbers or somebody typed an email address wrong. But those are all data issues that you cannot change.

But what happens is that, when you take that loyalty data, when you take that CRS data and try to basically fit it into some sort of a data warehouse or some sort of a data store and to make it fit into a certain schema - you're changing data. And while you're changing data, you're destroying the quality of the data.

So you get bad data as a result, but not because the system of record is giving you bad data.

| **Ira Vouk**

So, when you start dealing with those things when working with your customers, you see the results of those previous actions that happened on their side because they didn't know what they're doing?

| **Sekhar Mallipeddi**

That's right.

Or somebody had this rich data set but didn't have time to ingest all of the data, so they decided to drop all the data that they didn't care for and only use what they needed. That results in data loss. The data that actually was nicely coming through is not used. So when you make decisions like that, the quality of the data suffers, not because the source system is bad. But because somebody made a bad decision in the process.

| **Ira Vouk**

Because of the manipulations.

| **Sekhar Mallipeddi**

That's right. Or somebody created a data set that met a business user's reporting requirements. But they put in some business rules that changed the data to create that report, and that becomes the source of truth. The data is going to be only as good as the data architects and the data modelers that created it. If they made mistakes along the way, and implemented bad code or made wrong assumptions, the data will be bad. But if you go to the system of record, the data would always be good. And any mistakes in a system of record are not because of data quality issues, those are systemic issues that happen because of data entry or data ingestion.

To reiterate that point, you cannot fix the data quality in a data warehouse or a data lake. You can, but you're chasing a problem that you have no business chasing.

| **Ira Vouk**

So, the moral of the story for people who are going to be reading this book, executives of hotel companies, hospitality professors, software founders, what would you suggest for them to learn from what we just described in order to avoid running into these data issues in the future?

| Sekhar Mallipeddi

I would ask them to think about decisions they make that result in data quality issues. If you have data issues, you have to fix the source, don't try to fix it in the data warehouse or the data lake.

To summarize: essentially, if you're trying to mess with your data, you better know what you're doing.

New data mesh concept

I'll try not to make the next couple of sections too technical. But if you get lost while reading them - don't get discouraged. Just skim through and continue to the next chapter. It will get easier, I promise.

As we discussed above, the quality of your data is only as good as the quality of your data warehouse. And more importantly, the amount of legacy logic that you've built in the data warehouse over the last 20 years will reflect in your new data lake.

A **data lake** is a system or repository of data stored in its natural/raw format, usually object blobs or files. It can be established "on premises" (within an organization's data centers) or "in the cloud" (using cloud services from vendors such as Amazon, Microsoft, or Google).[118] And as discussed earlier, the world is moving away from "premise" to "cloud" at a rapid pace.

Taking it one step further, the new open **data lake house architectures**[119] are one thing that is critical for democratization of data (you can look it up or follow the article referenced in the footnote, for more information).

And then there's one new construct that has become popular lately that is called the **data mesh architecture**,[120] which talks about handling data in such a way that would allow you to create an architecture that can freely and openly scale and extend. Data mesh unlocks analytical data at scale. It is a new architectural and organizational paradigm that challenges the age-old assumption that we must centralize big analytical data in order to deliver value.[121] It's a concept of how to stop thinking about data analytics in terms of these monoliths, and start thinking about them in really open, scalable, and more importantly, agile terms.

Historically, data warehouses had very rigid schemas that everything had to fit into. So when you took highly complex objects, like stay or reservation objects, that are large, and tried to fit them into these rigid schemas - that resulted in degradation of data quality, which was part of the rigid structure.

---

[118]Wikipedia: Data Lake: https://en.wikipedia.org/wiki/Data_lake
[119]Databricks: Data Lakehouse: https://databricks.com/glossary/data-lakehouse
[120]Martin Fowler: How to Move Beyond a Monolithic Data Lake to a Distributed Data Mesh (May 2019): https://martinfowler.com/articles/data-monolith-to-mesh.html
[121]Thoughtworks: Data mesh (November 2019): https://www.thoughtworks.com/radar/techniques/data-mesh

So now we're dealing with these monoliths, huge teradata implementations. That made it very challenging to utilize that data for the benefit of the business. In the last 10 years or so, there has been some technology that solved some of these problems but they never took those inherent monoliths away and you still need 50-60 people on a six-month project to make them more usable in an effort to democratize that data.

By the way, this pattern described above doesn't apply to just legacy companies. This is a problem that nearly every hospitality company is struggling with and not just older companies. These days, 3 years worth of data is already a lot to deal with, because data is generated so fast in huge volumes. So if a company is 3 years old and it's technically still a startup, it's highly likely they have the same issues with their data monolith.

So I can only imagine how big of a deal that is for legacy companies. Their current single source of truth that they're running on premise in a data warehouse is not scaling, not meeting their needs. They can never catch up because their business requirements keep changing, because the schema keeps changing, because the data keeps changing. The good news is that in the new world of data lakes, you can be schema-less and manage your data in a much more efficient and scalable manner. So finally, in an effort to utilize those capabilities, these companies are starting to make a decision to move everything to the cloud to modernize their technology and their data (which is great). However, if you're just taking your monolith with you "as is" and bringing along all your dirty processes and problems to the cloud, you're not really leveraging the capability of the cloud.

So this new concept of data mesh is aimed to solve that problem. Essentially, it's about breaking this monolith into really small pieces so that a large number of small teams can own and deliver it rather than getting bogged down by all these unnecessary processes.

To avoid making this chapter too technical, I'm not going into the depth of explaining the details of this new concept. For those who are interested in learning more, please follow the links referenced in the footnotes.

I just want to draw the industry's attention to this new concept that has a lot of potential to solve many companies' data scaling problems and essentially allow us to evolve at a much more rapid pace. The bottom line of this concept is breaking down this monolith that takes years to build and reducing it down to literally weeks of work.

That requires changing the way companies think about handling data. If you think about programming code, people have mostly moved on to agile development. Nobody talks about software development that takes years anymore. It's all broken down into agile processes with delivery in two-week time frames. But when it comes to data, previously there was no formal way of breaking down these huge data assets into agile processes until this new data mesh concept was formalized.

This gives me hope, because investing in agile incremental re-architecting is a much easier business decision for any company than throwing a full team on a 12-month project. As a result, there will be more and more companies jumping on board to modernize their data architecture, which ultimately helps the whole industry because then the possibilities are infinite in terms of data analysis and optimal decision making.

Could we have done this 5 years ago, 10 years ago? Not really, because the technology did not exist. Now, things are possible.

Data decentralization

This is another construct that I want to draw the industry's attention to.

The introduction of blockchain technology[122] back in 2008 has completely altered the way we look at data sharing. Blockchain technology is most simply defined as a decentralized, distributed ledger that records the place of origin of a digital asset.

There are a myriad of use cases where this technology can be successfully applied to solve many of the data sharing and data security issues society is dealing with today. For example, as a result of the pandemic, digital health passports have been introduced that provide a form of digital proof of vaccination, negative virus test results, and/or positive antibody test results. This has been an important step towards getting the travel industry back to normal.

While the introduction of health passports greatly benefits the travel industry, use cases for decentralized digital data distribution expand way beyond that. The technology can (should and will) be used for any situation where consumers (travelers) need to provide personal information to businesses, and that will greatly improve the way businesses get, use, and retain that information. Some examples of these broader uses include validation of travel credentials (passports, visas, and programs like TSA Precheck and Clear), proof of employment or education, memberships, creditworthiness, and many others.

The key technologies that are responsible for making this happen are Self-Sovereign Identity (SSI)[123] and Distributed Ledger Technologies (DLT).[124] They can work in combination to put consumers in charge of their own data. DLT has been around for many years, but has been strengthened by recent advances resulting from the evolution of blockchain technology. SSI is younger and still evolving, but gaining a lot of interest.

As Doug Rice wrote in his article in March 2021, "*As with other technologies, other sectors will almost certainly lead the way. SSI is already appearing in the healthcare sector with digital health passports, and while that has become a high priority because of COVID, it is hardly the only application of interest. The finance and banking industries are not far behind... Many governments are looking at SSI as a way to modernize border controls, as are*

---

[122]Built in: Blockchain Technology Defined: https://builtin.com/blockchain

[123]Medium: Introduction to Self-Sovereign Identity and Its 10 Guiding Principles (January 2019): https://medium.com/metadium/introduction-to-self-sovereign-identity-and-its-10-guiding-principles-97c1ba603872

[124]Investopedia: Distributed Ledger Technology (DLT) (August 2021): https://www.investopedia.com/terms/d/distributed-ledger-technology-dlt.asp

airports to simplify check-in, bag-check, security, club access, and boarding."[125] Doug Rice believes that the effect of SSI will present "a generational change" for the industry and, ultimately, for the entire society.

I'm happy to report that we are already seeing first signs of introducing SSI technology in the hospitality industry. Germany recently launched a national SSI-based digital identity ecosystem[126] that now involves more than 60 stakeholders from the private and public sectors. With the digital hotel check-in, there is already a live use case for the hospitality industry. In addition, Germany and Spain have agreed to cooperate on building an ecosystem of digital identities across borders.

In his other article, Doug Rice wrote, "*In coming years, SSI will facilitate peer-to-peer communication between travelers and travel providers, which has the potential to reduce the market power of distribution intermediaries. Intermediaries may still play a role, but it may be a quite different one... Because travelers and providers will be able to easily bypass them with direct peer-to-peer conversations, there will be greater transparency of the value they add vs. the fees they assess to providers and to travelers.*"[127]

So this brings us from the discussion about decentralized identity and sharing sensitive customer data with a business into a slightly different realm: communication between travelers and travel operators that is related to planning and booking a travel experience, which involves access to what we call ARI data (Availability, Rates and Inventory). So now we're talking about the business sharing data with the traveler.

If you ask any hospitality tech and distribution expert who has been around for a while about the "ARI problem", they will inevitably twitch. Convenient real-time sharing of Availability, Rates and Inventory with the end consumer is something that the travel industry has been trying to solve for decades. However, we now finally have a chance to come close to solving it through the new blockchain-inspired decentralized data technology.

The issue of real-time rates and inventory distribution is more painful for brands that heavily rely on corporate bookings, than it is for the independents who mostly deal with leisure travelers and use a cloud-based booking engine and a channel manager connected to the property website as well as a myriad of OTAs (plus Google, as of last year).

But imagine if you are Hilton or Marriott or a smaller hotel company. How do you go about publishing your rates and inventory to GDS today? One would hope that CRS (Central Reservation System) solutions take care of it in a convenient real-time fashion. However, a lot of today's CRS systems have legacy technology. A lot of times, if a CRS is present, the data processing and publishing of the prices to the GDSs is not handled by them.

---

[125]HospitalityUpgrade: Definitely Doug 3/12/21: The Next Wave (March 2021): https://www.hospitalityupgrade.com/techTalk/March-2021/Definitely-Doug-3-12-21/

[126]The Federal Government: Germany and Spain push digital identity agenda forward (July 2021): https://www.bundesregierung.de/breg-en/news/digital-identity-ecosystem-1947474

[127]HospitalityUpgrade: Definitely Doug 7/30/21: Get On Your Surfboard, The Next Wave is Here! (July 2021): https://www.hospitalityupgrade.com/techTalk/July-2021/Definitely-Doug-7-30-21/

So each of these hotel companies has literally a team that publishes these rates and inventories on a daily basis, in the form of flat files. Manually. Every day. And then each GDS processes them and uploads them.

Every single hotel company still uses this ancient technology. Though, nobody really talks about it openly.

Airlines have a system that consolidates that data in one place and then sends it to everybody that needs it. Hotel companies don't have that capability. So what is happening right now is, "everybody has to publish to everybody". Currently, keeping your rates and inventory in sync, and making sure all channels have the right inventory, availability and rates - is a very tedious and inefficient process, especially for brands.

Thankfully, the concept of decentralized cloud data sharing is becoming more and more prominent. This new technology has already been applied in other sectors (airlines and retail) and has the potential to help us solve ARI data sharing problems in hospitality.

One example is a solution provided by Vendia[128] - they created the capability where companies can seamlessly share data across clouds, without having to do a lot of processing. And in the hotel industry in my opinion, this is one area where we really, really need help.

Vendia implemented it for a couple of airline companies. Airline Reporting Corporation uses it for settlements between agencies and airlines. BMW is using it for their supply chain. But technically, this technology can be used for any B2B or B2C data-sharing use case.

One idea for how this new technology can be applied to our industry is developing a system for real-time updates of rates and inventory, where permissions are granted to those who need access without having to do this heavy file processing on a daily basis. We could use this technology to solve our rates and inventory problem, for hotels, cruises, casinos and even car rental companies for that matter. We could solve the fundamental problem of publishing rates and inventory, and updating it easily without doing a lot of undifferentiated heavy lifting that happens today.

This new technology streamlines the process of sharing inventory and prices in real time and makes it simpler and more scalable. It's important to mention that these are low-code or no-code technologies, which means that it takes a small team of three or four people to orchestrate and manage it.

What that also means is that both sides, the publisher and the receiver of data, should play that game. They should agree to use that technology. And there has to be a central entity that needs to facilitate this. So while the technology already exists, the process of adopting it by the hospitality industry needs to be managed, perhaps, by a nonprofit organization that can adopt it and facilitate it without having to write code. Recently, I initiated a call with HTNG who added representatives from AHLA, AWS, Sabre, Amadeus

---

[128]Vendia: Share real-time data. Build universal apps: https://www.vendia.net/

as well as hotel companies like Hilton, Hyatt, Wyndham, MGM and others where we discussed this new technology and its potential to solve our data sharing problems. The conversations are already happening and this is very promising.

We're just in the beginning of these conversations and we will see where this takes us. But I believe exploring this is very beneficial for the industry, and the fact that this technology already exists, is a great first step towards solving our major data sharing problems.

This will be a long journey. But if we don't start it, we'll never get anywhere. And if we do get somewhere... this would be a breakthrough for the industry.

Conclusions

While companies like Google and AWS are on a whole different level of data handling, people who are running hospitality companies historically have not necessarily been very data oriented. But this is something that has been changing in the last few years and will drastically change in the future, and this is one of the main reasons why I decided to write this book.

It is also evident that the revenue management discipline (or whatever it shapes up to be and whatever name it is given in the near future) will be the key component of the new reimagined hotel operations, because this is really the only discipline in our industry that houses people who understand data. So hotel companies that want to succeed, need to allow those people to play a crucial role in the business decision-making process.

There is more and more data that we are gathering on a daily basis and it keeps accumulating every day, every hour, every second, and constantly increasing in volumes. There are so many examples where hospitality companies are sitting on pots of data gold without being able to properly use or monetize it. There's just so much more that can be done to utilize it to our advantage.

And in the end, it's the data analytics that is going to drive the value of these vast amounts of real-time data in our industry. The data needs to be simplified and usable. This is where analytical software companies as well as people with strong analytical skills (currently mostly hosted by the revenue management discipline) become real heroes of our future. More on that in the following chapters.

As machine learning applications (and data analytics in the hospitality industry in general) become more robust and more sophisticated, and the computing power increases as cloud solutions become more mainstream, we will be able to start addressing those issues and learn how to properly utilize data in our decision-making process, which will make our industry more efficient and successful. That's the bright future I'm painting and I'm going to stick to it.

Cobotics

As the industry continues evolving and the technology adoption increases, the decision making (especially the tactical, boring part of it) is falling more and more on the machine and less on the human.

As a result, technology will soon completely transform the way we do things.

A lot of the things that humans are doing manually right now should be (and will be soon) done by machines. Just like self-driving cars, there's no doubt it will be better for humanity.

So as automation increases - what happens to humans?

Naturally, the role of humans in hotel operations will be reimagined. How?

Mylene Young (Principal at Son Hospitality Consulting) helped me find the right name for the concept that has been shaping up in my head related to the new type of relationships between humans and machines. This is how it happened.

| **Ira Vouk**

Throughout my hospitality career, as I have been bringing various technology solutions to market, I have been facing a lot of conservatism from the industry and reluctance to adopt automation. And part of the reason is the fear of humans to be replaced by machines. But the evolution of technology is inevitable and unstoppable. How do we address this fear?

| **Mylene Young**

Have you heard of this new concept that is called Cobotics? You're going to love it!

| **Ira Vouk**

I have not. Tell me!

| **Mylene Young**

Cobotics is basically the relationship between people and machine-learning robotics. It is the combination of people and machines, it describes how they collaborate that results in much higher efficiencies than when either of them work on their own.

And this is to the point that you cannot have only machine learning or AI without the people. It's not like you put yourself in cruise control and you just go with it. You need the brain behind it to, for example, manage exceptions. You're still in charge of the strategy.

So instead of just being tactical, you become strategic. And that thing about Cabotics is really the collaboration of people and machines, and when you put both together, you come to something that is much greater than 1+1.

| Ira Vouk

I love it, you were right. That's the future and that's the word I've been looking for to describe the picture that has been shaping up in my head.

What Mylene mentioned above, becomes a very important aspect of incorporating automation, and in particular artificial intelligence, into our daily lives and addressing the fear of humans to be replaced by technology.

Cobotics is the collaboration between people and machines, or robots. The term is so fresh that it doesn't even have a wiki page yet.

When I say "machines" or "robots" I refer to an entity that uses artificial intelligence, not necessarily a metal box with legs and arms:

It can be a piece of software living in the cloud, talking to you through your computer or another intelligent device (think Siri):

As I already mentioned throughout this book, technology is designed to take away the most laborious and least pleasurable tasks from humans and enable them to focus their efforts on more rewarding and valuable work. So it's not a question of whether the machine or the human is going to take on a particular role in our businesses. **It's always both. It's a collaboration. It's teamwork.**

If we use my favorite analogy of self-driving cars: let's allow Tesla to do the heavy lifting (steering and controlling the speed) but it still needs the human component to enter the destination, request to avoid toll roads or ask for a pit stop in a few hours.

I couldn't have said it better than Ravi Mehrotra (Co-founder, President and Chief Scientist of IDeaS RMS):

I think all the discussions you might have in terms of AI and machine learning models, come down to a fundamental aspect of "what are the things that humans do well and what are things that machines do well?"

There are areas where AI and machine learning can be extremely effective and there are areas where humans will never be replaced.

Let me give you an example. If I were to give you 10,000 numbers to add, divide, subtract or multiply and I will not give you a calculator, do you think you'll be able to find the right answer? Well, even if you do find the right answer, what makes you think you'll be able to verify it? These are not areas where human expertise is extremely valuable. Humans can't do what certain algorithms can do. Those are best left to machines.

In those situations, technology should provide a decision support system. The system has to capture whatever data it can capture, present it to the person in whatever way possible to make it easier for the person to understand.

Without technology, we're expecting a human to perform that analysis, who we know is not necessarily prepared to deal with, for example, mathematical optimization, especially when the demand is so uncertain.

Compare that to providing a decision system, where you're going to consistently make thousands of decisions. You really want to let the machine make the optimal decisions and when the machine is not sure of certain things, you want to be able to let the machine tell you where your input can be most valuable. This way, you will only have to deal with exceptions or strategic decisions.

By focusing on the exceptions and strategic decisions, the grafts, charts, and reports are not even needed and will only waste your time. Machines should take away 99.8% of the work and only focus the attention of the humans where he or she can actually make a difference.

We just need to ask ourselves, "What are humans best at doing? What are machines best at doing? And how can you use the man and the machine together to work in a synergistic manner, which is going to be most effective in actually changing the future of all decision making?" Because remember, any company, any business, must make decisions hundreds of times a day and they need to consider the long-term implications of those decisions. Our actions today may reshape the future.

Mylene Young painted a brilliant picture of how cobotics can be incorporated into the revenue management discipline and how this reimagines the role of humans in hotel operations:

If you apply this concept, then as a human you can build a strategy moving forward with the marketing team, with the sales people, with the operations team and so on. So you still need people that understand the science of revenue management and can use all of that data and use all the recommendations to create a high level strategy where other departments will be involved.

So there should be no fear of humans to be replaced by machines because if you have mastered the data and you work with different technology platforms, you will be in a situation where you can be highly strategic and make the best decisions for the company. And when I say "decisions" - it's not how to price your Standard room for next Saturday. It's creating a high-level strategy for the property or the portfolio of properties, i.e. where you want to grow and what you want to achieve on all levels: rooms, F&B, golf, spa, you name it.

And from the technology standpoint, you have to be an ambassador of our discipline who is able to convince the finance department or the owners that we need the right technology in place. We need to be super passionate about that. We cannot take no for an answer. I'll say more: I would never work for a company that doesn't have the basic technology in place.

So will we allow machines around us to take more control of our lives and our work?

It is inevitable. It will happen slowly and naturally as we give up more and more routine boring tasks to automation. There are still all sorts of anxieties around it, but we will get used to it and will embrace it as soon as more and more of us see the value of those applications. And adoption rates will keep climbing.

Further development of technology will have an impact on jobs as they become redefined. As the number of traditional routine jobs may decline, new jobs are going to be created. Better information and forecasting will help optimize our industry and enable it to better manage downturns. As things evolve, and we learn to collect and analyze data from more sources to give us a better picture - humans will be removed from some parts of the decision-making process. Given defined and controlled parameters, machines will be making an increasing number of decisions. And they will be better at it than us. And humans will transition to strategic decision making.

As we discussed previously in the AI chapter of this book, there are many exciting applications of AI and automation in the industry. However, I'm most excited about the opportunities to use AI/ML in the area of data gathering, data analysis and decision making that results in enhanced guest experience, improved efficiencies of hotel operations and increased profits. And the best way to implement these technologies is through cobotics - collaboration and synergy of humans and machines.

Remember, this is not a competition! It's teamwork.

Redesigned operations

Breaking out of silos

As we have already established, we can't keep running our businesses the same way we were before. And one mistake we can't repeat is not having any synergy between departments (operations, marketing, sales, revenue management, finance, etc.).

You might recognize a typical scenario in a traditional hotel company:

Revenue Management

- Need dates are January 2nd to 31st
- Need to fill 50 rooms daily across need period
- Measures success using RevPAR

Marketing

- Running a promotion for the New Year's Eve weekend
- Budget is $5000 regardless of demand
- Doesn't know how to differentiate between displaced and incremental business
- Measures success using Rooms Booked per booking period

Sales

- Overbooks sold-out dates
- Is not familiar with how to calculate displacement
- Is not familiar with how to measure profit potential of a group
- Measures success using Total Revenue

Operations

- Doesn't fluctuate staff schedules with demand
- Refuses to oversell
- Measures success by cutting operating costs

Finance

- Looks at EBITDA

Owner

- Cares about cash flow

This has been happening in many organizations for many, many years.

Departments working in silos result in a situation described in an old Russian fable named <u>Crayfish, Pike and Swan</u>:

When partners have no accord,

Their business is hard.

Once, Crayfish, Swan, and Pike

Got hired to drag a cart,

Harnessed themselves, all three, and start

To move. It could be pretty light

for them, but to a river Pike is trying to drag,

While Crayfish, he is pulling back,

And Swan up to the clouds directs his flight.

'Tis difficult to say who is to blame.

Which place is now the cart? The same.

You get the point.

When there's no synergy and everyone uses their own performance metrics, the results are suboptimal.

So what should the organizational structure of a modern hospitality company be?

As we learned in previous chapters, it's all about data. And analytics is our future. And due to the growing importance of data, technology, and analytics, what we are witnessing today is that the role of the revenue management department is being redefined and reimagined to become a more central discipline that drives the decision-making for the entire hospitality business. The revenue management (aka Revenue and Profit Optimization) department is becoming a critical piece of the puzzle, that "glues" everything together and feeds the information and decisions to other parts of the organism, where in most cases, profitability is the ultimate goal, with all departments working towards the same metric.

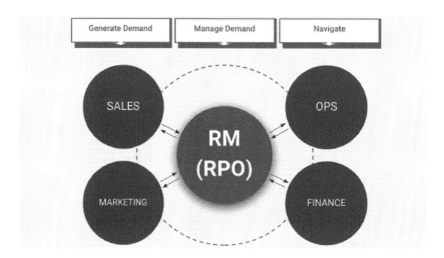

What we're also seeing is that the revenue management (or, revenue and profit optimization) discipline is evolving into something new and very different, broader and more comprehensive (hence the new name) that is going to help the industry move forward in a more efficient manner. As the distribution landscape becomes more complex and as technology evolves, RPO will continue growing in importance.

Marco Benvenuti (Co-founder of Duetto) had this vision long before the industry really started talking about it:

Whenever we were selling Duetto, we used to call it "Revenue Strategy Ecosystem". And of course the software is a big part of it, but then there is the whole culture and an operational side around it.

And getting all that is not always easy and it's not always immediate. But then when you get it, then all this stuff starts happening. And so it's not that you just make money on the top line, but all of a sudden you start saving on costs because your marketing costs actually go down or they stay the same, but they get relocated in a way that they deliver higher ROI. So you can make more money with the same marketing budget. Sometimes you make more money with less marketing, so your marketing costs get optimized.

And your labor costs go down. Because of course, by using open pricing, by having a strategy and by knowing better what your demand is going to be in advance, you can staff your hotel better. And we know that labor is the number one expense.

So when it's done right and you have the right people and all that, you're seeing a boost in revenue and decrease in costs. So the NOI repercussions of that are greatly significant.

There are already examples of companies that have successfully implemented this new, synchronized, profit-oriented way of running their businesses. We can learn a lot from those success stories. Take Sonder for example.

Francis Davidson (Co-founder and CEO of Sonder):

We have a handful of company goals every year, every quarter, and one of them is on increasing RevPAR and the other one is on increasing our operational efficiency. But the thing is that every single person in the company is responsible for driving progress on each of these dimensions. And to me, I never send a message that one goal is more important than the other. I think true creativity comes when people collaborate together and find a way to get both.

And so in order to ensure that we have the right strategy for profit maximization, our revenue management team will work very closely with our operations team to figure out exactly, for example, what is the delta in cost for housekeeping for a 3-night stay versus a 4-night stay and just ensuring that those departments are in sync.

It's just good organizational hygiene to ensure that during the planning process, especially in the context of dependencies, different departments co-create their roadmaps and global prioritizations.

So building a revenue and profit optimization culture in the organization is crucial as it is crucial to ensure that all "elements" are working in sync towards the same goal (or goals).

What do we need to get there?

1. **Use data for decision making.**

   Don't use your gut feeling, please.

2. **Rely on technology.**

   Having the right (modern) technology in place will help achieve closer collaboration between departments. Technology is not the barrier, technology is the solution. It helps streamline the use of data and enables the departments to cooperate.

3. **Have profit as your target throughout the organization.**

   Don't let each department use their own performance metrics. Use one that matters the most.

   Profitability should be the main centerpiece of the revenue management discipline (the Revenue and Profit Optimization discipline).

4. **Be agile, constantly revise your processes.**

We now understand how important it is to be adaptive. We need to establish the right business processes in our organizations that serve the ultimate purpose of ensuring access to the technology being deployed to help get that alignment among stakeholders that spans different departments of an organization.

We're at this point when we need to start questioning everything we do. Are we doing certain things just because we've been doing this for the last 30 years? Or is it actually justified from the ROI standpoint? Because things are changing so fast, we need to revise our processes at least every 6 months to verify that they're still relevant.

The reimagined role of a revenue manager

Professor Dave Roberts (Cornell University, School of Hotel Administration) recently shared during a CHR roundtable:

A revenue manager now spends less than half of their time doing traditional revenue management, they spend more than half of their time on stakeholder management. And that has accelerated during COVID. Now this is more like 60-65%. I think it's time for a reckoning on not just revenue management, but revisiting our business processes in general.

Previously, revenue managers were spending most of their time on pulling reports, aggregating data, analyzing data, and making tactical decisions, which is now delegated to machines and AI. As a result, as mentioned earlier, that role is expanding in the scope of responsibilities towards a higher level of strategic stakeholder management aimed at synchronizing different departments to ensure optimal decision making for the entire organization.

This is a trend that we need to embrace and allow the revenue management role to evolve to benefit the entire organization and ultimately, the whole industry. Here's how Bob Gilbert (President and CEO of HSMAI) describes this transformation:

I think the evolution in the future will be much more towards a commercial role where the integration of sales and marketing and revenue strategy, and loyalty strategy, and distribution strategy has to converge. And it will be someone like a DORM who will have the necessary skill sets to be able to step into those commercial functions or commercial leadership roles much easier than anybody who grew up in other disciplines. Because revenue leaders already have that holistic look at the business where others have a much more siloed look at the business. Those other functions will still be important but I think that the leadership roles in the future are going to be bright for revenue folks today, because they're the ones who have been shaped to really be commercial leaders.

We already have many examples in the industry of former revenue managers advancing into C-level roles and becoming successful strategic leaders thanks to their analytical skills, deep understanding of data, and ability to see how different actions by different departments affect the bottom-line profit and operating efficiencies of the entire organization.

I'm sure we will see an increasing amount of those examples in the near future. We're seeing more and more people with the title Chief Commercial Officer, which per John Burns, "*allows us to bring together sales, distribution, reservations and revenue management*".

John Burns:

So we have a new identity taking shape in the hotel org chart. And that's the Chief Commercial Officer. By virtue of being a "C", they have more clout, they have more responsibility, they have more people. They're going to have more opportunities to find and implement technology. So they'll have more money to spend and more opportunities to spend it. So I see a migration of a revenue manager to be a Chief Commercial Officer.

If you think of the people at the table: director of sales, director of revenue management, director of reservations, director of marketing and director of distribution - the person who stands out as analytical and who has proven themselves is the revenue manager. So I think in many cases, they're going to do well in terms of being able to steer choices for new systems. So I see hope there. It won't be with a revenue management title necessarily, it'll probably be Chief Commercial Officer.

And you can have that CCO effectively at the property level or at the brand level.

We should roll everything together under the CCO so the organization can work together rather than fighting internally, with a unified vision, unified message, unified budget, unified action plan.

So as a result, we're starting to expect a new set of skills from our RPO (revenue and profit optimization) professionals who want to grow into those CCO roles. And as the technology continues evolving, eventually the layer of human intervention will be minimized and we'll be focusing people on those elements where the combination of the human and the machine is unbeatable (#cobotics). And that dictates the type of individual we need to find for that role.

I've been teaching a class as a guest lecturer at some hospitality schools and universities lately where I try to prepare students for the real-life environment after they graduate. Here's the list of skills I tell them to master in order to be successful as a professional in the Hospitality 2.0 environment:

- **Understanding data**

Note that I don't say "knowing how to build a regression model" or "being a data analyst" because those tasks have been gradually delegated to machines, centralized or outsourced.

Data analysis and data science is not something hoteliers are traditionally strong at anyway. So good news for us: we're no longer required to do data modeling, data science and predictive analytics, but we need to be conversational in it in order to fit well in the new Hospitality 2.0 model. RPOs need to navigate very well in the data world, recognize patterns, know how to use data for optimal decision making and stakeholder alignment.

- **Being friends with technology**

This is a logical outcome of the increasing role of technology in our industry. We are now required to have more technical knowledge and navigate well in the hospitality tech ecosystem.

- **Strategic thinking**

As more routine tasks are delegated to machines and the role evolves, more time is now freed up for strategic decision making. Being a good strategist will help one become successful in our new environment.

- **People management**

Stakeholder management will continue to be a big part of RPO's responsibilities and will grow in importance. With that said, having people skills is no longer optional. While previously a perfect example of a revenue manager was a data-oriented nerd (like me) who mostly just communicated with an excel spreadsheet and sent reports via email, now we are expected to communicate with humans on a daily basis and those humans expect us to smile and be likable. It took me a few years to convert to an extravert but I think I'm doing okay. So the good news, it's definitely doable.

So a few things have now become evident. First of all, as we see, it takes a pretty sophisticated combination of skills to perform well in that new role. That explains why these people are not available in abundance. In addition, many of them left the industry because we didn't treat them right during the pandemic. So while we're dealing with a limited resource situation, we need to really work hard on training the new generation to be successful future revenue and profit optimization leaders growing into CCO roles.

What this also means is that we need to readjust the way we teach the new generation and the way we approach education. This is exactly what we talked about in one of the previous chapters (<u>Disconnect between the industry and academia</u>) and this is also what drives my initiative to bring my industry knowledge to hospitality schools all over the world. If you're a hospitality professor reading this book and would like me to visit as a guest speaker - please reach out via LinkedIn.

Proper education and training is more important than ever before. More and more hospitality schools offer a revenue management class (though some are already renaming it as we speak). And for those who are not planning to obtain a formal degree, there are other options available in the form of an industry certification. That's an area where that third-party designation really does make a difference in career paths for this discipline.

Here's a list of a few of the most prominent revenue management oriented certifications available in the industry today:

- CRME (Certified Revenue Management Executive) by HSMAI[129]
- CRMA (Certified Revenue Management Analyst) by HSMAI[130] - it gives students another badge on their resume to identify them as "revenue-ready" by HSMAI to go right into a revenue position
- Hotel Revenue Management Certificate by Cornell[131]
- CHRM (Certified Hospitality Revenue Manager) by AHLEI[132]
- CHIA (Certification in Hotel Industry Analytics) by AHLEI[133]

Success Story: citizenM

As we speak about redesigned modern operations in this chapter, we can't not mention citizenM... a company so revolutionary that their example doesn't yet fit in any familiar paradigm, which makes it so fascinating. They have completely reimagined operations (more like Hospitality 3.0, as you will see after you start reading) and, just like with their technology, they're on a whole different level or rather, a whole different planet, in terms of the way they manage their business. I find their story incredibly inspirational so I'm dedicating a portion of this chapter to my conversation with Michael Levie, Co-founder and COO of citizenM.

As one of my industry contacts mentioned to me once, "*I worked with Michael Levie for some time. He has always been about 30 years ahead of the rest of the industry.*" And I completely agree.

| Michael Levie

I always tell people that in the end, we're a hotel company like everybody else. We sell a room to a guest that travels, whether that's for leisure or business. What I think happens is that from there, everything is different.

So the best explanation is maybe Tesla or Amazon type of thinking whereby Tesla produced a car but they produced not only an electric car, not a gas or a diesel car,

---

[129]HSMAI Academy: Certified Revenue Management Executive (CRME): https://hsmaiacademy.org/certification-revenue-management-crme/

[130]HSMAI: Certified Revenue Management Analyst (CRMA): https://americas.hsmai.org/certification/certified-revenue-management-analyst/

[131]eCornell: Hotel Revenue Management: Cornell Certificate Program: https://ecornell.cornell.edu/certificates/hospitality-and-foodservice-management/hotel-revenue-management/

[132]AHLEI: Certified Hospitality Revenue Manager (CHRM) Online Program: https://www.ahlei.org/product/certified-hospitality-revenue-manager-chrm/

[133]AHLEI: Certification in Hotel Industry Analytics (CHIA) Online Course and Exam – Academic: https://www.ahlei.org/product/certification-in-hotel-industry-analytics-chia-online-course-and-exam-academic/

but they produced a completely different thinking. So how do you use your car? What are your needs when you use your car? What do you need to go to a shop? Can you wait for things to be done and do you have an office there?

So in the end, a Tesla owner decides to buy a Tesla car not only because they like the car but because of everything else around it as well: the ease of use, the automatic updates, everything that comes with it. It has four wheels, it has a steering wheel and it still moves the same way as any other car. But around it, everything is different.

And the same for Amazon. They rethought some existing, relatively traditional and cumbersome industries. So they started out with the book industry and they revolutionized that. And as they started rolling out different business processes, all of a sudden they became extremely successful.

And I think that if you look at citizenM, people see us as a mid-market player, they see luxury hotels, on the other hand, they see that we have limited service but it is very luxurious, but they don't get much further than that.

What I see is: we build modular. So our entire construction methodology is different and because of that, we were able to get value engineering not only from the cost but also from the functionality point of view. So if you see the first rooms we built and what we're building right now, we reduced fit-out time from 160 hours to 40 hours for a room. I mean, that is significant.

When we thought about being focused on guests at our hotels and having our teams be only busy with guest satisfaction, we said, "Okay, then we don't want to do the back of the house." Then, if we don't do the back of the house, then how do we do it? And thinking about it, I said, "We have facility companies that can clean, we have linen companies that we can rent our linen from or use them to clean our linen, so how about I ask a few friends in this industry to set up a company that sells a per-occupied-room cost to me to clean and do the entire back of the house? That includes purchasing, receiving, everything."

So imagine that our guest supplies and cleaning supplies go to the laundry plant, wherever we use them in the cities, and on the cart that travels anyway for the linen, it piggybacks and they do the logistics. It doesn't cost them anything. It doesn't cost me anything but it saves me huge money. Why? Because I don't have a purchasing department. I don't have a receiving department. I don't have store rooms on site.

So it's the rethinking and everything we did that was different about our company.

And in 2005, when we started the citizenM venture, for somebody to say, "I'm not going to sell by segmentation, I will only do channel management, I'm not going to do a corporate contract..." I mean, they almost locked me up and put me in an asylum.

So, we did some things that I would say are industry revolutionary. And we did that everywhere. Like with food and beverage: we don't have kitchens, we have pantries and we get everything fresh, delivered daily. So the whole thinking, the whole philosophy, technology, the digital, all the business processes behind it are different.

So all of a sudden when you start to look, yeah, we're a hotel like everybody else. But then if you really look at it closely, it's different.

And then the whole human resources, the way we find our teams, the way we onboard them, the way we train them, their responsibilities - that's different, too. So the line staff is responsible and accountable and sitting at the top of our pyramid. It's a reversed pyramid. So they are at the top and the rest of the organization supports them. And there's the whole incentive system that's behind that.

And what we do, our values are carried everywhere. And we end up with 92.5% guest satisfaction, system-wide for the last 10 years and our NPS score hovers between 58 and 64, which as you know, in this industry is unheard of.

So again, not everybody needs to know it from the inside. What our guests need to know is that they can just make a reservation, come in and enjoy our hotel. We honor our promise that we're an affordable luxury for the people. But behind that, we created new business processes and as such, maybe revolutionized the industry because a lot of systems and a lot of structures were not there before. So we had to create companies, bring partners along and initiate things. We did a lot of crazy stuff.

| Ira Vouk

This is fascinating. I didn't know the background story and really appreciate you sharing this with me.

So, since we're talking about the structure of your organization, I had a question related to that.

In a traditional hospitality organization (I'm referring to hotel companies or hotel management companies) what we see a lot right now is that different departments work in silos. For example, you have your operations, you have your revenue management department, you have marketing, sales, and finance. And what I'm seeing in the industry is that they don't really talk well to each other.

| Michael Levie

No, they don't.

| Ira Vouk

Right? They don't function as one living organism that is controlled by the head (brain), targeting some specific goal and working in cooperation. They're all kind of doing their own thing.

So is it something that you have been able to address through that different way of building your organization, using this new structure? Does it help you solve the problem that I'm describing?

| Michael Levie

What you're describing is actually the way organizations are structured, the process. So a lot of companies spend a lot of time on their content. And a lot of companies spend a lot of time on their process. But they do not necessarily look at the context in which they do this. And if you look at most hotel organizations, you will find that they operate from the top down.

What you see in modern organizations is either an inverted pyramid (what I described earlier) because sometimes they do need a structure, but it's reversed, so the decision making is done as close to the guest as possible. Or you see holacracy. And holacracy is working with circles of influence. There are still departments with specializations. But for a particular product, you invite people into your circle that can deliver. And hierarchy is the hierarchy of the circles, and the way you meet. It is an agile approach to production and everything else, but I think it is more the process behind it - how organizations can function.

So what we do is an inverted pyramid in our hotels, so the structure is relatively flat. You have line staff, you have a manager on duty and you have hotel managers, we have regions, and that is supported by the centralized office. And I think that if you look at it from a central office, the "support office" point of view there - there it is holacracy. We have a lot of specialists and because everything is in the cloud with us, we have everything centralized.

We just have a couple of support offices. The largest one is in the Netherlands where we started, but we have an office in New York, in Seattle, and in Hong Kong. And it could be that for certain disciplines, the person responsible is in one of those offices. It doesn't have to be in the Netherlands. So it's not like a headquarter type of system, it's support and it is carried by holacracy. And especially over the last year and a half with everybody doing digital meetings, it has become very easy and it has worked for us very well.

And I don't think there are any hotel companies that have changed the way they work and function, they all still are, for the most part, top-down and badly structured.

❙ Ira Vouk

So essentially you've adopted an agile framework to your organization and to how it functions. I'm a big fan of agile/scrum product development in the software space and it's very interesting to see how it could actually be adapted to the way an organization is functioning in general, not just from the standpoint of building software products.

❙ Michael Levie

Well, it's the same concept, right? If there's so much that needs to be done, if you break it down into manageable increments, and you sequence them, and you have the agile way of working - you become very efficient as an organization.

So, we started out with that philosophy and I think that the values that we have in our organization are carried by everybody.

And we also hire slightly differently in the hotels than in the support offices. So, in the hotels, we do casting days where we basically do workshops with people that we selected, and in those workshops, we observe whether they overlap 85% or more with our values. And if that's the case, I can give you the key to the hotel and you know how to run it, I just need to teach you some of our tasks.

In the support offices, that's different because you hire for a very specific, specialized talent. And that is more of a traditional selection process. Once you have made the final cut, you still need to interview with three random people at the office. That could be anybody at whatever level in the organization and the only focus there is whether we like you or not.

❙ Ira Vouk

So, cultural fit is more important than anything else?

❙ Michael Levie

Yeah, because who wants to work with people you don't like? I don't.

❙ Ira Vouk

Yeah, I don't blame you.

Very interesting. And I love the name you use - "support offices", you don't call it headquarters or corporate offices.

❙ Michael Levie

You know, from day one, we started correcting people that no, we don't have headquarters, till they started calling it "support office". So, everybody within our system thinks "support office". The scary part with headquarters is that they feel superior to everybody: "I'm from headquarters, I'm important". And we're absolutely not important, we're there to support. So if you're from support, then it's a different mentality that goes to the hotels and a different focus. So that's why we did that.

| Ira Vouk

So what role does the revenue management department/function play in your organization?

| Michael Levie

Revenue management has been at our core from day one.

We saw a need for a different kind of access to hospitality data – one that would be independent of any software provider and gave access and control back to the organizations that needed the data.

We started with the mission of breaking down data silos and being able to exchange data amongst departments, systems and properties.

So when it comes to revenue management, channel management, and understanding our data - that has lived with us for a while. We adapted very early on, gross revenue, cost of acquisition per reservation, net revenue. So we really understand the net contribution of that to our profitability.

| Ira Vouk

So, we spoke about people and processes. Now let's talk about technology. You built your entire tech stack from scratch. That must have been a very rough journey.

| Michael Levie

Well, there's a benefit in starting out from scratch. And the benefit is that I didn't have anything legacy. Now, obviously that was 14-15 years ago when we started. So one of the things that I said, "I want everything to be as modular as possible." So if I need to replace anything, if I need to do something different, I want to be able to do it.

So our whole tech thinking has been shaped in three silos, actually. One is on-premise and networks. The second one is hotel systems. And the third one is the commercial side (revenue management and those types of things). You could say there's also the fourth one, which is the guest facing tech. Because the digital sort of snug in there as well, right now.

So we set it all up to be as modular as possible and it took a couple of tries. But now, for example, we have in room CPUs that are basically room controllers that link into a network and the network is hooked into the hotel systems.

So we get the speed on premise but we also get to capture all the micro details so there is no transactional thinking from a PMS room-centric point of view, because we have made it guest-centric. And we have made it all about the guest profile. So if a guest checks out, that framing of the check-out allows us to look at the room setup, lighting, temperature, any specifics, television channels used, whatever it may be and that is stored in the guest profile.

So when a guest profile is called upon for a future check-in, it's very easy to set it up similarly and then when they walk in, it's comfortable for the guest. To realize this, we need the micro details. It simply can't be obtained with transactional interfaces. "On-premise" we need speed, but the rest of the systems are in the cloud, so our middleware allows for that.

As an owner-operator and having set all hotels up similarly, we sure have a head start. So, like Tesla, I can update my hotels overnight. It allows us to switch systems if we need to. And I even set it up with the middleware, so that if I'm forced to run two different PMSs at different properties, I could, because the middleware can neutralize the differences. So it's a pretty robust system.

Obviously, we grow fast. We have many different jurisdictions. But so far yeah, we're still ahead of the curve.

| **Ira Vouk**

This is mind blowing...

Role of the revenue management technology in the digital (r)evolution

As you see from the citizenM success story and other things we have discussed in the earlier chapters, technology is key to successful operations. And logically, as revenue management is gaining in importance and more is being asked of RPOs (Revenue and Profit Optimization professionals) - revenue management technology has a good chance of becoming the centerpiece of the hotel tech stack once it gains the necessary amount of functionality that targets profit maximization and stakeholder alignment. We also need a new name for it. For example, **Revenue and Profit Optimization System**. RPOS. Let's use that, why not.

These days, RM tech providers are challenged to do more, faster and be more innovative. As a result, we are seeing increased investment in the discipline and acceleration of its growth and development.

Wouter Geerts (Skift) recently wrote in one of his reports, "*As data has turned into the new gold, more data will become available and affordable to hotels... revenue management systems have an important role to play here, to partner with hotels and ensure they get the best available data to improve the short-term pricing and long-term revenue strategy. While historical data remains paramount in the industry, it is likely that the future growth area will be forward-looking data that allow hotels to be more proactive in their fight for the customer."*[134]

When it comes to the existing revenue management software vendor landscape, John Burns described it beautifully in a few paragraphs:

In regards to adoption of RM technology, we've had a few waves, a few generations of entrants.

We had the originals: EzRMS and IDeaS. And then some new entrants, 2 or 3 other smaller ones. Then we had new entrants come along like Duetto and bring in some very interesting ideas, especially related to outside influences and this aspiration to have 1 to 1 personalized pricing. That was disruptive.

Then a third generation of revenue management technology came along. We can call it "revenue management light" - systems like Atomize and Pace and Revenue Analytics. Their value proposition is that it takes a remarkable amount of a DORM's day to manage older RMS tools. So how can we break away from that? An RMS should be more automated, it shouldn't require that much hands-on management. Which is very relevant considering that we're at a time when we don't have enough people.

If you're looking for a detailed list of revenue management solutions available on the market, Skift research from 2019[135] references the most complete list at the time of publication (there have been a couple new vendors since then but in general, that report is still very relevant). This is by far the most comprehensive study of the revenue management software space that I have encountered in my entire hospitality career. I am proud of the fact that I was able to contribute to the development of 3 products on that list (iRates, PIE and Duetto).

So as the revenue management discipline evolves and the way we manage our businesses is being completely reimagined, that puts more pressure on RMS vendors to provide more comprehensive solutions to ensure they're aligned well with the new Hospitality 2.0 model.

That means they need to:

- Help achieve closer collaborations between departments by breaking them out of their silos
- Aid with stakeholder management
- Support profit-centric approach, aimed at profit maximization and total revenue management (not revolve around RevPAR alone)
- Incorporate machine learning using true external forward-looking market data to objectively assess future demand potential

---

[134]Skift: The Hotel Revenue Management Landscape 2019 (April 2019): https://research.skift.com/report/the-hotel-revenue-management-landscape-2019/

[135]Skift: The Hotel Revenue Management Landscape 2019 (April 2019): https://research.skift.com/report/the-hotel-revenue-management-landscape-2019/

- Seamlessly integrate with the systems of record in real-time
- Be user-friendly and intuitive to minimize time spent in the system, thus freeing up users for more strategic decision making
- Provide better enterprise functionalities to strategically manage entire portfolios
- Be agile and support continuous innovation

I'm also working on my third book that will attempt to describe how to build a new-generation Revenue Management System (or rather, Revenue and Profit Optimization System). Stay tuned.

Leif Jägerbrand (founder of Atomize RMS) shared his point of view:

RM tech will take a bigger responsibility. Now it's about maximizing the revenue, down the road it will be about maximizing profit, the total profit, taking everything into consideration, including additional revenue streams and all the costs and so on. And RMS systems should also be able to optimize both for the short term and the long term.

And the more hotels become confident with using an RMS, the more we can grow and innovate.

As he rightly noted, increased adoption rates will make tech companies more successful, which will ultimately result in higher investments and, in turn, drive more innovation in the area of revenue and profit optimization.

Now that we have talked about the reimagined hospitality industry from different aspects (data, technology and operations), here comes the most important part of the book that describes what the future holds and what the main areas of opportunity are.

PART 4: **INVESTMENT OPPORTUNITIES**

"Change has never happened this fast before,

and it will never be this slow again."

Graeme Wood

Throughout this book, I talked about various challenges in the hospitality space and hotel tech specifically, described major disruptors that have shaped the industry, and painted the picture of the new Hospitality 2.0 model - the future that is already here. In this chapter, I will highlight the areas of value creation and **opportunities for investment**, and not only financial investment (though this is the most critical element) but also investment of our talent, time, and resources.

As we have seen in the previous chapters, the market opportunity for hospitality technology is tremendous. We looked closely at high-growth areas that are currently developing around new technologies, cloud computing, big data, machine learning, as well as business intelligence and revenue management. There are also many areas of opportunity in the way we run our businesses, build our teams and approach customer acquisition and retention.

Let's start with Technology as this is clearly where the revolution is happening and where most changes are going to take place in the next 5-10 years in our industry.

Technology

Traditionally, the hospitality industry has not been on the forefront of technological change. And I don't think that's going to change, but because of all the factors described in this book, technologies are being developed more rapidly and our industry is being forced to start catching up with the rest of the world.

B2C

When it comes to the consumer side, I believe the industry will mature at a faster pace than ever before. Technology like mobile apps, remote check-in and check-out, etc. - all of that seems to be much more readily available and accepted now as a result of the pandemic and other factors, and it's likely to continue evolving. Although, I recently had a painful experience attempting to check in at the Marriott through the app. The mobile key must have been shipped all the way from China and got stuck in the Suez Canal because it never arrived, so I had to check in at the front desk and get a physical key. But someday, Marriott will catch up and make it happen. I'm a believer.

Many other industry leaders agree that there are many opportunities in the B2C space that enhance guest experience.

Bob Gilbert (HSMAI):

I think the biggest opportunity for technology is going to be in anything that interacts with the consumer. A lot of the texting tools and such. Something that gives the consumer an ability to instantly talk to somebody at the front desk or to text them for directions while they're in route to the hotel, whatever it may be - the things that really enhance the guest experience, the age old things that frustrate the customer, those types of things that provide instant or live response.

Jan Freitag (CoStar / STR):

I think what COVID pushed forward very, very quickly was that everything has to be touchless. We're using our phone to plan, book, check in, pay, check out and then review - everything is happening on this device and that's not going backward. So the technology in the sense of interacting with the consumer is all going to be mobile.

Michael Levie (citizenM):

The guest is not going to put up with this nonsense. So if they are used to retail being up to par, if they're used to the airline industry being up to par, and they're used to Google, and everything is within reach and it sits in an app and they can use it on their smartphones, they simply are not going to accept anymore that some brands still have an extensive check-in processes. And unless I carry my own frequent stay program card, they will not know who I am. I mean, it's just not going to happen anymore. They need to get digitally better and they can only do that when they improve their tech architecture.

Michael, I feel your pain!

I predict that more and more hotels will be using AI-driven customer service and data analytics that will redefine industry standards on providing a personalized guest experience. It is already happening. And one day Marriott will deliver my mobile key to me.

B2B

For B2B, the future is in systems that will be highly optimized with little or no human intervention using real-time data and seamlessly integrated into our daily work, systems that will take over most of the operational functions.

The main transformation will be happening in the area that allows us to build better, more coherent workflows that aid in building synergies between departments and allowing the whole organization to be aligned and achieve better operating efficiencies.

Mylene Young (Son Hospitality Consulting):

I think the opportunity is that we have more and more systems that connect different departments together so that you have a suite of products. If you're still working in silos - that is a major headache.

So I think there is an opportunity for hoteliers to understand that your tech stack is something that you need to pay a lot of attention to. You need to ask an expert to really look at the big picture based on what you're trying to achieve, and look at the connectivity and whether those systems work well together. At the end of the day, if your goal is to make 2-3 million dollars more per year and be more efficient - how you're going to do that and what kind of expertise you need in order to understand the tech stack a hundred feet above is where the opportunity lies.

Jordan Hollander (Hotel Tech Report):

We now have all these tools like zapier[136] and coda[137] and airtable[138] that connect to each other, with automated messages and sign-up flows and all this stuff that feels like it's us, it's an extension of us. And I think ultimately hotels are moving in that direction, too.

From the author: Zapier is a product that allows end users to integrate the web applications they use. Coda is a new doc that brings words, data, and teams together. Airtable is a platform for building collaborative applications. Technology exists that allows us to build seamless collaborative workflows in organizations. It won't be long before we start adopting it in our industry.

In addition, there's an opportunity for technology vendors to introduce new functionalities that will allow hotel operators to properly measure, track and forecast profit-related metrics as well as build optimal revenue management strategy that maximizes overall profit and not just top-line room revenue.

When it comes to the hierarchy of the B2B ecosystem - that seems to be changing and opening up opportunities for RM/BI (Revenue Management and Business Intelligence) solutions to take on a more central role in the hotel tech stack. What will end up happening, is when hoteliers make technology buying decisions - they will inevitably start looking at RM/BI capabilities first, and then work backwards to what PMS connects and integrates best with those capabilities.

---

[136]Zapier: http://zapier.com/

[137]Coda: https://coda.io/

[138]Airtable: https://www.airtable.com/

Legacy PMS companies will start losing market share if they don't open up their APIs to other companies to connect with, because integrations are becoming a key decision factor for buyers. PMS alone is no longer enough for a hotel to operate efficiently. So eventually, we will be in a situation where if your legacy PMS doesn't connect with all these tools that you need to optimally operate your business, you will be going to the newer cloud-based providers. Maybe they have a smaller market share, maybe slightly less functionality in the core product, but they have all these connections through an open API that you will be able to pick and choose from an easy-to-use self-serve app marketplace.

Data handling and data analysis

As we discussed in the previous chapters, the largest potential in this area arises from the fact that the amount of data available for our decision making is multiplying by day, by hour, and even by minute. At the same time, machines have become more effective in many things that humans have done in the past manually. Humans and machines work best in tandem (#cobotics) when humans capitalize on their own creativity and intuition, while machines handle data gathering, analytics and algorithms.

Compute and storage, and tools in the cloud are becoming more and more available and easy-to-use. And as people start to use those capabilities with various cloud providers to execute innovation, there will be some very interesting opportunities for customer experience and improving operations. But the key here is that hospitality companies have to find a way to cut loose from legacy systems and legacy processes to be able to do this. And if you can do that, there are a lot of very interesting innovations that can be achieved.

Data analysis is also the area in which AI is being utilized more and more widely within the hospitality industry. In this capacity, the technology can be used to quickly sort through large amounts of data and draw important conclusions for optimal decision making. There is no doubt artificial intelligence will reach wide adoption in our industry in the near future, and especially in the area of data analysis. There's no way to stop that trend. And those companies that ignore that trend, will fall behind.

A lot of opportunities also lie in the ability of AI to help us with **data standardization**.

Jan Freitag (CoStar / STR):

We have all these data lakes - how can we make them talk to each other? Because the words we're using are not the same. The concepts are the same but the words are not. This is called a regular room in this hotel and in that hotel it's called a standard room but they're most likely the same. And that's where we need technology to align and come up with actionable definitions that allow us to utilize the data better. So that part I think is also going to make huge leaps as computing power gets cheaper.

There are also huge opportunities in **new ways of building our data architectures** (data mesh concept referenced earlier) and **decentralized data sharing** (also described in one of the previous chapters) that could be used to solve the ARI sharing problem as well as sharing sensitive customer data.

When it comes to forecasting and optimization, more and more data sources are becoming available to us (like forward-looking market data) that will allow analysts (and mainly analytical tools) to **build better forecasts and make better optimization decisions** that maximize profits for hotel owners. More and more companies are starting to incorporate new data into their traditional models, or rebuilding those models altogether. And we can't do it successfully using our old mathematical models, this is where the value of AI and ML is maximized.

The **new types of external market data** that are interesting to explore: OTA search volumes, flight search and booking volumes, car rental search and booking volumes, Google search and booking volumes, events intel, OTA ranking and visibility, VR competitive data, and more. Data sharing between industries is also something that could open up many interesting things. The possibilities are infinite.

As volumes and value of data increase, **Data Brokers and Data Aggregators** become key elements of our ecosystem and that's where another huge area of opportunity lies.

Consolidations

There's also a lot of room for consolidations among existing tech vendors in order to drive the creation of comprehensive end-to-end solutions, both for businesses and for travelers as well, that will eventually simplify the cumbersome hotel tech ecosystem and make it a more comfortable environment for all players.

This is another trend that results in many opportunities for hospitality companies and investors. The growth of innovative companies in the hospitality ecosystem leads to mergers and acquisitions by large players. Many of them see gaps in their solutions portfolio (for example, a PMS product that lacks an RMS component). Many smaller players emerge who have figured out bits and pieces because the larger players have been too slow, and so the large players have started buying the small pieces to complement their existing product offering. This becomes an appealing environment for early-stage investors in this field.

Bob Gilbert (HSMAI):

I think those legacy companies either have to develop those features or they're going to acquire, which is what you're seeing with larger players like Amadeus and Sabre. They're acquiring and they're also trying to develop on their own because they have to. They have to because the legacy systems alone, by themselves, won't survive without these new features that are critical to manage the complexity of how hotel businesses operate today.

I think there's going to be a market for a certain number of companies targeting different segments, but there will probably be consolidation there as well. And I believe that will be good for the industry because if somebody goes from a brand, to a management company, to an ownership group, there would be the continuity of the same system at the unit level of the hotel that everybody will embrace. And there's not going to be the risk or the need or the desire to jump from system A to system B when a new management company comes in and dictates their tech stack. Those transitions are just disruptive. So, consolidation could be good in this scenario.

John Burns (Hospitality Technology Consulting):

We have big companies making a big difference.

We have several private equity companies that are currently rolling up companies. So we've got three or four or five standalone hotel technology vendors now under the same PE company. That's going to change things. I see hope in terms of the emergence of new vendors. So, that's good news.

We're also noticing that categories are blurring between different products (both in B2C and B2B) as many vendors are starting to offer more comprehensive solutions. As a result, our ecosystem will start looking more and more integrated and less cumbersome, with less categories. We will see more companies moving to the cloud, more mergers and acquisitions, and more collaboration between departments at properties to work together towards addressing the complete customer experience: from looking to booking, to departing and returning.

To conclude this section: clearly, at the end of the day, the best investment opportunities are going to be driven by very well-defined problems that technology will help solve for our industry: increased productivity, profitability, reduced guesswork, less human error, and increased guest satisfaction.

For many companies, venture capitalists and other investors, it's important not to wait too long, but to embrace the opportunities that lie behind hospitality technology. Hopefully, this book has helped you build an understanding of the space, its challenges and its opportunities.

People

The entire industry is suffering from lack of human resources as a result of the pandemic and other factors. Many people were laid off and many of them are not coming back. So we need to rethink many things: the way we educate, the way we recruit, the way we build teams and the way we treat our talent. We also need to redesign many operational roles that previously had responsibilities that are now delegated to machines and algorithms.

Michael Levie (citizenM):

After COVID, it has become harder to find staff. People are simply not attracted to our industry.

And it's because we're all dinosaurs and we don't pay enough. It's not sexy anymore. So I think that eventually we will see that people need to get savvy in the way they use culture, people and the way they organize themselves. And it needs to happen fast. There will be a lot of mistakes made in the beginning but that will improve also in the next five years.

Jan Freitag (CoStar / STR):

One of the things that will shape the hotel industry, and in the US specifically, is labor. Right now, we have this huge issue of access to labor and lack of labor. This is not new. This has a lot to do with immigration reform. Because traditionally, the hospitality industry has always been an entry-level industry that attracted people who come to this country and want to make it. It's an entry level job.

So I think without comprehensive immigration reform and visa reform in the United States, this idea of lack of labor is not going to go away. And so therefore we may need more technology to figure out what jobs we can eliminate or whether we need to cut down services, just like we see with the housekeeping piece.

And the asterix to that is going back to the alternative accommodations discussion, they have trained their audience so well to accept "Pay for cleaning". A cleaning fee is standard for alternative accommodations. And I really wonder if five years from now a cleaning fee will be in hotels. And yes, of course we clean it when you check out but if you want something while you're there - we're going to charge you for it. Question mark.

Jordan Hollander (Hotel Tech Report):

The general trend that I see in hotels is that there is more automation and that automation creates new roles and it also changes old roles. And so what we're seeing more and more is that a team of 10 people on property can do what 50 people did 20 years ago.

And so the biggest innovation I think is in having people who are entrepreneurial, who could wear multiple hats, and who can use different types of tools and having those tools available through open APIs, interacting with each other.

There's of course some "old world" infrastructure that needs to play out of the management companies but we're definitely seeing this trend in more entrepreneurial midsize hotels and independents in Europe. The younger generation of owner-operators are really getting engaged and start building that technology-oriented culture within the organization. They want to automate customer acquisition, integrate with all the different software systems, etc. So then you don't need all the on-property teams to run these functions. And that corporate office can pay people better, which attracts more talent, which ultimately makes everything operate smoother.

So I think, as much as the technology is enabling it, the innovation is actually coming from rearranging roles and being able to attract better talent.

And as Mylene Young (Son Hospitality Consulting) rightly noted, education is at the base of everything when it comes to our talent. Many opportunities exist for hotel schools to update their curriculums and hospitality organizations to offer certificate programs in different areas to raise awareness and improve the knowledge level in the industry.

Universities with hospitality programs should have a required set of courses devoted to technology and data, and faculty should be incentivised to teach and focus on the area. For example, companies like Expedia, Google, AWS, and major hotel chains could fund endowed chairs and research in the area of hospitality technology.

Max Starkov recently commented on one of my LinkedIn posts after I taught a class at San Diego State University, *"Education is the only way forward to move our beloved industry from a technology-averse, real estate-minded, number-crunching industry to a 100% digital technology-enabled industry powered by online, mobile, cloud, IoT, AI, robotics and blockchain tools and applications, an industry where digital technology has made its way into every aspect of the industry: hotel operations, guest services, communications, revenue management, distribution, CRM and marketing."* I couldn't agree more!

Customer acquisition, customer service and retention

While this is mostly enabled through technology, it definitely warrants a dedicated discussion, that's why I'm separating it in its own section.

Marco Benvenuti (Duetto):

Definitely I think the biggest change we will see will be in the way that people book and consume travel. When I started in this industry, we were moving from calling hotels or going to a travel agent to book a trip, to going online. And that was a pretty seismic shift. And so now there's going to be another one. I don't know exactly what it's going to be, but it's going to be in that arena. Someone will figure something out that will change the way that we consume travel, especially now accelerated by the fact that we're coming out of a pandemic. 9/11 did it for the OTAs.

John Burns (Hospitality Technology Consulting):

We need to pay more attention to e-commerce. We still don't take e-commerce seriously. Airbnb does a much better job, OTAs do a much better job. For us, it's 5% or 10% of our budget, which is very insignificant.

Francis Davidson (Sonder):

Take a long list of services that you have in a hotel. I think it's a worthwhile exercise to look at all of them and think about what is the best way to deliver them in 2022. And our view is that very little is left from the traditional hotel operating model.

We call it like putting the lobby on your phone. So take all hotel services and ask, "What is the digital equivalent of them?" And I think that's going to liberate a lot of the cost structure so the guests can then self-select into the services they want without it being pushed on them and also allow them to just get a nicer space and a better location. So there's kind of a value equation trade: give me less kind of manual service and give me more of what I need. Everyone should stay in a suite and everyone should stay in the best location, and they can actually do it at a Holiday Inn price, if you really look at each of the cost drivers. And so in our view, it is the biggest opportunity for the hospitality industry.

To conclude, in addition to adopting the right technology, a big opportunity for the industry lies in learning how to improve our value proposition to avoid losing our customers to the "not-so-alternative accommodations" sector as well as rethink our services and amenities to be more in line with the new generation of traveler.

Climate and Environment

Many industry leaders are talking about environmental changes and their effects on the travel industry.

Jan Freitag (CoStar / STR):

The biggest influencer on the global hotel industry will be climate change. I don't think that there's a close second. I think climate change will impact the way we travel. It'll impact the way we design. It'll impact the way people stay in hotels. What will become very important is how we make hotels more resilient, with access to water, electricity, internet, etc. And then, do we want to go to places that have wildfires, that have tsunamis, that are impacted by weather phenomena?

Climate change, then sea level rising - that has a huge impact on our industry. Mauritius, Bora Bora, places like that - they may not be available to us the way they used to.

So to me, it is the main influencer that will shape and impact the global hospitality industry going forward.

Michael Levie (citizenM):

Ownership is very eager in ESG (environmental social governance) and it comes from the financial institutions backing them. The top banks and even private equity are leaning more and more into the ESG.

OTA landscape

Many of us agree that we may see some changes in the OTA arena that will present opportunities for hospitality organizations in the next 5-10 years. There are some big players that are potentially going to make a big difference and change the distribution landscape, so hotels will eventually need to learn how to readapt to the new environment. And clearly, everyone needs to keep a close eye on Google.

John Burns (Hospitality Technology Consulting):

I don't know what's going to happen with Google. They have a path, they have a roadmap. They don't tell mere mortals like you or I but they're in a position to be important. They already are important. They very subtly control the buying process, a big part of the buying process. They are already influencing us and they will continue to do so even more.

Marco Benvenuti (Duetto):

I think that in the next five years, we're going to see something different coming out in the agency world. Whether it is going to be Airbnb that becomes a full-fledged OTA. Whether Expedia or Booking.com will become something different. Whether it's Google that will come in and destroy everybody else, or Amazon.

As you see from the above discussion, the industry has transformed a lot and it keeps transforming very fast. And that presents a wide array of opportunities for investment. As John Burns mentioned:

I see a great deal of change. I see more change in the next five years than in the last 20. I see a new generation of technology leadership doing really aggressive things. So, I don't know, so much can happen, and really, if you dwell on it - it's frightening, but I choose to think it's exciting. There's just so much. And most of it is going to be good.

Can't be as bad as 2020, right? We shouldn't be frightened because all of these exciting revolutions (not just transformations but revolutions) make our lives more fun. They make our businesses more profitable. They make our operations more efficient. And they make our guests happier. They're here to help us.

As the industry recovers, we will see rapid growth and more technology adoption, there's no question about it. And this comes with a tremendous amount of opportunities for investment of our money, our time and our talent.

Notably, the common denominator of the successful hospitality companies (the ones that I used as examples in this book and also many, many more) is heavy investment in technology.

I think there will always be some of the larger infrastructure and legacy technology issues and it takes decades for industries to transform, it doesn't happen overnight. But, if you look at the changes this industry has experienced just in the last 10 years, that are described in this book, we've accomplished so much! It just takes a while for an industry as big and as diverse as hospitality, to make a major turn, but it will happen. It is already happening and there are tremendous amounts of opportunities that lie ahead.

Let's build a brighter future for our industry through technology and education!

CONCLUSION

"Sometimes we are like a point in a circle and we're trying to get out,

and no matter which direction we go, we hit the circumference

until we realize that the only way is to hop over, to go into the third dimension."

Ravi Mehrotra, IDeaS

The world has changed. And the hospitality industry has drastically changed as well in the last 10 years. And it will keep changing at a more rapid pace.

That means that we can't keep doing what we were doing for decades and keep making the same mistakes. We need to readapt to the new environment in order to be efficient, successful, profitable and also attractive for the new talent.

Many things that we're doing now (the way we build our teams, the way we approach customer acquisition, the way we segment our business, the way we forecast, etc. etc.) are done out of habit. But do we really understand why we're doing these things in this particular way? Is this optimal and does it actually drive ROI and improve operating efficiencies? Does the new reality dictate a new approach? Can we do better?

We need to ask ourselves these questions critically so that we are able to truly understand our behavior and take a very different, more optimal approach, to ensure that it corresponds with the new Hospitality 2.0 model.

And when we ask these questions, we need to understand that all answers are in the data, not in Tarot cards, not in the movement of celestial bodies, and not in coffee grounds. We need to turn to data to help us make the right decisions. And for that, we need to understand how to find the right data, how to access it, how to analyze it and how to store it. And technology will help us with all those things. Imagine all the possibilities that will open up as cross-industry data becomes available, as we learn more about our consumers, as we gather more information about their behavior on property and actually learn how to use that information to improve our businesses and at the same time, dramatically increase guest satisfaction. The possibilities are infinite.

Revenue management will be reimagined as the only data-driven discipline and will take on a central role in hotel operations. A business simply can't be successful without having a proper revenue and profit optimization culture at the core. Those hotel companies who have been operating without this in mind are the ones who suffered the most during COVID-19 and many of them will never recover. Gradual transition towards profit management is inevitable. "Survival of the fittest" is what we recently experienced in many industries as the pandemic introduced a mechanism of natural selection. In addition, profit optimization technology will no longer be considered an expense, but an investment that will allow hotels to navigate the situation better and thrive, not just survive.

Technology will also help us with many other aspects of the business, and artificial intelligence will play a very important role in our evolution. Technologies can solve very real problems while improving processes. Hospitality companies that succeed in the new environment will be those who are agile and those who heavily invest in new technologies in the next 5-10 years.

Tech adoption rates will inevitably continue climbing as technology becomes more and more accessible and widespread. It could be helpful if tech vendors worked together to do broader education about use cases, data quality, optimization, machine learning, and how to look at the hotel business as a whole. I find that vendors spend more time trying to compete against each other as opposed to educating hoteliers and the industry on a broader level, which would benefit all of the companies and hoteliers themselves.

What will also help tech vendors increase adoption rates is designing tools that are user-friendly, intuitive, and automated, as well as completely redefining their sign-up and onboarding processes, from manual to self-service SaaS model that can be easily scaled via app marketplaces.

When it comes to formal education, we have to rethink the way we teach and find a way to bridge the gap between academia and the industry. There are many ways to do that and I'll continue my attempts to help in that area.

Throughout the last 20 years that I have devoted to hospitality, my main goal has been contributing to its success on a larger scale and helping the industry become more successful, more efficient, more modern, and more in line with the 21st century. This book will hopefully be able to make at least a slight difference in the evolution of our industry and move us closer to this goal. I'll be happy and very grateful if this happens.

Besides this publication, I will continue to work on improving the world of hotels and hospitality - through education, consulting, and building innovative software solutions. I will continue to learn how we, together, can improve the state of the art of hospitality and encourage others, especially the younger generation, to devote their energy to doing the same.

I'm very excited to see what the next 5 years hold for us. The possibilities are indeed infinite and it's all in our hands. All we need to do is embrace the change.

Thank you for joining me on this journey.

ACKNOWLEDGEMENTS

Tony Mangano. Nearly 20 years ago, he hired an international student from Belarus for a summer job in the housekeeping department at a little Ramada in Syracuse, NY. With that, he opened the door for me into the hospitality industry, the industry that adopted me, allowed me to contribute to its success, helped me find my passion, my path, and realize my potential as an immigrant in this wonderful country. Tony, I would like you to know that I will always be grateful for the opportunity you gave me many years ago.

Dana Blasi. One person who has been my biggest influencer since the beginning of my hospitality career, my former employer, my mentor and my best friend. Dana is the President of a local San Diego hotel management company, a hotel owner who has been contributing to the industry for decades. He gave me my first lessons on revenue management when I was still in Belarus. He believed in me, in my potential and taught me a lot of things about the hotel world. He guided and supported me throughout my entire career. He helped me build an RMS company with my business partner and generously offered his hotels as guinea pigs for the algorithms to learn on their data (we thanked him by increasing his RevPAR by 30% YOY the next year when his hotels adopted the newly built RMS). He celebrated my success and my achievements as I was growing as a professional and a human. I credit him with the idea for writing my first book on revenue management that went on to become quite popular, as well as many other great ideas that have shaped my life since I moved to San Diego. He is the reason for my growth and success in this country and in the hospitality industry.

I'm very grateful for the contribution he has made to my success. He will be the first person getting a signed copy of this book.

Daniel Obodovski. I'm sure he will be surprised seeing his name on this list. But I can't not mention him because this book wouldn't have been born if I hadn't met Daniel just a few months ago. Daniel co-authored a fascinating book titled <u>The Silent Intelligence, The Internet of Things</u>[139] that became a hit back in 2013 when it was published. I'm one of those lucky owners of a signed copy. The book provided me with such inspiration as it described the complex world of the emerging M2M/IoT industry, the challenges it was facing, the stages it was going through, and the incredible potential that the evolution of intelligent devices could bring very soon. As I was reading his book, I started finding so many similarities with what the hotel tech industry had been going through, which inspired me to start writing about hospitality from the same aspect - the digital transformation journey that would very soon evolve into something new and revolutionary. This is how the idea of this book was born, at 3 o'clock in the morning as I was dwelling on the recently consumed pages of 'The Silent Intelligence'. Daniel was also very supportive throughout the process of working on my book and gave me valuable advice from his perspective of a published author, professional speaker, an experienced executive and just a very bright and talented person. I would like to thank him for his contributions to this book and to many other ideas that emerged in my restless head after our conversations.

---

[139]Amazon: The Silent Intelligence: The Internet of Things: https://www.amazon.com/Silent-Intelligence-Internet-Things

Mylene Young. I want to thank her for her support and friendship. When I meet people who I can learn from - I hold on to them and try not to let them go. Mylene is one of those rare wonderful people who has shared her wisdom with me and has been a good friend since we met. Mylene is a Co-founder and the Principal at Son Hospitality Consulting. I always marvel at how much she knows about the hotel world and how well she navigates in this space. She is also a wonderful person that I adore tremendously.

There are many other people who I couldn't thank enough for running into me at different stages of my life and making me who I am today. Many of them don't even realize how much influence they had on my personal growth. Thank you everyone from the bottom of my heart.

And of course, I want to thank everyone who agreed to participate in my research.

Industry leaders interviewed (in alphabetical order):

Amanda Belarmino, PhD: University of Las Vegas (Assistant Professor)

Bob Gilbert: HSMAI (President, CEO)

Francis Davidson: Sonder (Co-founder, CEO)

H. G. Parsa, PhD: University of Denver (Professor)

Jan Freitag: CoStar Group (National Director)

John Burns: Hospitality Technology Consulting (President)

John Tilly: Aggregate Intelligence (Founder, CEO)

Jordan Hollander: Hotel Tech Report (Co-founder, CEO)

Leif Jagerbrand: Atomize RMS (Founder, Chairman of the Board)

Marco Benvenuti: Duetto RMS (Co-founder)

Michael Blake: HTNG/AHLA (CTO)

Michael Levie: citizenM (Co-founder, COO)

Mylene Young: Son Hospitality Consulting (Founder, Principal)

Ravi Mehrotra: IDeaS RMS (Co-founder, President and Chief Scientist)

Ravi Simhambhatla: Google Cloud (Managing Director/CTO, Digital Transformation - Travel & Transportation)

Scott Shatford: AirDNA (Founder, CEO)

Sekhar Mallipeddi: Vendia (Managing Director)

Timothy Webb, PhD: University of Delaware (Assistant Professor)

Made in United States
Orlando, FL
19 May 2022

18003698R00152